Online Customer S~~~~
For Dummies~

C000067420

Traditional service principles in an online world

To achieve world-class online customer service, you need to honor the traditional principles of service excellence. You'll build your company's reputation for being customer-friendly if you:

- **Stand for real values**. Ultimately, the success of your enterprise has more to do with your core values, and a commitment to delivering them, than it does with the latest business or technology trends.

- **Value customer loyalty**. By some estimates, gaining a new customer costs five times more than keeping a current one. Studies show that, on the Internet, the cost of getting visitors to come to your site once is significantly heavier than the cost of keeping them coming back. The more you do to retain your customers, both online and offline, the more satisfied and lucrative they will be.

- **Build relationships**. Put an equal amount of attention on building relationships as on developing products. Software and hardware must be designed and used with a focus on service. In the end, a strong relationship between company and customer can overcome most temporary service problems.

- **Stay close to your customers.** Online, you can assess each individual customer's needs, ask for input, and suggest new products or services suited to the individual. Having a direct line to your customers is a new, exciting opportunity for any company that knows the value of listening and staying close to its customers.

- **Make it personal**. Investing in e-business software solutions does not guarantee the personal touch. People like doing business with people. Best-in-class companies demonstrate their caring attitude by using technology to support their relationships with people, rather than to replace human-to-human relationships with human-to-computer ones.

Using technology to serve core customer needs

The application of CRM and other technologies has made it easier than ever to fulfill customers' core needs, including:

- **Personalization.** With the information you gather through CRM, you can tailor the service you offer to an individual customer. CRM helps you to predict what new products a customer is likely to buy or concerns a customer is likely to have.

- **Convenience.** These days, it seems that everyone, including your customers, has more to do and less time to do it in. Always being accessible to your customers, via the Web and a call center, keeps you from missing valuable business opportunities and helps your customers.

- **Responsiveness.** Whenever a problem occurs, most of us want to be able to take immediate action to resolve it. Through self-service Web interactions, your customers are able to verify the most up-to-date information on their account and often solve the problem online. When they can't, a Please Call Me button that puts them in touch with a service agent provides a prompt response.

- **Understanding.** Service agents, by using software that allows them to view customer data and history on their screen, have all the needed information at their fingertips and don't have to ask the customer basic questions in order to get up to speed with the issue at hand. As a result, customers feel that their situation has been immediately understood.

- **Speed.** In this fast-paced world, whenever we want something, we usually want it NOW! Giving customers the option to conduct business transactions via e-mail, voicemail, and the Web provides an alternative to the traditional mail and telephone methods that usually take more time than do the new options.

Online Customer Service For Dummies®

Winning Web content

Given the vast choice of Web sites out there, what can you do to inspire a Web surfer to take the time to visit yours? The content you offer on your site is one way to provide value to your customers and keep them coming back for more. Some of the things to consider adding to your site include

- ✔ **White papers.** A generic term used to define any document your company has created and posted on your Web site. They are usually research-based and detailed.
- ✔ **How-to articles.** These articles provide value to your customer by giving them relevant and valuable information in bite-size chunks.
- ✔ **Relevant links.** Links to other companies that are complementary with your business add value and convenience.
- ✔ **Online tools.** The content on your site doesn't have to be limited to passive print. You can also provide your visitors with an online tool, such as a self-scored test.
- ✔ **Advice.** If your business has a particular expertise, offer a Q&A section or full-blown advice column where typical questions a visitor may have are answered.
- ✔ **E-mail newsletters.** A newsletter is a way to provide valuable information to your customers and promote the commerce side of your business at the same time.
- ✔ **Live chat/Web-cast interviews.** The interview is hosted on your site, set for a specific date and time, and features a guest who is of interest to your audience. A moderator facilitates questions from the online audience. The more advanced version includes audio and video with concurrent PowerPoint slides.

Six keys to becoming a customer centric company

The key to long-lasting customer loyalty and retention is to go beyond the application of technological solutions to embracing the commitment to becoming a customer centric organization. Becoming customer centric is a process that requires focus, effort, and action in the following key areas:

- ✔ As a manager, take a top-down approach by walking what you talk in the arena of quality service.
- ✔ Ask for feedback and utilize it by regularly surveying your customers and staff.
- ✔ Train and educate all your staff and managers in service excellence and the skills they need to be part of a customer centric company.
- ✔ Design customer centric processes and technologies that are focused on the customer's convenience rather than your own.
- ✔ Set consistent service standards that are measurable, specific, and spell out the actions that express the service qualities you value.
- ✔ Reward and recognize service excellence in both formal and informal ways. Remember, what gets rewarded is what gets done!

Hungry Minds™

For Dummies™: Bestselling Book Series for Beginners

Praise for Online Customer Service For Dummies

"Filled with down-to-earth advice and infused with a commitment to service excellence, *Online Customer Service For Dummies* is an important tool for mastering the new economy. Karen Leland and Keith Bailey adapt their practical advice for the e-business world. Anyone committed to service excellence will benefit from this book."

> — Konrad S. Alt, chief public policy officer, Providian Financial

"Outstanding! *Online Customer Service For Dummies* is the most important element in any good e-commerce site. . . . *Online Customer Service For Dummies* gives you the tools to build the right experiences for your customers."

> — Debbie Lutkenhouse, vice president, Applied Biosystems

"This is a very 'in the bones' guide for virtually every aspect of e-business in the 21st Century. The anecdotes make their tools easy to use in real life situations. It's the only book you need!"

> — Raz Ingrasci, president, the Hoffman Institute

"Karen Leland and Keith Bailey understand deeply what it takes to deliver effective and lasting customer service. . . . The key is the practical ideas and examples that illuminate the important concepts to which they are committed. I particularly liked their advice on how to get results using e-mail. I learned a lot myself!"

> — Giles H. Bateman, cofounder of the Price Club, former non-executive chairman of CompUSA

"Leland and Bailey have done an excellent job of focusing business and customer satisfaction in the world of e-business. . . ."

> — Charles P. Kendig, vice president, Quality/Customer Satisfaction, Oracle Service Industries

"This book is a must-read-and-follow for customer service organizations that are in the midst of either creating and/or maintaining online support to enhance operational effectiveness and/or customer satisfaction. Once again, Karen Leland and Keith Bailey have compiled a fun to read, informational book that can help a traditional service organization transcend into one that is proactive and leading edge!"

> — Bo Wilson, senior director of Internet Services, VeriSign, Inc.

"In *Online Customer Service For Dummies*, Karen Leland and Keith Bailey introduce a well thought-out, logical and fresh approach to improving online customer satisfaction by making the user's experience simpler and more efficient. Readers will relate to the straightforward, engaging and rich techniques introduced by Karen Leland and Keith Bailey. *Online Customer Service For Dummies* delivers high quality, up-to-date information, tied in with time-proven customer service tips, that will help assure that your customers continue coming back for more!"

> — Jim Smith, Real Estate Investment Mangers (RREEF)

"Karen Leland and Keith Bailey's work is the best in their field. Use these potent techniques and ground breaking ideas to take your company to a whole new level."

> — Marcia Wieder, author of *Making Your Dreams Come True*

"Chisels down the complexities of technology and gets to the core element of providing effective e-service — keeping the human connection!"

> — Jun Young, training solution architect, Microsoft Corporation

"This gem of a book is a *must* for anyone who uses the Web and e-mail in business. Karen Leland and Keith Bailey give us the *do's* and *don'ts* of online communication. This book is a refreshing mix of practical hands-on advice and a research oriented understanding of customer service."

> — Michelle B. Blieberg, Blieberg Consulting

™

BESTSELLING BOOK SERIES

References for the Rest of Us!®

Do you find that traditional reference books are overloaded with technical details and advice you'll never use? Do you postpone important life decisions because you just don't want to deal with them? Then our *For Dummies*® business and general reference book series is for you.

For Dummies business and general reference books are written for those frustrated and hard-working souls who know they aren't dumb, but find that the myriad of personal and business issues and the accompanying horror stories make them feel helpless. *For Dummies* books use a lighthearted approach, a down-to-earth style, and even cartoons and humorous icons to dispel fears and build confidence. Lighthearted but not lightweight, these books are perfect survival guides to solve your everyday personal and business problems.

> *"More than a publishing phenomenon, 'Dummies' is a sign of the times."*
> — The New York Times

> *"...you won't go wrong buying them."*
> — Walter Mossberg, Wall Street Journal, on For Dummies books

> *"A world of detailed and authoritative information is packed into them..."*
> — U.S. News and World Report

Already, millions of satisfied readers agree. They have made For Dummies the #1 introductory level computer book series and a best-selling business book series. They have written asking for more. So, if you're looking for the best and easiest way to learn about business and other general reference topics, look to For Dummies to give you a helping hand.

Hungry Minds™

1/01

Online
Customer Service
FOR

DUMMIES®

Online
Customer Service
FOR
DUMMIES®

by Keith Bailey and Karen Leland

Hungry Minds™

HUNGRY MINDS, INC.

New York, NY ◆ Cleveland, OH ◆ Indianapolis, IN

Online Customer Service For Dummies®

Published by:
Hungry Minds, Inc.
909 Third Avenue
New York, NY 10022
www.hungryminds.com
www.dummies.com

Library of Congress Control Number: 00-112180

ISBN: 0-7645-5316-X

Printed in the United States of America

10 9 8 7 6 5 4 3 2 1

1O/RW/QU/QR/IN

Distributed in the United States by Hungry Minds, Inc.

Distributed by CDG Books Canada Inc. for Canada; by Transworld Publishers Limited in the United Kingdom; by IDG Norge Books for Norway; by IDG Sweden Books for Sweden; by IDG Books Australia Publishing Corporation Pty. Ltd. for Australia and New Zealand; by TransQuest Publishers Pte Ltd. for Singapore, Malaysia, Thailand, Indonesia, and Hong Kong; by Gotop Information Inc. for Taiwan; by ICG Muse, Inc. for Japan; by Intersoft for South Africa; by Eyrolles for France; by International Thomson Publishing for Germany, Austria and Switzerland; by Distribuidora Cuspide for Argentina; by LR International for Brazil; by Galileo Libros for Chile; by Ediciones ZETA S.C.R. Ltda. for Peru; by WS Computer Publishing Corporation, Inc., for the Philippines; by Contemporanea de Ediciones for Venezuela; by Express Computer Distributors for the Caribbean and West Indies; by Micronesia Media Distributor, Inc. for Micronesia; by Chips Computadoras S.A. de C.V. for Mexico; by Editorial Norma de Panama S.A. for Panama; by American Bookshops for Finland.

For general information on Hungry Minds' products and services, please contact our Customer Care department; within the U.S. at 800-762-2974, outside the U.S. at 317-572-3993 or fax 317-572-4002.

For sales inquiries and resellers information, including discounts, premium and bulk quantity sales and foreign language translations, please contact our Customer Care department at 800-434-3422, fax 317-572-4002 or write to Hungry Minds, Inc., Attn: Customer Care department, 10475 Crosspoint Boulevard, Indianapolis, IN 46256.

For information on licensing foreign or domestic rights, please contact our Sub-Rights Customer Care department at 212-884-5000.

For information on using Hungry Minds' products and services in the classroom or for ordering examination copies, please contact our Educational Sales department at 800-434-2086 or fax 317-572-4005.

Please contact our Public Relations department at 212-884-5163 for press review copies, or 212-884-5000 for author interviews and other publicity information, or fax 212-884-5400.

For authorization to photocopy items for corporate, personal, or educational use, please contact Copyright Clearance Center, 222 Rosewood Drive, Danvers, MA 01923, or fax 978-750-4470.

About the Author

Keith Bailey and Karen Leland are co-founders of Sterling Consulting Group, Inc., an international management consulting firm specializing in off and online quality service. They have a combined 30 years of experience in this field and have worked with over 100,000 executives, managers, and front-line staff from a wide variety of industries including high tech, retail, transportation, hospitality, financial services, and consumer goods.

Their consulting and training work in corporations, and their public speaking engagements have taken them throughout North America, Southeast Asia, and Europe. Their clients have included such companies as AT&T, American Express, Apple Computer, Avis, Bank of America, Bristol Myers-Squibb, The British Government, Dupont, S.C. Johnson Wax, Lufthansa German Airlines, Microsoft, Oracle, Pacific Bell and Xerox, to name a few.

In addition to their consulting work, Keith and Karen are sought after by the media as experts on quality service. They have been interviewed by dozens of newspapers, magazines, and television and radio stations including The Associated Press International, The British Broadcasting Company, CBS, CNN, *Executive Excellence*, *Fortune*, *Management Today*, *Newsweek*, *The New York Times*, *Sales and Marketing*, *Time Magazine*, and *The Oprah Winfrey Show*.

Sterling Consulting Group offers a variety of training programs, consulting and key note speeches on how to create a customer centric company and how to improve customer service via the Web, e-mail, phone, face to face, or carrier pigeon. Among the programs that SCG offers are:

The Service Advantage: a one-day workshop for front-line staff focusing on principles, skills, and techniques necessary to provide excellent customer service.

Essential E-mail: a half-day workshop for executives, managers, and employees for improving online productivity, enhancing electronic communications, and creating e-mails with impact and style.

Keeping the Human Connection: a keynote speech focusing on how executives and managers can achieve a healthy balance between being technologically up-to-date and customer focused.

Creating Service Partnerships: a keynote speech that explores the three essential steps leading to excellent service. Filled with practical tips and techniques, this presentation is valuable for any manager or employee whose job involves frequent contact with customers.

Core Competencies for Working in a Wired World: a two-day program designed for managers and their staff to improve individual and team productivity and performance. Participants will learn four skills vital to success in today's rapidly changing marketplace.

Building a Winning Quality Service Strategy: a one-day program for executives and managers designed to help them evaluate the current customer focus of their organization and develop a strategy for creating a more customer centric company.

The Quality Service Audit: a comprehensive survey and evaluation that helps a company or division to identify how customer-centric they are currently and to target specific areas for improvement.

If you would like more information on the services we offer, please visit our web site at www.scgtraining.com. If you are interested in booking a speech or training, please contact Karen Leland/ Keith Bailey at: Sterling Consulting Group, Inc. , 180 Harbor Drive, #221, Sausalito, CA 94965; phone (415) 331-5200, fax (415) 331-5272; e-mail: service@scgtraining.com

Dedication

Keith's Dedication:

To my wife Deborah, a shining light whose love and spirit enriches my world, and to my three grandchildren, Angelo, Alex, and Lauren, for teaching me to look anew at everything — even when I'm tired.

Karen's Dedication:

This book is dedicated to my girlfriends. Over the years, I have had the good fortune to be surrounded and supported by these women through all the ups and downs in my life. A deep heartfelt thank-you to Liza Ingrasci, Joanne Fox, Joanne Kellert, Deborah Coffey, Randy Martin, Shelley Simon, Irene Dayan, Suzanne Saxe, Anat Baniel, Karen Druck, Gayle Canton, Sharon Roe and Diane Morrison.

Authors' Acknowledgments

First of all, a very big thank-you to all our clients who continually remind us that everything is always changing, and who provide us with endless opportunities to adapt and learn with them.

Much appreciation goes to our trainers and staff who made it possible for us to spend time writing this book. A special thanks to Eddie Oliver and Irene Dayan, our senior trainers who bring professionalism, enthusiasm, and commitment into every class they teach, and to Jean Cabonce, our office manager, who supports us with her organizational skills, steady focus, bright smile, and great sense of humor.

A special thanks to Kathy Welton and Mark Butler of Hungry Minds, who suggested that we write this book. Over the years, they have been great supporters and champions of our books. We value their friendship, guidance, and expertise.

We are also indebted to our editor, Marcia Johnson, whose flexibility and feedback were invaluable and whose voice of reason guided us through the turmoil of research, writing, and deadlines.

Thanks also to Jon Leland (Karen's husband and Keith's friend) for allowing us 24/7 access to his Web development expertise and for being such a valuable source of ideas, feedback, and information for this book.

We owe much gratitude to Wayne Pryor, who has been our client for many years and who was generous enough to serve as the technical editor for this book. We couldn't think of a person we would rather have do the job!

A special thanks to our unofficial board of advisors: Giles Bateman, Stewart Emery, Celia Rocks, and Suzanne Saxe. They have all been most generous with their valuable time and sage advice.

We are also very grateful to everyone who contributed their expert opinions and guidance to the pages of this book. We are especially thankful to: Gerry Barber, Jean Bave-Kerwin, Brad Cleveland, Nathan Fierman, Robert Gray, Susan Hash, John Jessen, Dick Kennedy, Jon Leland, S. B. Master, Carl Oppedahl, Howard Rheingold, Celia Rocks, Jim Smith, Larry Wasserman, and James Zeldin.

Publisher's Acknowledgments

We're proud of this book; please send us your comments through our Online Registration Form located at www.dummies.com.

Some of the people who helped bring this book to market include the following:

Acquisitions, Editorial, and Media Development

Project Editor: Marcia L. Johnson

Senior Acquisitions Editor: Mark Butler

Copy Editor: Ben Nussbaum

Acquisitions Coordinator: Lauren Cundiff

Technical Editor: Wayne Pryor

Editorial Assistant: Carol Strickland

Cover Photos: © Eric Kamp / Index Stock / PictureQuest

Production

Project Coordinator: Dale White

Layout and Graphics: Amy Adrian, Jackie Nicholas, Jacque Schneider, Kendra Span, Brian Torwelle

Proofreaders: John Bitter, Andy Hollandbeck, Jennifer Mahern, Angel Perez, York Production Services, Inc.

Indexer: York Production Services, Inc.

General and Administrative

Hungry Minds, Inc.: John Kilcullen, CEO; Bill Barry, President and COO; John Ball, Executive VP, Operations & Administration; John Harris, CFO

Hungry Minds Technology Publishing Group: Richard Swadley, Senior Vice President and Publisher; Mary Bednarek, Vice President and Publisher, Networking and Certification; Walter R. Bruce III, Vice President and Publisher, General User and Design Professional; Joseph Wikert, Vice President and Publisher, Programming; Mary C. Corder, Editorial Director, Branded Technology Editorial; Andy Cummings, Publishing Director, General User and Design Professional; Barry Pruett, Publishing Director, Visual

Hungry Minds Manufacturing: Ivor Parker, Vice President, Manufacturing

Hungry Minds Marketing: John Helmus, Assistant Vice President, Director of Marketing

Hungry Minds Online Management: Brenda McLaughlin, Executive Vice President, Chief Internet Officer

Hungry Minds Production for Branded Press: Debbie Stailey, Production Director

Hungry Minds Sales: Roland Elgey, Senior Vice President, Sales and Marketing; Michael Violano, Vice President, International Sales and Sub Rights

◆

The publisher would like to give special thanks to Patrick J. McGovern, without whom this book would not have been possible.

Contents at a Glance

Cartoons at a Glance

By Rich Tennant

page 5

page 215

page 101

page 163

page 33

Cartoon Information:
Fax: 978-546-7747
E-Mail: richtennant@the5thwave.com
World Wide Web: www.the5thwave.com

Table of Contents

Introduction

Over the past several years we have seen a dramatic change take place in the business world. More and more of our clients have shifted their attention away from the big-picture of creating a customer-focused organization and instead stress the narrow need to implement service strategies in the online world.

We think both a focus on becoming customer centric — as an entire company — and a service-oriented online presence are necessary for any company that wants to survive and thrive in the coming years. In order to help you achieve both of these objectives, we have written *Online Customer Service For Dummies*. This book is designed to be a manual that shows you how to deliver excellent customer service in harmony with today's remarkable business technology.

While the Internet can (when used effectively) make communicating with your customers cheaper and easier, it also makes it more challenging to personalize the service that you offer. Survey after survey shows that the traditional values of customer service, such as responsiveness, product knowledge, friendliness, and accuracy, are more important now than ever. The challenge is to learn how to deliver these traditional values in an online environment.

Online Customer Service For Dummies presents new ways for you to get close to your customers while using a medium that is often perceived as cold and distant. The book helps you understand — and master — the challenges of building relationships in a digital world so that your customers remain happy and loyal. Among the many topics covered in this book are

- Generating a sense of caring in an e-mail message
- Extending a courteous and warm welcome when customers enter your Web site
- Using the principles of CRM to streamline your service delivery process
- Exploring ways to make your company more customer centric
- Creating a user-friendly Web site
- Solving problems as a team via e-mail
- Making your online service world class
- Dealing with customer complaints and service breakdowns
- Redesigning your IT department to better serve your internal customers
- Retaining staff and improving morale

We wrote this book with a broad range of readers in mind. Whether you are technologically challenged or a demon techno-wizard, an entrepreneur, a manager in a high growth start up, or an executive at a well-established Fortune 500 company, the information in this book shows you how to improve the quality of your online service.

How to Use This Book

This book does not have to be read cover to cover. For those of you who know the specific area of online service you want to learn about, we recommend you find that part and head right to it. If you are interested in getting an overall picture of the world of online service, we suggest that you start with the section of the book that seems to be calling to you and then read all the chapters in that part before moving on.

How This Book Is Organized

Online Customer Service For Dummies is organized into five parts. Chapters within each part cover specific topic areas in detail. Each chapter has lists of what to do, what to look for, and easy to follow instructions so that you can turn good ideas into actions.

Part 1: The Heart of Online Customer Service

In this part of the book, we explore how technology has impacted the basic philosophy of customer service excellence and changed your customers' expectations. In order to empower you to deliver superb online service consistently, we take a step back and look at the big picture of online service. You'll be able to evaluate how your company's online service rates today and discover strategies for becoming more customer centric in the future.

Part II: Turning the Theory into Practice

In this part of the book, we explore the infrastructure that provides the everyday backdrop to service delivery. We define CRM (customer relationship management), separate the hype from the reality, and show you how to harness CRM's principles to work for your business, big or small, without breaking the bank! Whether you're working at a help desk, a call center, or in an IT department (or supervising any of these), you can learn the best-in-class secrets for raising service levels head and shoulders above those of your competition.

Part III: Web Wise and Customer Friendly

Here you get all the information you need for creating and maintaining customer-friendly Web sites. Every step — from choosing the right domain name to working with a Web developer — is presented with tips and techniques for making sure that your online business entices and keeps customers.

Part IV: Essential E-Mail: Building Online Relationships

E-mail is rapidly becoming the most popular form of business communication, so it makes sense to know how to write, manage, and use e-mail messages to create positive and powerful impressions. We show you how to manage your mailbox so that you avoid common pitfalls associated with e-mail communication and how to use this new medium to create rapport and closeness — even with customers or colleagues you've never met!

Part V: The Part of Tens

This part of the book contains a huge amount of how-to information in quick, easy-to-digest bites for managers, salespeople, and front-line staff. It is a quick and easy way for you to learn some key points that make the difference between mediocre and world-class online customer service.

Appendix: Grammar Reminders for E-Mail Perfection

This straightforward reference section gives you useful grammar tips to help you avoid common mistakes that could diminish your (and your company's) image. We cover making nouns plural, creating new words with suffixes, understanding when to use *me, myself,* or *I,* as well as the proper use of numerous punctuation marks.

Icons Used in This Book

The tip icon provides you with general recommendations on how to make your customer service better — or your life easier.

This icon flags any potential pitfalls that you need to be careful of.

This is the stuff that you don't want to forget.

This icon marks examples of online service that go above and beyond customers' expectations.

Part I
The Heart of Online Customer Service

The 5th Wave   By Rich Tennant

CUSTOMER PHONE SERVICE AT DISNEY CORP.

In this part . . .

*H*uman beings never get tired of relating with other human beings. If you realize that people want to be treated as people — not extensions of a computer — then you are already halfway to the heart of online customer service.

In this part, we present key principles for creating a solid foundation for customer loyalty via the Internet and compare how predigital values translate in today's faster paced and computerized world.

So that you can be sure that the money and time you spend implementing your software and hardware pay off, we show you the keys to creating a customer centric company.

Chapter 1

Keeping the Human Connection

● ●

● ●

*W*e are at a turning point in business today. Tools such as e-mail, voice-mail, and the Internet have become an integral part of our everyday workplace. The influx of technology into almost every facet of business has created a streamlined workplace. But what happens to human contact?

Over the past five years, we've interviewed over 25,000 business people, asking them to identify the single biggest challenge they face in today's business environment. Time and again, we hear variations on the same theme: How do we keep the human connection with our customers in a high-tech world? When doing business through the often impersonal means of technology, people want — and many need — the reassurance of personal contact.

Traditional bricks-and-mortar businesses kept the human connection and distinguished themselves from their competitors by consistently delivering quality products to their customers with efficiency, caring, courtesy, and personalized service that was maintained over time. Today, if you do any business over the Internet, your company's reputation can be made or lost in the time it takes to click a computer mouse. The challenge today is providing added value in a minute rather than in an hour and understanding the impact that your online presence has on your customers.

Although the way companies do business is changing rapidly to stay in step with evolving technologies, the fundamentals of excellent customer service have not changed. In fact, traditional service values are more relevant than ever in a world where a passion for technology seems rampant — and a passion for service excellence is rare. Too many businesses fail to listen to their customers and, instead, get caught up in the new and better service strategies that change faster than teenage fashion.

We're not suggesting that you ignore changing markets or new ways of serving them; we simply believe that delivering excellent customer service online doesn't require that you wave goodbye to everything familiar. In other words, don't forget everything that you know about making customers happy just because you're now providing customer service through wires and circuitry instead of face-to-face. Delivering service online requires a change in context rather than a change in the content of customer relations.

Providing excellent online customer service requires that you embrace the traditional principles of service excellence while adopting new practices to fit the technological times. The principles presented in this chapter can help you stay on track.

Standing for Real Values in the Virtual World

If you look through the shelves of your local bookstore or search for the key-words "customer service" on your favorite book seller's Web site, you'll find a long list of titles to choose from (including our very own *Customer Service For Dummies*). The books spell out customer service strategies for making it in today's high tech world. But service strategies — like the seasons — come and go. Ultimately, the success of your enterprise has more to do with your core values, and a commitment to delivering them, than it does with the latest and greatest business trends.

Amid the hubbub caused by new and better technology, the businesses that will differentiate themselves as customer centric are those that will see online service as an exciting opportunity for delivering their *existing* values of service, quality, and excellence to a wider group of customers. The root of these values is a genuine customer-care attitude that compels companies to create a feeling of closeness with their customers and use technology to design systems with their customers' concerns and convenience in mind.

From the way an e-mail is worded to the design of a Web page, winning companies are constantly standing in their customers' shoes and asking: "Does this convey to our customers that we care?"

Valuing Customer Loyalty

Numerous studies have concluded that one key to cyber success is developing customer loyalty. One study concluded that the cost of gaining a new customer is five times greater than the cost of retaining a current one!

When it comes to e-commerce, the cost of enticing customers to use your online service is heavy at the front end and light at the back end. In other words, the longer you keep your e-customers and the more loyal they are, the more lucrative they become!

Placing a high emphasis on customer loyalty isn't a new phenomenon — even though many books and magazines seem to trumpet loyalty as if it's a recent innovation. Adapting your customer satisfaction efforts to a digital world will be easier if your company already values customer loyalty and is experienced in creating it.

Building Relationships

Many analog years ago, service gurus counseled senior executives to create customer centric organizations. Becoming customer centric often meant moving from putting an intense focus on product development to putting an equal amount of attention on relationship development. After all, even great products fail occasionally, and a strong bond between company and customer can overcome most problems.

If you're a business owner today, you still need to develop trusting relationships with your customers. The difference between today's business world and the business world of the past is the tools that are at your disposal. The courteous voice on the end of the phone and the friendly face across the counter are still important — they're just so expensive that they have to be rationed. In their place are software and hardware which, when designed, integrated, and used with a focus on service, can be as rewarding to your customers as they are to your company's bottom line.

Staying Close to Your Customers

Customers rarely describe doing business over the Internet as a warm and fuzzy experience. The absence of face time is, for many, the downside of online commerce. However, never before have businesses had an opportunity to be in such direct contact with their customers. The Internet allows your company to be in direct communication with every one of your customers — no matter where they reside on the planet (as long as they have an Internet connection, that is).

You can assess individual customer's needs, apologize, say thank you, ask for input, and suggest new products or services suited to the individual rather than to a whole demographic group — all online. Think of the Internet as a direct line to your customers. It's a new, exciting opportunity for any company that knows the value of listening and staying close to its customers.

Making It Personal

In a wired world, your company must find ways to communicate caring through computer screens and digital technology. The field of e-business technology uses sophisticated software programs to track inventory, accept payments, trace deliveries, predict customer needs, and send thank-you notes. In short, it attempts to automate the personal touch — thus making the most efficient use of your human resources — by minimizing human interaction. At the same time, e-business technology offers fast, convenient, "personalized" service.

Ultimately though, investing in e-business software solutions does not guarantee the personal touch — and remember that people like doing business with people. That's not to say that customers don't like quickness and convenience — they do. But they also crave a real human who can help them when they have a question or concern that doesn't fit in the templates of an online help desk. Best-in-class companies demonstrate their caring attitude by using technology to support their relationships with people. *They don't use technology to replace human relationships, only to enhance them.*

This book is designed to guide you as you make the transition to online customer service excellence. The chapters in Part II suggest concrete ways to practice excellent customer service in your company's daily activities. Part III suggests strategies to ensure that your Web presence is both useful to your customers and beneficial to your company's service directives. The chapters in Part IV present the ins and outs of effective e-mail use. And Part V — The Part of Tens — offers useful information in easily accessibly form that didn't fit elsewhere.

Chapter 2

Jumping the Digital Divide: From Traditional Customer Service to E-Customer Relations

Service strategies — like the seasons — come and go. Ultimately, the success of your enterprise has more to do with your core values, and a commitment to delivering them, than it does with the latest and greatest business trends. We're not suggesting that you ignore changing markets or new ways of serving them. We simply believe that jumping the digital divide doesn't mean waving goodbye to everything familiar (and analog) and forgetting all that you already know about making customers happy.

Jumping the digital divide is really more about a change in context than a change in basics. In fact, traditional service values are more relevant than ever in a business world where a passion for technology — without a passion for service excellence — seems rampant. Too many businesses fail to really listen to their customers. Instead, they get caught up in the "'new and better'" service strategies that change faster than teenage fashion.

Amid all the hubbub, the businesses that will separate from the pack and become truly customer centric are those that see online service as an exciting way to expand their existing commitment to service and value and reach a wider group of customers through e-mail and the Web.

The Digital Age

In 1995, for the first time ever, personal computers outsold televisions. According to some, this was the beginning of the digital age. By the middle of this decade, experts predict that we'll be spending more waking hours online than offline — and much of that time will be spent servicing, selling, and listening to customers. Online customer service is about harnessing technology so that its immediate and global capabilities improve service to your customers and your bottom-line. It is learning how, without the traditional and trusted tone of voice or eye contact, you can develop and maintain responsiveness, consistency and courtesy using a medium that can all too easily come across as cold and impersonal.

Savvy businesspeople will always be able to adapt and integrate new and improved approaches to listening to and addressing customers' needs. For those of you who are too easily enticed by the current buzzword or the latest acronym, we include a quick look back over past business trends. Hopefully, they'll remind you that, regardless of the different labels, customer service has always been rooted in a genuine desire to keep your customers happy — and loyal.

Service — The First Two Thousand Years

In the old days, nobody wrote books about service. It was simply a way of life. The pace of business was slower and people had more time to talk and listen to one another. Mr. and Mrs. Smith could go to their corner grocery store to buy a pound of Muenster and count on a warm welcome, friendly service, and familiar faces.

Then came the great depression. Price, always an important factor, became even more important. Life was about survival. Quality and service — never high on Maslow's hierarchy of needs — disappeared from everyday life and was reserved for the rich and infamous. In the more prosperous 1940s, consumers began to consider value in addition to price as part of the service equation. By the 1960s, quality became important, with most customers willing to pay more for higher quality products and services. The era of convenience began in the 1970s with quick and easy foods, stores, banks, and so on. Today, all of these characteristics have converged; we want a competitive price, good value, convenience, customer service and we want it yesterday!

Then, in the middle of the 1980s, service became a hot topic.

TQM — The first service acronym

In the 1980s, *Customer Service* and *Quality Improvement* were the buzzwords of the moment and *TQM* (Total Quality Management) became the most popular acronym since BLT. TQM — implemented to enhance customer service through delivering quality products — helped bring about modern manufacturing techniques.

We were told that we could have the edge over our competitors by establishing optimal production processes, conforming to standards, and empowering our staff to blow their whistles when they spotted a defect. Well, time passed and we found that it was too expensive to give everyone a whistle. TQM faded into the sunset — often better in theory than it was in practice.

MOT — The second service acronym

Behind the noise and fanfare of TQM's moment of fame, Jan Carlzon, who was the CEO of SAS Airlines, quietly published his book *Moments of Truth.* The book created a new acronym, MOT. It's an account of how the airline, under Carlzon's leadership, asked exactly what influenced its passengers' perceptions of service. What the airline found was that perceptions of service depended on how customers remembered very discrete encounters they had with the airline. These encounters — moments of truth — could either be memorably positive experiences or memorably negative experiences. Each one would play a critical part in the individual customer's future purchasing decisions. For example, a two-minute phone conversation could influence a customer's opinion about the entire enterprise — even more so than a two-hour flight!

The MOT approach still lives on because its premise can be applied to any business, large or small, and any medium, such as voicemail, e-mail, and so on. The MOT method of thinking about customer service still holds up because, no matter what your service or product, your customers are, more than ever, making quick judgements based on fleeting contacts. It may not be fair that your organization is so quickly judged — but it is customer logic.

Imagine that a customer receives an e-mail from your company that has no greeting and several spelling mistakes. The sloppiness and carelessness of the e-mail, for many customers, could signify that your staff members are not professional, your company doesn't care, and the quality of your product is questionable!

MOT introduced the business world to the radical idea that customer perception is reality and that service excellence, to a large degree, is managing your customers' perceptions and expectations. This theory is the primary driver behind many of the technology tools that are being developed to enhance online service.

SOM — The third service acronym

With Share of Market (SOM) gaining renewed strength in the early 90s we forgot about all the process improvement mumbo jumbo and got on with the job of dominating the world by capturing every available customer on earth. Around this time the speed of business began to increase exponentially. Fax machines, overnight delivery, and a very young Internet were beginning to present new customer communication opportunities. E-mail soon joined the established channels of phone, mail, and fax. The Web was promising to change business life forever.

As technology advanced by leaps and bounds, more and more magazine articles and business books were being devoted to the "new" idea of developing deeper relationships with customers. We were told that viewing each sale as a transaction was shortsighted. Customers are, after all, a finite commodity and many markets were maturing. Business pundits suggested that we use every customer touch-point as an opportunity to establish a dialogue and create customer loyalty. It made sense; after all, since it costs four times more to acquire a new customer than to keep a current one, why not increase efforts to retain established customers?

SOW — The fourth service acronym

Eventually, we began to learn more about one-to-one marketing. Even though it was labeled "marketing" it was essentially a smart approach to service excellence. By listening to our customers and providing them with the services and products they really wanted, we could move away from traditional Share of Market strategies and focus on something far more compelling — Share of Wallet (SOW).

In a sense, quantity was being replaced by quality. Every interaction with a customer, or potential customer, became an opportunity for gathering feedback, searching out needs, and implementing changes that would make the organization more customer centric. For service champions, the idea of converting transaction buyers (customers whose purchasing criteria is solely price and who have no vendor loyalty) into relationship buyers (those who value a long-term vendor partnership) was possibly the most important service development since Jan Carlzon's moments of truth. But we began to notice that the transaction to relationship conversion had a couple of costly flaws:

- ✔ Some transaction buyers were just shopping for price. They liked being transaction buyers and didn't want to join the flock. They didn't want a relationship and it was pointless to spend money convincing them otherwise.

- ✔ Some relationship buyers just weren't profitable (nothing personal, they were nice people). They purchased too little or too infrequently. Their loyalty to our companies was costing us too much in overhead.

It quickly became evident that one-to-one marketing was only profitable if you could be sure that the "one" you were one-to-oneing with was likely to become a long-term customer and therefore justified your marketing investment. This view formed part of the foundation for a newly emerging customer care process: Customer Relationship Management.

CRM — The latest service acronym

Welcome to the present! CRM (Customer Relationship Management) is the acronym that customer service professionals are using today. Simply put, CRM is the marriage of process and technology for tracking every contact point that customers have with your organization.

Many companies believe that the CRM strategy is the digital key to becoming customer centric in a fast-paced world. For the small and medium-sized enterprise, CRM can smack of hype or be too confusing to really understand. However, if you dig deeply enough there are valuable lessons to be learned from CRM — lessons that can improve your bottom line, such as discovering specific, and often unspoken, customer needs that enhance both loyalty and sales.

See Chapter 4 for a thorough discussion of CRM. We tell you what to take from CRM and what to leave behind. We extract and simplify the key elements so that you can move beyond the acronym-of-the month to the real, leading-edge issues. New technology presents new opportunities and new challenges that will, no doubt, impact your business's ability to provide great customer service in the years ahead — so read on!

Chapter 3

Creating a Customer Centric Organization

In this Chapter

▶ Identifying six key ways to create a customer centric organization

▶ Measuring how important the customer is to you

▶ Becoming more customer centric

*R*egardless of whether your company is large or small, the key to successful customer relations is infusing your company to the very core with the principles of quality customer service. This means that in order to deliver first-rate service to your customers, you have to instill a commitment to service in every person who works for you. "Like begets like" or "Practice what you preach" — however you say it, the key to ensuring that your customers receive excellent service is to create a customer centric organization. In order to do so, you have to establish a company culture in which a dedication to service is paramount. Keep the following points in mind as you consider how you might guide your company toward realizing the goal of being customer centric:

✔ The way you treat your employees has an impact on how they treat their customers.

✔ Front-line staff need to be trained in soft skills (interpersonal and communication skills) as well as in technical ones (process and problem-solving skills).

✔ The most effective managers model the service skills they want staff to demonstrate.

✔ Internal procedures should be designed with customer convenience in mind.

In this chapter, we show you how to sharpen your company's focus on quality customer service. We present you with the rationale and the specific strategies for adopting a company-wide customer centric mentality. We also show you how to evaluate how customer centric your company is now.

Putting Your Customers First — Always

In today's one-to-one, CRM-impacted, Internet-inspired world, one of the hardest lessons for business leaders to learn is that neither excellent product quality nor the latest, greatest technology is the panacea that will cure all their customer relationship ills. (See Chapter 4 for more on CRM.) Ultimately, the key to long-lasting customer loyalty and retention is to go *beyond* the mere application of technological solutions. The key to making customers stick with your company is to embrace the idea of becoming a customer centric organization. Becoming customer centric is a process that requires focus, effort, and action in the following areas:

- ✔ Taking a top-down approach
- ✔ Asking for feedback and utilizing it
- ✔ Training and educating staff and managers in service excellence
- ✔ Designing customer centric processes and technology
- ✔ Setting consistent service standards
- ✔ Rewarding and recognizing service excellence

Take a top-down approach

Most business owners, executives, or senior managers, if asked, will nod their heads in complete agreement that excellent customer relations is the cornerstone of a successful business. In the final analysis, however, it's not what they say but what they *do* that matters. A manager's actions can greatly enhance the staff's commitment to providing improved service.

Many managers express their commitment to service by taking a roll-up-your-sleeves approach and modeling excellent service skills. Examples of this approach include

- ✔ Executives at a well-known communications company who took complaint calls in the customer service department once a month. They personally followed up on all calls until the issues were resolved.

✔ Executives at a rental car company who took a trip, every week, on a shuttle from the rental location to the airport terminal to speak with passengers and get their impression of the service offered. Each of the executives would bring stories and suggestions back to their monthly management meetings.

✔ A general manager in a transportation company who started holding informal lunch gatherings on a regular basis. The meetings gave the employees a chance to ask him questions and make comments or suggestions related to improving the conditions at work and the quality of the customer service they offered.

No quicker way exists for an executive to hinder a company's progress towards becoming customer centric than by promoting service excellence with her words and expressing mediocrity with her actions. For example, a senior manager who recommends service training for employees, but refuses to participate in the training herself.

Ask for feedback and utilize it

Many companies mistakenly assume that they know what their customers want. One of the first and most important steps in becoming customer centric is to take steps to find out — rather than just assume that you already know — what your customers want and expect of you. You need to discover whether you're meeting, and hopefully exceeding, their expectations. You can put your fingers on the pulse of your customers' experience by conducting surveys and focus groups.

Leading astray by example

One of our clients worked for a large multinational that had received dozens of complaints regarding the handling of telephone calls at corporate headquarters. Specifically, the complaints centered around people not picking up ringing telephones, not returning voicemail messages, and general discourtesy. In response, the senior management asked the Human Resources department to design a ½-day training seminar on customer service to help resolve the problem.

The HR department set up a seminar and invited all of upper management to attend. The idea behind the invitation was twofold: to allow the managers to underline their support for a new way of thinking by being present at the seminar and to provide training for some of the worst offenders — the members of upper management! Upper management responded by saying that they didn't have time to attend the program and that they didn't really need the training anyway — only the lower ranks needed it. This lack of participation from senior management created the impression that the training provided by the seminar wasn't all that important after all.

After you gather and analyze the data, be sure to close the loop by communicating any appropriate findings back to those surveyed. At the conclusion of the surveys, after you digest the feedback, you can get in touch with your customers any number of ways, including

✔ Sending a letter thanking your clients for their feedback, outlining your major findings, and proposing next steps

✔ Sending an e-mail, no longer than 3 to 4 paragraphs, that summarizes the findings from the report and highlights any actions you plan on taking

✔ Inviting those customers who participated in the survey to a meeting where you present the overall survey results and conclusions.

As a byproduct of conducting the survey and sharing the results, both good and bad, your company can enjoy an enhanced image and greater prestige among the customers who played an active role in the evaluation process.

 Gathering feedback from staff is another significant step in discovering where you stand as a company. We often begin our consulting work with a client by conducting an employee survey that focuses on how the company treats *its own staff.* This "cultural X-ray" is an inside look at the organization's internal focus and provides insight into how the current company culture is affecting customer service. A company that treats its staff poorly can't expect the staff to treat customers like royalty.

Train and educate staff and managers

Your front-line staff has the greatest amount of interaction with your customers. Many times, however, these are the people in the organization who get the least service training and education. In this context, *service training* means formal, classroom-style sessions whose objective is to build skills and awareness in specific areas of service excellence. *Education,* in this context, is any process which illuminates how service improvement relates to specific jobs, tasks, and behaviors.

Know thyself! (and know thy customers!)

As part of a survey we conducted for one division of a large multinational, we asked senior executives, middle managers, and front-line staff to choose from a list of 100 service qualities those that they felt were the most important to their customers. We then asked its customers to choose from the same list. The three qualities the supplier thought were most important were ranked, by the customers, as the least important service qualities on the list. The three items listed by the customers as the most important were listed by the supplier as the least important!

Education can take the form of newsletters, briefings, meetings, videos, and so on. Although the areas of education and training are often managed by different departments and serve distinct and separate purposes, they both contribute to the staff's awareness of the importance of service. Maximum effectiveness is gained when education and training are combined — as in the following case:

> One company waited two years before introducing service skills training into its cultural change program. It waited this long to ensure that the staff was informed (educated) about the company's long-term sales and service strategies as well as some planned changes in the organizational structure and systems. By preparing the soil in such a way, the formal service training, once initiated (with sessions focusing on such topics as dealing with difficult customers, going the extra step, and so on) took root quickly. This approach produced immediate positive feedback from customers who noticed a definite attitude change.

Training the managers of your company in how to create an environment for service excellence is also important — at least as important as training the front-line staff, if not more so. Training front-line staff alone isn't enough to create a customer centric company. "Train those people, and the wheels of the corporate machine will keep running smoothly" is a mentality we run into in our seminars. "Those people" are normally not the managers. Partial training rarely leads to improved service.

The enthusiasm generated by participants in a workshop is fragile — it's easily extinguished by the environment that they return to. The manager must take steps to reinforce what was learned in the workshop, or the training may be quickly forgotten and the money spent for naught.

Establish customer centric processes and technology

In our work, we see that *in-focused systems*, those systems that work favorably for the company but unfavorably for the customer, are the fulcrum on which a successful move towards being customer centered rests. Companies must be willing to examine and change these systems in order to be customer centric. Until the inherent service problems caused by such systems are resolved, any service improvement is limited.

The prospect of creating customer centric systems can be overwhelming. Part of the problem lies in the tangled web of procedures, policies, and actual technology that make up the systems and act as a blueprint for the way a company does business. Systems, while obviously indispensable, can help or hurt your customers and staff depending on how they are designed.

Using a broken ceiling to boost morale

In an earthquake in San Francisco a few years ago, downtown businesses sustained a lot of damage to their offices. In one case, most of the ceiling tiles in the customer service department crashed down on the staff's desks. No one was hurt, but the place was a mess. The manager, wanting to lift his staff's morale, took one of the ceiling tiles, spray-painted it gold, and inscribed it "The Mover And Shaker Award." Each month, he put the award on the desk of the best performing customer service representative. This manager proved that it isn't the award that counts as much as the spirit in which it's given.

Some systems are set up with the objective of protecting the company from having employees or customers take advantage of it. For example, the delivery procedure for a large consumer-products company involved customer-delivery personnel having to call back to the distribution center for authorization to accept merchandise for return to the warehouse. The call to the distribution center was then routed to the warehouse manager, who then called the sales manager for approval, and so on, ad nauseam. This time-consuming procedure would delay the driver and consequently make him late for his next delivery. This inefficiency was further compounded by the fact that permission for the return of merchandise was granted in nine cases out of ten!

The customer suffered as a result of a system that made returns unnecessarily difficult and prevented drivers from completing their routes on time — even though the company derived some benefits from (slightly) reducing the amount of returned merchandise.

Other systems still exist because they're the way the company has always done business. No one questions their validity or effectiveness. One woman in a workshop we led put it perfectly when she said, "In our company, adhering to the procedures and policies overrides common sense!"

Quality groups work well when developing procedures and processes. They empower the staff to take ownership of the new procedures and processes and ensure that staff members, who are the closest to the customers and know the most about the issues, are integral in brainstorming service solutions. Remember that changes in processes and technology should be based on customer and employee feedback. After you have feedback, then you can utilize quality groups to design the new procedures and processes.

Set consistent service standards

Friendliness, courtesy, responsiveness, accuracy — worthy goals, but how do you achieve them, given that they mean different things to different people? If you ask ten people what being friendly to a customer means, you'll more than likely receive ten different answers. You have to quantify *service quality* by developing specific, objective, and measurable *service standards* that translate service qualities into specific behaviors and actions. Service standards allow objective evaluation of staff performance and ensure consistency in treatment of customers across the board — but you must clearly communicate to your staff the behaviors that are required to meet these standards. For example:

> A manager at a large hotel chain we were working with had received multiple complaints from customers that his senior front-desk clerk was difficult to deal with. In an attempt to remedy the situation, the manager explained to the clerk the importance of being friendly. Much to the manager's dismay, none of his coaching produced the desired result. Finally, the front-desk clerk asked the manager to detail specifically what he should do to appear friendly. The manager realized that he had wrongly assumed the clerk knew how to translate the service quality of *friendliness* into specific behaviors. Obviously, he did not, so the manager explained how the clerk should smile, make eye contact, use the customer's name, and so on. Within a few weeks, the manager received numerous compliments from customers on the front-desk clerk's friendly manner.

Reward and recognize service excellence

In a company's culture, what gets recognized and rewarded is what gets done. Every recognition program should have three important elements:

- ✔ **A formal recognition program.** Formal recognition can be department-, division-, or company-wide. It should provide rewards for the individual or team that best fulfills the specified service criteria. The rewards could include cash, movie tickets, vacations, and so on.

- ✔ **An atmosphere of informal recognition.** This is the casual, everyday acknowledgment of staff that's often expressed by the manager's spontaneous gestures, such as thank-you notes, pizza parties, sharing customers' complimentary letters, and so on.

- ✔ **Salary and advancement.** In the final analysis, all staff have to see some personal benefit in increasing their sensitivity towards customers. If providing quality customer service isn't central to the possibility of advancement in pay and position, then the gospel of service becomes just so much hot air.

For more detailed and specific information on ways to focus your company on your customers, check out *Customer Service For Dummies,* 2nd Edition (Hungry Minds). It features ready-to-use surveys, templates, and detailed plans for making your company more customer centric.

Fish stinks from the head down

An old Dutch saying goes, "Fish stinks from the head down." We had firsthand experience of this when we were invited to present our ideas on how to create a customer centric organization to the senior executives of a large and well-known manufacturing company. They had just completed a two million dollar, two-year overhaul of their manufacturing capabilities aimed at improving overall quality. While they were pleased with the progress they had made so far — especially in product quality — they were scratching their heads in wonder at the results of their most recent customer and employee surveys. They were still getting relatively low scores when it came to their overall responsiveness to customer and staff problems and concerns. They asked us to meet with them to help figure out why and strategize a plan to address the problem.

As soon as the meeting started, it became apparent that both the president and his senior management team were uncomfortable with our core beliefs on what it takes to create a customer centric organization. At almost every turn, they took issue with the guiding principles of a customer centric organization. They were ambivalent about modeling service from the top down, making meaningful use of feedback, educating every person about quality service, setting service standards, and recognizing employee service excellence. (Rest assured: These principles are explored in detail in this book.)

Realizing that we needed to give them a bit of time to digest what we were saying, we took a break. During the break, one of the senior vice presidents shuffled us into a dark corner of the boardroom. He said, with fear in his eyes, "Are you trying to tell me that the way I treat my staff has an effect on how they treat their customers?" "Yes," we said, relieved that our message had, at last, gotten through to one person. Unfortunately, we were mistaken. In disgust, he shook his head, lit his pipe, and wandered off through a billowing cloud of smoke.

As the meeting went on, it became crystal clear to us why this company had the problems it did. The final straw came when we boldly (in their opinion) dared to put forth the idea that there might be a direct connection between their survey results and their lack of focus on the quality of service the customers received. The body language of the group said, unmistakably, "Heretics!" The day eventually ended. Much to our relief, the company did not call us again.

Measuring Your Customer Centricity

The questions presented in this section are meant to give you an idea of how customer centric your company or department is today. You can complete this questionnaire on your own, or you may want to gather together four or five of your coworkers and, as a group, discuss the questions and reach a consensus on the score you give yourself for each one. More often than not, the ensuing conversation — including each person's reasons for their rating — proves to be as valuable as the scores themselves. In fact, many people view the survey as basically an excuse to talk about the state of the company's customer service.

Another option: You may want to complete this questionnaire yourself, then give a copy of it to some of your coworkers to complete on their own. Schedule a time to get together to discuss and compare answers.

Before you begin

The 38 questions that follow are designed to be applicable to the evaluation of an individual department or of an entire company. Before you begin, decide whether you are going to focus on a department or the company. Some general guidelines to keep in mind as you go through the questionnaire include

✔ DO be honest and discerning in the ratings you give.

✔ DO go with your gut feeling when responding to each question.

✔ DO base your ratings on where things stand today.

✔ DON'T base your ratings on what you're planning to do in the near future.

✔ DON'T base your ratings solely on other people's opinions — although building consensus when working as a group is fine.

✔ DON'T overestimate where your company is.

Using the following rankings, consider each question separately and assign a score that you feel reflects where your company is today. Each question should receive a score of 0 to 3, according to the following criteria:

0 = Not at all

1 = To a small degree

2 = To a moderate degree

3 = To a large degree

As you read the questions, you may find yourself thinking, "Aren't these subjective?" Of course they are! This questionnaire is designed to give you a feel for where you stand today and to highlight some key areas for improvement. This questionnaire is not meant to replace formal customer and staff surveys, which give you hard data about the way your customers and staff view your company.

Ask yourself this!

___ Is it customary procedure to regularly survey our customers to find out how satisfied they are with our service/products?

___ Do we have a written, clearly-articulated mission statement that stresses our commitment to providing our customers with quality products and an excellent level of customer care?

___ Do we have specific, long-range goals for improving and enhancing customer satisfaction within our company?

___ Do we make day-to-day decisions that are consistent with our customer satisfaction goals and stated mission?

___ Does taking care of our customers have a higher priority than the internal politics of our company?

___ Do we collect data on the aspects of our service that are statistically measurable, such as telephone waiting times, e-mail response time, the percent of deliveries that are made on time, defect dates, and so on?

___ Do we focus an equal amount of attention on service excellence and cost-cutting to increase our profits and earnings?

___ Do our managers consistently demonstrate, in their everyday dealings with their staff and customers, the service attitude and skills we expect our staff to show towards our customers?

___ Do we have an effective process for handling complaints, so that the feedback we receive is translated into preventive measures?

___ Do we regularly survey our employees to find out how satisfied they are with their jobs, their managers, and the company?

___ Is it customary procedure for us to meet with our employees to get their ideas on how our service and products can be improved?

___ Do we provide our staff with job descriptions that include specific, measurable criteria and standards for service excellence?

___ Do we collect and make available data on the effects of poor service (mistakes, waste, redoing work, lack of communication, lost customers) and what it costs our company in terms of time, effort, money, and morale?

___ Do we regularly meet with staff members to keep them updated on relevant objectives, changes, and plans within the organization that affect their jobs?

___ Do we have a means of internal communication, such as a company newsletter, that regularly focuses on service excellence as the key to our company's success?

____ Do we train our managers to fulfill their roles in creating a service-oriented organization?

____ Do we train front-line staff in effective telephone, face-to-face, and e-mail customer relations skills?

____ Do we educate internal service staff about the important role they play in customer care and satisfaction?

____ Do we put new hires through an orientation program that stresses the importance of service excellence and their role, as individuals, in creating excellence?

____ Do we consistently look for ways to reduce bureaucracy, red tape, and other obstacles that get in the way of our staff being able to best serve the customer?

____ Do we promote those staff members who demonstrate excellent service and people skills to management positions?

____ Do we have an organizational structure that minimizes the number of levels between the customer and senior management?

____ Do we have telephone systems that reduce the amount of customer waiting time and allow our customers to get through to us easily and quickly?

____ Do we have an atmosphere that informally recognizes employees who provide service excellence to customers?

____ Do we have computer systems that enable our staff to provide fast, efficient, and responsive service to our customers?

____ Are our current policies and procedures customer-friendly and centered around the customer's convenience as well as our own?

____ Do we have a process in place that allows us to make specific changes in our policies, procedures, and systems, based on customer feedback?

____ Do we have minimally acceptable customer care standards in place for customer satisfaction?

____ Do our performance reviews evaluate the degree to which staff members are meeting the specific standards set for service excellence?

____ Do staff members understand the connection between our mission statement, their jobs, and the established service standards?

____ Have we established an executive task team to review the status of service within our organization and to create a plan for its continued improvement?

____ Do we use the feedback we receive from customers as the basis for determining what our service standards will be?

___ Do we periodically review and update these standards of performance?

___ Do we have a formal recognition program that rewards excellence in customer care and service?

___ Do we discipline and council those employees who are not demonstrating the desired service attitude and skills or who are not performing up to the established standards?

___ Do we have examples of individuals in our organization who have gone beyond what was expected to perform an almost heroic act in order to serve a customer?

___ Do our senior managers make a point of regularly meeting with customers?

___ Do we go out of our way to acknowledge staff for their efforts on behalf of customers, rather than reprimand them for going beyond the scope of their authority?

___ TOTAL

Scoring your responses and making improvements

Add your numbers up for all of the questions and get a total score. Look at the list below to determine what stage your company or department is currently at in regards to being customer centric.

- **Stage one:** Awareness building (0 to 26 points)
- **Stage two:** Education and training (27 to 57 points)
- **Stage three:** Process improvement (58 to 83 points)
- **Stage four:** Organizational infrastructure (84 to 114 points)

The primary activity you need to work on to further develop the customer centric focus of your organization is listed next to each stage.

Stage one: Awareness building (0 to 26 points)

Thank goodness you bought this book! Even though you may have invested some time in improving the quality of the service your company or department is providing, most of your time and effort is focused on other priorities and goals. At this stage, chances are that your company has probably been more oriented towards bottom-line results, such as revenue generation, cutting cost, and budgeting, with more attention going to quantitative rather than qualitative aspects of the company. We recommend you:

✔ Conduct formal surveys with your customers to determine overall satisfaction levels and assess the main service issues. Benchmarking your starting point before you begin any service improvement program is essential. Various methods you can use to gather feedback include

- Telephone interviews

- Mail surveys

- Face-to-face interviews

- E-mail surveys

- Complaint analysis tools

- Lost account surveys

- Focus groups

✔ Create an executive task team to champion the service improvement effort. Executives should tie a portion of their compensation to qualitative and quantitative performance in these areas.

✔ Determine the overall objectives and goals of the service improvement effort, including a timeline and accountabilities. Many companies have a vision to "serve the customer," but few have articulated a specific strategy to accomplish this. Using the survey feedback, the executive task team should develop an overall strategy for service improvement, including:

- Setting specific goals for customer satisfaction. For example, achieving a 90 percent excellent rating on all product review forms.

- Deciding on specific actions to be taken in each of the key areas involved in creating a customer centric organization. For example, putting all staff and managers through a training program that improves their basic customer service skills. (See the first part of this chapter for the six key elements of creating a customer centric organization.)

Stage two: Education and training (27 to 57 points)

At this stage, your company or department has recognized the importance of quality service and there's talk in meetings and memos about the need to take better care of customers. Your senior management team may have even taken one or two highly visible actions to this end.

What's missing is a well-planned process and a specific structure to get all managers and employees (regardless of department) educated about and participating in the company's goal of becoming customer centric. We recommend you:

✔ Hold an all-company meeting or a series of smaller meetings to introduce an initiative designed to make you more customer-friendly.

✔ Implement organization-wide service training for staff and managers in all areas of the business. Long-term service improvements won't happen without training your staff and managers in:

- Customer service skills (for front-line and backroom staff)

- Service management skills (for all managers)

- Team-oriented problem-solving skills (for all employees)

Stage three: Process improvement (58 to 83 points)

Companies or departments that are in stage three are actively engaged in the process of becoming customer centric and genuinely see providing excellent service as a priority. Even though you still feel you have a ways to go, your commitment to service has been manifested in everyday policies and behaviors that are noticeable to staff and customers alike. At this stage, the goal is to dive into the work of evaluating and redesigning (where needed) the major processes and procedures that affect your customers. We recommend that you:

✔ Implement an employee-centered continuous improvement program, that includes such elements as quality groups, task teams, or brainstorming sessions, to focus on process improvement within the company. Front-line staff can provide you with invaluable input on how to make your policies and procedures more customer centric, so be sure to draw on the expert knowledge of these groups when reviewing major procedures and design standards.

✔ Review major procedures and processes that impact the customer and redesign those that are in need of improvement. Although every company has a multitude of systems, the key systems to be examined when striving to become a more customer centric organization include

- Sales/ordering systems

- Supply/logistics systems

- Accounting/payment systems

- After-sales service systems

- Complaint procedures

- Crisis/contingency systems

- Telephone/computer systems

- Web/e-mail interfaces

- Contact management (CRM) systems

✔ Design and implement standards for service excellence throughout the organization. Remember, standards are specific and measurable. For example:

- Answering the phone within three rings

- Responding to all e-mail inquires within 48 hours

- Returning all customer calls within 24 hours

- Filling all orders within one day of receipt

Stage four: Organizational infrastructure (84 to 114 points)

If you scored at this stage, your company or department has already achieved a strong customer centric business culture. In fact, service excellence seems to have taken on a life of its own and has been translated into specific standards and procedures and permeates the daily operations of your company. Quality service has become, for all intents and purposes, a way of life. Because of the groundwork you have already laid, any efforts you put into further building your company infrastructure to improve service will be relatively easy to implement and will produce a high return within a reasonable amount of time. Recommended actions include the following:

✔ Conduct performance evaluations using established service standards.

✔ Formally recognize individual and team efforts for improvements in service excellence.

✔ Redesign the hiring process to screen applicants for a customer-friendly orientation.

Part II
Turning the Theory into Practice

In this part . . .

Customer Relationship Management (CRM) is the fastest growing e-business segment because it provides automated ways to stay in touch with customers. No matter what size your company, in this part we show you the principles and practices that the really big players use to improve their online customer service and how you can adapt these to your business.

Managers and staff of call centers, help desks, and IT departments can discover techniques and tools for increasing their productivity, satisfaction, and service ratings.

Chapter 4

CRM: Automating the Personal Touch

*N*ot so long ago, only large companies — because of the economies of scale — could harness technology to create a useful customer database. Mainframe computers would laboriously hum and eventually spit out a list of customer names and related information. The information was costly, and it was often outdated before the direct mail reached the mailbox or the service representative could initiate the sales call. Now, more computing power is in a laptop than was in many of the old mainframes. Fast, inexpensive, and easy-to-access technology has hatched a new world of customer tracking possibilities. Any size company can now maintain a database and effortlessly track all the comings and goings of its customers.

Technology is at everyone's fingertips. Customers are saturated with technology that's often a hindrance — rather than a help. In this chapter, we look at the latest online customer service technology — CRM, for *customer relationship management* — and give you ideas for using its principles in your business, big or small, so that it serves you, rather than vice-versa.

Defining Customer Relationship Management

Customer relationship management (CRM), when used in conjunction with a customer centric business strategy, allows your company to track every aspect of the customer relationship. You can determine who bought what and when they bought it. When you have a profile on each customer, you can transform each business interaction into a dialogue. In effect, you can talk to the customer as if you know him or her. By using CRM technology to understand the customer's relationship with your company, you create a one-to-one relationship with hundreds or thousands of customers at a time.

Too often, the relentless pursuit of higher profits is the sole driver for many CRM initiatives. A corresponding commitment to customer care is sadly lacking. Customers become frustrated and disheartened by companies who mistakenly believe that every human interaction can be replaced by technology applications. Customers love technology when it resolves a problem quickly; they're not so crazy about it when it hinders progress and creates an even bigger problem. After all, most of us have lost brain cells through the stress of trying to navigate a poorly designed voicemail system!

Successful CRM requires more than an investment in software and hardware. It also requires a commitment to developing a customer centric strategy, then investing in the people and training that will deliver it.

More and more companies are investing in CRM. Experts estimate that, by the year 2003, companies worldwide will spend $38 billion a year on CRM implementation. Dick Kennedy, VP of Worldwide Customer Support for Peregrine Systems (www.peregrine.com), one of the leading providers of CRM technology, told us that CRM "helps provide more efficiency because you don't lose any important information about your customers and you don't have to continually ask them the same questions, such as, 'Who are you?' or 'What did you buy from us?'"

The fundamentals of online customer service are the same on this side of the digital divide as they were on the analog side. Quality customer service still consists of listening to customers, doing everything you can to fulfill their needs, and knowing what to do when you can't.

Customers who feel that they're in a dialogue with your organization — who feel as if they're listened to — become lifelong customers. As the relationship matures, they spend more and more of their money with your company while requiring little or no incentive to continue purchasing. The more you understand about CRM, the more the line blurs between sales and service.

One example of this blurred demarcation is *up-selling*. Say that a customer has a problem with your product. Your sales rep is able to solve the problem and spare the customer the effort of contacting your service department. That customer is now far more likely to buy services and products that the agent suggests. The service rep becomes a vital player in opening up new revenue streams with existing customers. Remember also that your current customers are easier to contact and sell to than prospective customers are. CRM systems gather information customer trends and needs — information that is invaluable to your sales department.

Developing Trust and Loyalty Online

When implemented effectively, CRM can add tremendous value to your company by helping you to create and retain loyal customers. This loyalty is developed through the types of experiences customers have with your company. If you can consistently provide competent and immediate service, you increase the likelihood that your customers will stay with you.

CRM in a perfect world

In a perfect world, CRM is

- Immediate — allowing your customers instant gratification, whether the interaction involves processing a request or solving a problem

- Personalized — enabling you to tailor each interaction to your customers' unique needs and preferences

So, whether you're selling dog collars or offering cleaning services, CRM can help you make every customer encounter positive and rewarding. And that's good for business!

In the following scenario we demonstrate how CRM technology, when implemented well, can have a positive impact on cyberservice by creating satisfied, loyal customers. The interaction is a practical balance between providing a set of personalized help options to the customer and maintaining an efficient, low-overhead support process for the company. Here goes:

Imagine that you receive your monthly bank statement in the mail and discover that your balance is less than you expected. You're close to being overdrawn. You look through your register and discover that a deposit you made two weeks ago isn't recorded. You do some of your banking via the Web, so you access your checking account online by entering your account number and password.

Customer profiling has provided the bank with a detailed understanding of how you use its Web site and what information you're usually seeking. The bank has customized its presentation of your information by providing you with easy access to the functions that you use the most. Running across the top of the screen are special introductory offers for investment opportunities to help with future education and schooling costs. Data mining (seethe sidebar later in this chapter) has shown the bank that given your age, income, family situation (two young children), and zip code, you're very likely to be looking for investments that will help cover your children's educational needs a few years down the road.

As you scan your online statement, you discover that the deposit isn't recorded there either. The Web site provides a Please Call Me button that initiates an immediate telephone call back from the bank. You click the button, enter your phone number and a few other details, and wait.

The request is automatically sent to a customer service agent within the bank's call center who specializes in bank statement inquiries from the specific customer segment to which you belong. The computer screen that notifies the agent to call you also supplies him with your personal information, your history with the bank, the reason for your call, and what Web page you were looking at when you initiated your request for a call back.

With the press of a button, the agent returns your call. You speak with an agent, who, having all the relevant information in front of him, has an immediate understanding of the situation.

The agent scans your other accounts and discovers the money was mistakenly deposited into your money market account. He then apologizes for the mistake and the inconvenience it has caused, corrects it, and suggests that, for a small monthly fee, you purchase overdraft protection so that money from one account can automatically be transferred to another account, thereby avoiding costly overdraft fees. The added security makes good sense to you and you decide to sign up.

The agent explains that, if you sign up via the Web, the first month's fee for the service is waived. You agree, he directs you to the site and asks if you would be willing to fill in a brief customer survey regarding your satisfaction with the service you've received. You go to the survey page, fill in a brief questionnaire, and then sign up for overdraft protection. The Web pages explain the details about the service, how it works, and what it costs. You fill in the application form and press the Submit button.

The following morning, to your surprise, your receive an e-mail from the agent. He apologizes again for the mistake and assures you that everything has been taken care of as promised. You're impressed with the service and, when you arrive at work, talk enthusiastically about your bank and what a good job it does. You forget completely that it misplaced your money.

The scenario above shows how you can effectively use the information you gain through CRM to provide better service. The result? Satisfied customers.

In order to gain a deeper understanding of how the balance between customer needs and company benefits is achieved, let's take a look at the scenario from both sides of the equation.

Customer needs

Assume that you're the manager of the bank. You need to decide whether your investment in CRM is paying off. Thinking about the earlier example, you see that the integration of CRM technology and your commitment to delivering excellent service has fulfilled a number of customer needs:

- ✔ **Personalization.** With the information you gather through CRM, you can tailor your customers' experiences according to what they routinely request. CRM helps you to predict what new products they're likely to buy or concerns they're likely to have. The bank has designed its Web site to change its appearance per the individual customer's unique usage patterns.

- ✔ **Convenience.** Everyone is busy these days, including your customers. Always being accessible to your customers ensures that you'll never miss a business opportunity. In the bank scenario above, both the Web site and a call center response are available 24 hours a day, seven days a week.

- ✔ **Responsiveness.** Whenever a problem occurs, most of us want to be able to take action to resolve it. At the beginning of the scenario, the customer is understandably concerned regarding the missing money. Through a self-service Web interaction, he's able to verify the most up-to-date information and easily contact — by using the convenient Please Call Me button — a service agent.

- ✔ **Understanding.** We all need somebody to lean on. The service agent, through viewing pertinent data on his screen, is able to immediately ascertain why the call has been made. As a result, the customer feels that his situation has been immediately understood.

- ✔ **Expertise.** When you've got a specific question, you need a specific answer. In the scenario, the call is routed to an agent who specializes in the area of the customer's query.

- ✔ **Speed.** Whether it be purchasing a new sweater or solving a troublesome problem, in this fast-paced world, when we want something, we usually want it *now!* Because the agent in the scenario is familiar with the customer's circumstances, he doesn't have to ask the customer questions in order to get up to speed with the customer's issue.

- ✔ **Resolution.** Knowing that something is taken care of is always satisfying. If customers feel that they are in good hands, they're very likely to stick with you. In the scenario, the agent resolves the issue by seamlessly transferring the money to the correct account without having to ask the customer for account numbers.

Electronic loyalty

Recently, Bain & Company (www.bain.com), a consulting organization, completed a study on loyalty and electronic commerce. It reports that Web customers are less flighty and fickle than you may expect.

According to Bain, earning your customers' trust is the first step towards creating loyalty. In a medium that lacks a high human-touch factor, trust is the result of consistently keeping your promises, period. The article reports that Web sites that are fast to load, simple to navigate, and cater to a carefully-defined audience reap the benefits of loyalty. Those that try to be everything to everyone, with the goal of scooping up massive market share, miss the boat. In the frenzy to increase their visitor capacity, they overlook the opportunity to increase their share of wallet.

Casting too wide a net on the net inevitably leads to missing out on potential business and explains why the average site only reaches an estimated 30 percent of its full sales potential.

The study also found that the typical pattern in the business world of early losses followed by profits that increase over time is more exaggerated on the Web. You can expect fairly dramatic losses while you're first acquiring Web customers, but, assuming that you use technology wisely and quickly gain the loyalty of your customers, you can expect profits to accelerate at a faster rate than in traditional markets.

Profit-making momentum develops when customers trust your Web site. Their trust leads to them sharing more personal information with you, which helps enrich your knowledge of them and their needs, which, in turn, allows you to provide ever more tailored products and services, which increases trust! (This cycle is often called the *virtuous circle*.)

Ultimately, however, the study finds that the four primary sources of customer loyalty come from old-fashioned customer service and not the bells and whistles offered by technology. The four basics are

- Quality customer support
- On-time delivery
- Compelling product presentations
- Convenient and reasonably priced shipping and handling

One key element affecting customer loyalty is specific to the Internet: having a clear and trustworthy privacy policy.

Company benefits

One of the biggest benefits of CRM to a company is that it creates happy, loyal customers. But other benefits to your company exist too, such as:

- **Feedback.** Whenever you can get insight into your customers' experiences with your company, you have an opportunity to improve your service. The customer in the scenario, delighted with the efficiency with which the bank resolves the problem, willingly fills in a short survey.

- **Up-selling.** Offering an existing customer new services is more effective on inbound calls. The agent uses the interaction in the earlier example to better service the customer and to generate a new revenue stream for the bank.

✔ **Marketing.** No company can ever have too much exposure. During the banking interaction above, targeted banner ads are displayed by the bank and its third party vendors or partners.

✔ **Referral.** Hardly any better advertising exists than a satisfied customer. The customer in the scenario, pleased with the overall experience, considers the bank to be very customer-centered. He becomes a walking referral.

Clearly, the bank in the earlier scenario has developed a strategy and trained its people with the overarching goal of keeping its customers happy. As a result of that commitment, the bank has saved time, enhanced the customer's service experience, and reinforced customer loyalty so that promotions and offers by competing financial institutions are less likely to erode the relationship. Your company can benefit by implementing some of the following CRM strategies:

✔ **Preempting a voice call.** Any time you enable your customers to help themselves, you minimize cost. The customer in the scenario initiates his or her own inquiry by using the Web. Information you post on the Web can, in many cases, resolve the problem without the need for any further contact.

✔ **Automating the inquiry.** Having the call diverted to an agent automatically maximizes use of personnel.

✔ **Routing the call.** Eliminating the need for multiple transfers by having a customer's call go directly to an agent who specializes in the problem at hand provides faster service to your customers and conserves personnel resources.

✔ **Specializing the agent's expertise.** Having agents specialize in a particular customer segment (in the case of the scenario, 30-something urban professionals with a family who hold numerous investment vehicles within the bank) increases their effectiveness.

✔ **Preparing a response.** Time is money. Service agents can save call time by knowing the details of an inquiry prior to beginning a conversation.

✔ **Providing self-service.** Having the customer fill in a Web application for new services requires no investment of personnel.

When creating a new Web site, making it more than simply an online brochure is important. The more value your site adds to your customers' experience, the more loyalty it will generate.

When customers aren't able to resolve their issues or answer their questions through the self-service features of a well-designed site, they're going to be calling your agents for some personal assistance. The bad part of having a great CRM system is that your customers are going to be asking your staff or telephone reps more and more difficult, sophisticated questions. Being prepared to answer these in a quick and knowledgeable way is important. Such responses do a lot toward enhancing your company's image as competent and caring.

Consider conducting in-depth training with your staff so that they can answer the complex questions that aren't answered on the Web site.

Cyber nightmares — the dark side of CRM

You may be thinking that the earlier banking scenario had the potential to become a cyber nightmare. In the example we use, everything goes smoothly and CRM enables the service representative to give the customer great service. However, any of a number of problems could have occurred. Without a well-trained staff and committed management, the following problems could arise in the banking scenario:

- ✔ **Frustration.** The Web site is difficult to navigate and frustrating to use because it's not designed from the customer's perspective.

- ✔ **Anger.** By the time the Please Call Me button is pushed, the customer is upset or angry — swearing that he hates technology and that the Web marks the end of service on our planet.

- ✔ **Unresponsiveness.** The call back never comes — or, it comes days after the customer requested it.

- ✔ **More frustration.** The service agent asks the customer for his account number and password again. The customer explains that he's already entered all this in to the Web page, but the agent mumbles something about how "It didn't come through."

- ✔ **Eroding credibility.** The agent asks the customer what the problem is. The customer explains that he entered this information in the Please Call Me dialogue box. Again the agent mumbles, a bit grumpier this time, "Well, that didn't come through either."

- ✔ **Lack of confidence.** The agent, clearly frustrated by his inability to access information, is terse, unfriendly, and comments that "This new system was brought in a year ago and it's never worked."

- ✔ **Impatience.** The agent takes to long to figure out what statement the customer is looking at and takes even longer to resolve the problem.

- ✔ **Negative venting.** The customer agrees to fill out the customer response form because he wants to express his total dismay at how he's been treated. Doing so is more an opportunity to vent than anything else, because the customer has a strong sense that this complaint will be lost in cyberspace, never to be read by anyone.

🖊 **Looking for new bank.** Instead of signing on for overdraft protection, the customer is looking for another bank.

🖊 **Word of mouse.** The customer tells several work colleagues and friends about this terrible experience, and then sends an e-mail about it to the 27,000 people in his newsgroup!

Hello . . . is anybody out there?

The sad news is that the majority of companies are not even close to delivering excellent customer service over the Web. WizardMail Marketing Systems just completed a one-year research project where it measured the responses received from e-mail inquiries. All e-mails requested pricing and delivery information and were designed specifically for the company that received them. Each company was contacted up to four times, if necessary, in hopes of getting the requested information. The e-mails were sent to:

🖊 200 Fortune 1000 companies

🖊 300 random e-commerce Web sites

🖊 400 industry specific Web sites

🖊 100 home business and multi-level marketing organizations

Getting everyone on board

The Customer Marketing Institute (www. customermarketing.com), an organization that specializes in CRM implementation for small- and medium-sized businesses, advises clients that consultants don't implement CRM. The real CRM implementers are

🖊 Sales managers

🖊 Marketing managers

🖊 Service managers

🖊 Call center managers

🖊 Back-office managers

🖊 IT managers

CRM fails because:

🖊 Top management says, "Let's make it happen!" Then they go on to more important things.

🖊 The staff says, "This too will pass." Then they go on to more pressing things

🖊 Middle management says, "Help! We're trapped between a rock and a hard place!"

To succeed at CRM:

🖊 Get middle-management consensus on CRM plans before they're announced to the staff.

🖊 Train CRM skills to middle managers before you train the staff.

🖊 Provide training and coaching on change management.

In all, over 4,000 e-mails were sent over a period of four months. The results were staggering: Only 20 percent of those companies that were contacted ever responded to the e-mails! Table 3-1 shows the responses.

Table 3-1	Business responses to e-mail inquiries	
Number of Responses	**Type of Response**	**Percent of Responses**
575	Generic answer	14%
260	Specific response	7%
3,165	No response	79%

We're all doomed! Maybe

What do the statistics in Table 3-1 mean? Either that we're all doomed or, on the brighter side, that there's plenty of room for improvement. CRM *can* be harnessed to fit your business and used to sustain the service values that have always created relationship, and value with your customers. Stellar online service providers are few and far between. Those companies that are committed to looking for new ways of molding technology around their service vision and their strategic intent can quickly become leaders of the pack. But keep in mind that cyberservice winners are separated from cyberservice losers not by competitive pricing but by the caliber of the relationships they build and by the amount of trust they engender in their customers.

Using CRM to help achieve cyberservice excellence takes time, commitment, a strategy, and research. Most importantly, however, it requires a champion, a senior manager with the clout and dedication to stand by the project from the initial start through the inevitable roadblocks. The manager needs to pave the road to completion.

The successful outcome of your project largely depends on getting everyone on board and promoting the benefits of CRM from an enterprise-wide, rather than a departmental, perspective. See the sidebar, "Getting everyone on board," for more information.

Learning from CRM

No off-the-shelf, generic CRM template perfectly fits every company's needs. However, regardless of your organization's size and future plans for CRM, every savvy business person should understand the principles that are part of its successful implementation. The following two areas are common denominators among companies where online service is flourishing:

- ✔ Segmentation of the customer base
- ✔ Consistency across communication channels

Although not every company is big enough to implement CRM, these two elements can help any business offer better online customer service by making products and services more customized and more accessible.

A few good resources to check out on the latest and greatest in CRM technology include

- ✔ www.crmguru.com
- ✔ www.crm-forum.com
- ✔ www.zdnet.com/intweek

Segmenting your customer base

SOW makes more financial sense than SOM. (That was a test. See Chapter 2 if you need a refresher course on Share of Wallet and Share of Market.) As a result, you need to view cyberservice as strategic customer care, where investment in tools, training, and resources helps you to determine your customers' needs and helps you to deliver the appropriate goods or services at the appropriate time. In fact, 35 percent of all CRM investments are for reengineering and improving customer care — focusing on areas such as call centers and Web sites.

Because of the newly developed ability to "industrialize" the trust and loyalty building process with customers, business people are required, as never before, to analyze which customers they should spend resources on and which ones they shouldn't. It makes sense to only invest heavily in those who have a high probability of being lifelong and profitable. This prioritization is the heart of customer segmentation.

Investing in customer loyalty (see the sidebar earlier in this chapter) takes place heavily at the beginning of a new customer relationship and diminishes quite dramatically as the relationship between you and your customer cements and matures into loyalty.

A segmentation strategy is a three-part process that sorts those customers who meet the criteria you set for gaining a return on your investment. The criteria may be based upon how much a client spends with your business in a year, the average dollar amount the client spends per purchase, or the potential growth rate of the client (which, in a business-to-business situation, signals increased sales for your company). Segmentation then categorizes these potential spending habits in a way that makes it easy for you to create distinct customer populations.

Each distinct customer population can be offered very specific products and services that may be too expensive to offer to your entire customer base. A simple example is a company that offers free delivery to those customers who purchase goods over a certain amount. Or the credit card company that offers you a lower-than-advertised rate because of your repayment history (and, no doubt, the strong possibility that you will use the card extensively). Twenty percent of the CRM investments companies make go towards the loyalty-building aspects of profiling customers and segmenting markets.

The 80/20 rule, which states that 20 percent of your customers are responsible for 80 percent of your revenues, is accurate for almost every business. If you take this analysis one step further, the 1/10 rule reveals that about 1 percent of your customers account for about 10 percent of your profits. These numbers are a good place to start when segmenting your customer base according to profitability.

Step 1: Sort your customer base into profitability segments

Select the customers that you're making the most money off of. Say you have a customer base of 5,000. Using the 1/10 rule, select the 50 customers that contribute the most to your profitability. These are your premium customers, and you'll probably discover that you're garnering most of their business already. However, the true value of CRM is that it isn't only about getting more business from your customers, it's about finding ways to better serve them and to deepen their loyalty to your company.

Here are some of the key traits, other than their contribution to your bottom line, of customers in this primary segment:

- They have the potential to become customers that you make an even higher profit from.
- They are market-savvy and are also interested in establishing strategic partnerships with their suppliers.
- They are profitable and financially sound.
- They are industry leaders.

Next, sort out the 40 percent of your customers that you don't make tons of money off of but that could become lucrative accounts with diligence and cultivation. Creating a dialogue with these customers will more than likely give you rich information regarding why they give some of their business to your competitors. By discovering what they need in the way of service and products — and supplying what they need — you help move them towards the most-profitable bracket. For a company with 5,000 customers, approximately 2,000 customers would be in this secondary segment. As well as the key traits for high-profit customers, medium-profit customers also have the following characteristics:

- ✔ They are innovative and flexible.
- ✔ There is a high possibility for cross-selling.
- ✔ Your product or service is significant to their business.
- ✔ They show a trend towards increased revenues.

Then come the customers that are marginally profitable. In the sample customer base of 5,000, about 3,000 customers would be in this category. We believe that giving every customer the highest possible level of service is important. We also feel that good business sense requires you to carefully consider who your premium customers are and, when appropriate, offer them premium services that may be too costly for you to offer to smaller or less-frequent buyers. In other words, the highest possible level of service that you can give to an occasional customer that has a tendency to pay you late and is rumored to be going out of business is probably not real high. But for the big accounts, the highest possible level of service means pulling out all the stops.

Assuming that you have a limited amount of online service resources to devote to developing customer loyalty, we recommend reviewing how much overhead you're spending on low-profit customers. Ask yourself if changing your current spending ratio in order to capture a higher share of business from the most profitable 50 percent of your customers is appropriate.

After you know which customers you're going to invest in, the next job is to understand what it is they need from your organization — not only now but also in the future. You learn this information as you implement the second part of your segmentation strategy.

Step 2: Segment the markets and functions of your customers

The more refined your customer segmentation, the better able you will be to determine your customers' specific needs and tailor your services to them. In this second step, you initially need to segment the vertical markets of the companies that you serve into categories such as:

- ✔ Financial
- ✔ Engineering
- ✔ Manufacturing
- ✔ Healthcare

Next, segment the specific customers from each of these markets into functional responsibilities, such as:

- ✔ Executive
- ✔ Management
- ✔ Marketing
- ✔ Sales
- ✔ Clerical
- ✔ Accounting

Sort this list of individuals by their areas of responsibility, such as:

- ✔ Corporate
- ✔ Division
- ✔ Department
- ✔ Individual

By doing this vertical segmentation, you are better able to hit the mark when it comes to product design, marketing, and sales. For example, a training company that has identified a large customer segment of, say, corporate-engineer managers, may design and market a seminar that deals with the specific concerns and issues that it knows to be of interest to this group.

Step 3: Segment the habits of your customer base

Obviously, your customer database is the central tool for CRM. New database technologies such as data warehousing, that allows you to store information in a single place, and data mining, that enables you to retrieve specific information about your customers, have brought about a new sophistication in forecasting what your customers will want from you. (Data warehousing and data mining are explained later in this section.) The purchasing habits of your customers can partially be predicted by customer information such as:

- ✔ Products purchased previously
- ✔ Frequency and volume of purchases
- ✔ Zip code
- ✔ Gender

Online service presents a means for more comprehensive customer profiling and data collection. Many companies are now collecting customer information that helps provide a deeper knowledge of customers so that interactions are smoother. These areas of familiarity may include

✔ How many times the customer has encountered a problem with a product or service

✔ How many times a customer has called in or e-mailed a product-related question

✔ How much working experience the customer has had with the product

✔ How many company-offered product-familiarity courses the customer has attended

✔ The customer's personality over the phone (chatty, curt, bitter-and-twisted, and so on)

Although building your customer database is the beginning of the segmentation process, it is *only* the beginning. The average organization has about 10 separate databases, and these disparate systems needs to be brought together into one place — a *data warehouse*.

A data warehouse is a database that is used to store information that originates from the many different corporate databases and external market data sources. Because of the way information technology has evolved, most companies have different databases, in different formats, using different languages. The process of bringing all this information together is data warehousing.

Given the need to have all departments (reception, sales, marketing, credit, manufacturing, and so on) access and update the same customer information, the data must be manipulated and "cleansed" so that it is consistent and compatible with the format developed for the warehouse. Once this consolidation has taken place, special software programs can be used to sort through the data. This process is data mining.

Data mining allows users to sift through large amounts of data, using specialized software tools, to uncover data content relationships and build models to predict customer behavior. Predictive modeling can segment and profile customers and this information, if appropriate, can be integrated with other marketing-oriented applications.

Maintaining consistency across channels

The second element in assuring effective CRM is maintaining consistency across communication channels. A channel is any avenue that allows you and your customers to communicate with each other, including:

✔ The Web

✔ E-mail

✔ Fax

✔ Telephone

✔ Face to face

CRM has brought into sharp focus one of the most distinctive aspects of online service — the multiplicity of channels. These channels are used for the many different aspects of running your business, including:

✔ **Distributing information,** such as the specifics on your product or service. This information may include models, colors, characteristics, availability, the warranty, pricing, and service agreements.

✔ **Communicating** by answering customer inquiries about products and services, for example.

✔ **Making transactions,** including sending invoices and payments.

✔ **Distributing** products in innovative ways. Many software companies, for example, allow you to download the software directly from a Web site after you've paid.

✔ **Providing service** through the many channels makes it easier for your customers to connect with you.

Finding help to ease the transition

If you want some help implementing CRM within your company, many organizations are ready and waiting to assist you. Here are some to consider:

Applix Inc. www.applix.com

Clarify Inc. www.clarify.com

Commence Corp. www.commence.com

eGain Communications Corp. www.egain.com

E.piphany, Inc. www.epiphany.com

GoldMine Software Corp. www.goldmine.com

ISky www.isky.com

Kana Communications, Inc. www.kana.com

Multiactive Software Inc. www.multiactive.com

Neteos Inc. www.neteos.com

ONYX Software Corp. www.onyx.com

Oracle Corp. www.oracle.com

Quadstone Inc. www.quadstone.com

Peregrine Systems www.peregrine.com

SafeHarbor.com www.safeharbor.com

SalesLogix Corp. www.saleslogix.com

SAP AG www.sap.com

The Saratoga Group www.saratoga.com

Trilogy www.trilogy.com

ServiceSoft Corp. www.servicesoft.com

Siebel Systems, Inc. www.siebel.com

Unica Corporation www.unica.com

The Vantive Corp. www.vantive.com

Your organization's reputation for being customer-centered will hinge largely on your ability to create a consistent service level regardless of what channel your customer chooses. If you're not convinced that you need to be strong across all channels, consider this: Forty percent of online shoppers in a recent survey say that they would use more than one route to obtain customer service. It's not just phone calls anymore.

Many bricks-and-mortar companies who have moved into Web sales are having a hard time serving customers across all channels. They aren't in the habit of keeping up with the details of customer interactions. One scenario in which a customer gets bad service is if a customer calls a catalog company about a recent store or Web purchase only to be greeted by a service rep who has no record of any previous purchases via other channels.

Although realizing that customers value consistency across all channels is extremely important, the most successful online service providers also know that different customer segments have different channel preferences. These preferences can change depending on circumstances. For example, customers who normally use the Web to ask questions will make a telephone call if they need an answer quickly.

Your customers assess the level of service they receive largely by how easy it is for them to change channels and still be treated with consistency and responsiveness. Your Web-based customer service may be terrific. But if your other channels are lackluster, the customer's overall impression is going to be negative.

When your company uses multiple channels (the Web, e-mail, phone), you provide your customers with the means of getting the information and the responsiveness they want. But you need to be sure that customers get the service they want using every channel. Your customers aren't automatically able to change channels easily and still receive exemplary service; you need to devise and implement a strategy.

Developing a multi-channel strategy

Although many different methods exist for developing a multi-channel strategy that suits your organization, the first step is always to survey your different customer segments to discover their needs and their loyalty drivers — those things that keep them coming back for more!

Part 1: Create a customer survey

Hold a brainstorming session with key staff members to come up with a list of interview questions. You may wish to create a slightly different set of questions for different customer segments. The following list can get you started thinking about potentially useful questions:

✔ Do customers have access to the Web, or at least to e-mail?

✔ What is their preferred channel for receiving new product information?

✔ What is their preferred channel for obtaining answers to questions regarding products or services not yet purchased?

✔ What are their invoicing and payment preferences?

✔ Do they have concerns or feedback regarding privacy and security?

✔ What are their preferred channels for technical support and problem resolution?

✔ How satisfied are your customers and what impacts their loyalty?

✔ What products or services do your customers not know about?

✔ What are their future spending plans and via which channel?

✔ What services would you need to supply in order to get a greater share of their spending?

Be sure to keep your survey brief. Regardless of whether they're responding to a live person or filling in a form online, customers soon get weary of answering questions.

Part 2: Conduct customer interviews

Once you develop the questionnaire, decide on how the surveys will be delivered to your customers. The fastest and least expensive method will undoubtedly be e-mail. However, because e-mail questions are so cut and dry, no opportunity is created for the in-depth dialogue that can, potentially, spin off from a live conversation. For some of your clients, the expense and time of a live interaction with an in-house person who has knowledge of the client's history may be worthwhile.

We recommend that interviews generally be conducted in the following way:

✔ **Face to face.** For big accounts and accounts with great potential

✔ **Telephone.** For medium-size accounts

✔ **Writing.** For small accounts that will probably stay small

✔ **E-mail or the Web.** An increasingly popular method that can be used, if appropriate, with small and medium-size accounts

Part 3: Use collected data as a basis for your strategy

The next step is to analyze the information that you collect from your survey and begin building a channel strategy. Your strategy will be unique to your products, your services, and your customers' needs. Some things to keep in mind include

✔ Some customers use the Web far more than others. Because Web interactions require dramatically lower overhead than voice interactions, many companies offer incentives for Web ordering. For example, airlines may offer mileage bonuses, retailers an across-the-board 10 percent discount, and so on.

✔ Many customers prefer a dialogue with a real person, which translates into an agent-assisted telephone call.

✔ Some customers prefer an automated voice response system, so that they can push buttons on their own telephone to get the recorded information that they need.

✔ Everyone wants the option of switching channels when they require fast problem resolution. Companies that do not provide alternative contact information on their Web sites and e-mails score low marks with customers.

Real-time customer service

According to a survey by Jupiter Communications, 40 percent of online customers prefer to speak with a live human being when they have questions about a product or service. More and more companies are responding to this desire by complementing their e-mail and FAQs with real-time customer service over the Web.

Internet telephone tools are one option for doing so. By using software products from companies such as Speak-2-Talk (www.speak2talk.com) and Digiphone (www.digiphone.com), your customers can use their computer like a phone and speak with a live agent without disconnecting from your Web site. This technology is becoming more and more popular as connection speeds get faster and bandwidths get larger. The downside, currently, is that not all computers come with built-in microphones, sound cards, and the necessary software.

Another option for real-time customer support comes not in voice but in words. Using technology that provides a chat room–type interface, products from companies such as LivePerson (www.liveperson.com) and HumanClick (www.humanclick.com) allow online customers to have an interactive dialogue with a service rep via a small window that pops up on whatever page is being viewed. Some of these tools monitor your site, identify repeated user actions, and then trigger onscreen messages that offer on-the-spot customer support.

Larry Wasserman, VP of Marketing at LivePerson, explains the popularity of their product: "Servicing customers over the Web is about creating a brand for the customer. Trust, value, usability and service level create the brand of a Web site, from the customer's perspective. Users can go from Web site to Web site in seconds — but only a few sites differentiate themselves by providing real-time answers in seconds."

Because e-mail and Web solutions are so cost-effective, some companies have set up interactive e-mail and sophisticated bulletin boards and chat rooms. Customers can access these online communities and ask questions of other users of the same product or service. Although finding the right answers may be a little more hit-or-miss, some people report that persistence often produces a more in-depth answer than could be obtained from a service agent.

Note: The average cost of a service call that takes place over the phone is $5. If the call is answered by some kind of voice response system that presents menus and answers to frequently asked questions, this cost goes down to 50 cents. The same interaction conducted over the Web costs 3 cents.

Ultimately, the success of your channel strategy will depend on your understanding of your customers' needs, your ability to deliver products and services along the appropriate channels to meet those needs, and the development of new strategies for enticing customers towards the channels with the lowest overhead.

When you consider CRM, keep in mind that successful CRM implementation is as much a people process as it is a technology process. Having the right tools without a top-down commitment to training and motivating staff is a recipe for failure. As David Sims, a frequent writer on CRM, puts it, "The worst scenario is when a company purchases CRM software, opens the box, and then says 'Okay, now what are we going to do with it?'"

Chapter 5

Help Desks: The AAA of the Cyber Highway

*H*elp desks come in many shapes and sizes. The smallest "help desk" is the helpful coworker in the nearby cubicle who always seems to know what to do when you can't pull up a report that you need.

A help desk may also be a part of the IT (Information Technology) department. These help desks exist to support the internal workings of a whole organization. They aid employees who need assistance with their software, computer, or peripheral hardware.

Help desks also exist for the purpose of providing technology support to the customers of a company. These help desks may be staffed by a few people or by many hundreds of people. They deal with issues as simple as replacing a battery or as complex as creating a work-around for a software bug.

Regardless of their size or their purpose, help desks are the AAA of the cyber highway. They come to the rescue whenever a user has a technology breakdown. As we show you later in this chapter, dealing with service breakdowns is similar to dealing with automotive breakdowns. The people who need the services of a help desk aren't all crazy, desperate, and ready to throw the computer out the window — but many are. Use the information in this chapter to make your help desk a paragon of excellence — even when the going gets tough!

We address this chapter to people who work at a help desk, to managers who supervise help desks, as well as to executives who make decisions about the help desks in their organizations.

Dealing with an Angry Caller

Imagine the following scenario. You are driving down the freeway to visit an important customer. Today is the day the customer signs the contract for a very large order with your organization. As you drive down the freeway, thinking about the meeting and the profit that the new order will create, you notice that something's wrong with your car. You pull over — miles from any exit — and see that your passenger-side rear tire is flat. Your journey to the meeting has been interrupted unexpectedly — and you're frustrated, angry, and uncertain what to do next.

Similarly, when customers call into your help desk, they're trying to reach an important destination or attain an important objective. Your help desk may serve internal customers who need to print an urgent report, design an overhead presentation for a sales meeting, or crunch some spreadsheet numbers for a meeting with their boss. Or it may serve external customers who are experiencing difficulties of one type or another. Whatever the goal — and however mundane or insignificant it may appear to anyone else — your customer considers it important and he expects the help desk to respond in a concerned and caring manner.

One key to dealing with an angry or frustrated caller is to listen through a *service filter* — an attitude of empathy for the troubled customer. Sometimes, help desk workers mistakenly interpret customer behavior. For example, they may decide that a customer who asks a certain question is arrogant or that a caller who seems to be upset is stupid. Such negative assessments can affect what they focus on when listening to customers. When they listen to customers through a negative filter, they are mostly listening to their inner dialogue *about* the customers, rather than listening *to* the customers — making it difficult to get to a speedy resolution of the problems.

Using a service filter is a great technique. It takes your attention off the negative aspects of the person you're talking with and puts your attention back on the real needs of the customer. When you notice yourself having unconstructive thoughts about a customer, slide in the service filter. Ask yourself: "What does this person need and how can I provide it?"

As soon as you insert your service filter, your attention goes back to the caller's real needs and turns away from your negative perceptions. For more information on negative filters and service filters, see *Customer Service For Dummies,* Chapter 9.

Letting Frustrated Customers Vent

As you stand by the side of the freeway, staring at your flat tire, you feel worried, then upset, and then maybe you even start saying things to yourself, such as, "I can't believe this!" or "Oh no! I can't be late for this meeting!" Although these emotional responses don't move you towards your destination, they are natural reactions to your predicament.

When customers (and your own employees calling your own help desk are also considered customers) call your help desk with a problem, they are often emotional and unreasonable because their printer, software, CPU, or whatever isn't doing what they expect and need it to do. Some customers are very expressive and demonstrate their emotions with volume and force; others are quieter and more subdued. Both types of customers need to vent in their own way. Help desk practitioners must understand that venting is a natural part of dealing with frustration and must not take it personally.

When customers are venting, the best thing to do is keep quiet and listen. Don't hold the headset away from your ear — really listen! From time to time, use a *verbal minimum* — that's the official word for "uh-huh" or "mm-mmm." Verbal minimums work well because they let the customer know that you are there and paying attention, yet they don't interrupt or distract from what the customer is desperate to communicate. Once the customer has vented and calmed down, you can apologize and gather the information that you need for resolving the problem.

Customers cannot listen very well when they're venting. Attempting to quiet upset customers or asking them to calm down is equivalent to throwing a gallon of gasoline onto a fire — stand back! The technical solution to a customer's problem can only be presented *after* the customer's emotional response. Help desk practitioners usually must exercise their basic human-relation skills before they show their exceptional technical know-how.

Controlling Your Talk Time

Imagine going to the trunk of your car, pulling out the jack, and then noticing that your spare tire is also flat. Oh boy! You have another emotional outburst — you curse at the guilty tire and then graduate to laying the blame on someone else:

> "They should have checked this when the car was serviced!"

> "That's the last time I let my kid use the car!"

> "Why do I have to take care of everything!?"

Help desk customers are often in a similar predicament. For example, they may try and fix a software problem themselves by changing, say, the preferences on the program. Then they find that they've accidentally changed or erased all of the work they've done so far. By the time they call for help, they may be far more stressed and upset than seems logical — and even vent for so long that they forget the purpose of their call.

Remember that customers often vent more if they've been waiting in the phone queue forever or have been transferred to several people before arriving at the help desk. Be aware that emotions can run amok when callers encounter new problems in trying to resolve their current problems. They may talk on and on and on about their issues.

When customers vent excessively and begin repeating themselves, use a *verbal bridge* to get the conversation moving towards resolution. A verbal bridge is a polite interruption that refocuses the conversation on resolving the problem. Bridging is an important technique for help desk staff because it reduces the amount of time that they spend helping an upset customer.

Imagine that a customer is venting about a printer that keeps breaking. "This is the fourth time I've had to call you about this. I just want a new printer. I keep asking for a new one and they promise me a new one but do I get a new one? No. This is the fourth time — it is costing you more money in man-hours to talk to me than it would cost to buy me a new printer. Four times it's broken . . ."

Obviously, this call needs to move forward. The key to a polite interruption is waiting for the customer to take a breath and then cutting in with an empathic phrase, such as, "I can see why you feel that way." Empathic phrases soften the interruption and demonstrate understanding and concern, without agreeing or disagreeing with what the customer is saying. Other useful empathic phrases include

- ✔ I know what you mean.
- ✔ I understand your point of view.
- ✔ I recognize how upsetting this must be.

After the empathic phrase, make a bridge by asking the customer an open-ended question, such as, "How long since the printer was last fixed?" Open-ended questions tend to evoke answers that require the customer to think and recall the factual information that can lead to problem resolution.

Save closed-ended questions — questions that evoke one-word answers such as "yes" and "no" — for when you're dealing with a confused customer or want to double-check your understanding of what a customer has said.

Helping Your Customers Help Themselves

The role of the help desk staff is to serve as the roadside assistance representative — to listen to the sad story, to empathize, and then to ask questions to determine the level of service that the breakdown requires. Before sending a tow-truck out to fix a flat tire, try to determine if there is anything that your customer can do to resolve the problem herself. If she has exhausted every option, extend help as soon as possible.

When customers can fix the problem with minimal or zero assistance from the help desk, everyone benefits. The fix is usually faster and the help desk saves time and money because the interaction is much less involved. Several ways exist to provide your customers with tools that encourage self-help:

✔ Publish FAQ (Frequently Asked Questions) pages on your Web site.

✔ Offer fax-back services. To do so, present a phone menu of specific service problems. When the caller selects a specific number, he is instructed to punch in his fax number and within minutes receives a fax with possible solutions.

✔ Establish e-mail support.

✔ Make problem resolution databases available to internal customers.

✔ Set up IVR (Interactive Voice Response) systems that help callers perform common tasks.

Creating Reasonable Service Expectations

Distressed drivers don't want to sit by the side of the road waiting forever to be rescued. Similarly, customers who call your help desk assume that a representative is there, waiting, ready to assist them. The longer they wait, the more upset they may become. They don't care or even consider that they're just one of the many people who are calling for help. Customers who reach a live help desk representative within five minutes or less perceive themselves, for the most part, to be in the good hands of a caring company that will help them get back on the road again.

To ensure that your customers never feel neglected, establishing realistic service expectations is important. A *service level agreement* (SLA) is a written document that clearly defines the agreed-upon services to be provided and the measurable targets to be met by the help desk. Share the SLA with your customers. An SLA can go a long way toward promoting your customers' trust that you will always be there to help.

For internal customers, the following areas should be included in your SLA:

✔ **Hours of operation.** Include operating hours, such as Monday through Friday 6:00 a.m. to 8:00 p.m., or 24 hours a day, seven days a week. Include information on what support is available in emergency situations.

✔ **Customer access channels.** Clarify how customers can contact the help desk. Include specific phone numbers, e-mail addresses, self-service Web pages, fax numbers, and pager numbers for after-hours service, if appropriate.

✔ **Call prioritization methods.** Assign a priority to all the calls the help desk receives, for example:

- Priority one: Critical component down

- Priority two: Critical component corrupted

- Priority three: Non-critical component offline

- Priority four: All other questions and requests

✔ **Response time standards.** After the priorities are defined, assign a response time for each priority:

- Priority one: Respond within 10 minutes

- Priority two: Respond within 30 minutes

- Priority three: Respond within 2 hours

- Priority four: Respond within 6 hours

✔ **Resolution time standards.** Resolution times define the maximum target time for problems to be resolved once received, for example:

- Priority one: Resolved immediately or as soon as possible

- Priority two: Resolved within 3 hours

- Priority three: Resolved within 8 hours

- Priority four: Resolved within 12 hours

✔ **Escalation procedures.** Escalation procedures define the different courses of action to be taken when response or resolution targets are not met, for example:

- Level one escalation: Help desk manager contacted when response times are not met.

- Level two escalation: Director of Operations contacted when no response is received within one hour of level one escalation.

- Level three escalation: VP of Operations contacted when no response is received within 2 hours of level two escalation.

After service levels are set, the help desk can measure its performance against the defined service levels and coach customers as to their responsibilities regarding agreed-upon access channels, times, escalation procedures, and so on. Establish service levels for external customers using a similar format as the one outlined above.

Chapter 6

Call Center Fundamentals

In This Chapter

▶ Redefining customer expectations in a multi-channel environment

▶ Exploring the differences between phone and e-mail

▶ Motivating your call center staff

▶ Outsourcing your call center

*T*he first contact many customers have with a company is through the *call center.* You know — those places where you get put on hold for so long that you forget who you're trying to call. Fortunately, companies today are more aware than ever that their call centers are key customer touch-points and the hub of almost all inbound customer communications.

To remain competitive, companies are slowly updating their call centers so that the call centers offer customers a wider range of options than just waiting on the phone for "the next available operator." The options often include going to the company's Web site, sending an e-mail or a fax, and so on. Whether it be making an airline reservation, ordering an item from a catalogue, contacting a financial institution, or finding technical assistance for a new computer, customers like the option of helping themselves rather than having to rely on telephone conversations and the long waits often associated with them.

Business owners love the dramatically lower costs associated with Internet communications and the possibility of reserving more costly, one-to-one interactions for those customers who really need individual attention. (Although, so far, self-service is a bit of a myth — the Internet has not diminished incoming phone call volumes as much as anticipated.)

Offering customers all the multi-channel communication options associated with improvements in technology lets the company listen better. Integrating the Internet into the call center helps companies transform a brief, individual customer contact into a loyal and trusting relationship.

The big three call center tools

ACDs (Automated Call Distributors)

ACDs are highly sophisticated call-handling tools that are an indispensable part of any call center. ACD systems have been evolving over the past three decades and continue to play a key role in facilitating voice-to-voice customer contacts as well as facilitating the relatively new areas of e-mail and Web contact. An ACD system can

- ✔ Route and prioritize e-mails

- ✔ Bring forward e-mails that need an immediate response

- ✔ Hold a phone call in a queue

- ✔ Route a call to the most appropriate agent

- ✔ Determine the identity of the caller

- ✔ Play messages

- ✔ Send auto-response messages to received e-mails

- ✔ Provide productivity measurements

IVR (Interactive Voice Response)

IVRs, sometimes called *VRUs* (Voice Response Units), are really super-cyber-turbo-charged answering machines. They are used to obtain information and give it to the customer in response to prompts inputted by customers, who either say words or punch numbers on their telephone. IVRs diminish live agent interactions by offering a menu of prerecorded messages and options that, with a touch of a telephone button, can provide

- ✔ Account balances

- ✔ Credit card activation

- ✔ Stock market transactions

- ✔ Airline arrival and departure times

- ✔ Much, much more

CTI (Computer Telephony Integration)

CTI is the general name given to the integration of computer and telephone technology. It includes both ACD and IVR components. CTI applications include

- ✔ A menu of prerecorded solutions to common customer problems

- ✔ Sending faxes from a staff member's PC

- ✔ Call conferencing

- ✔ Transferring multiple message types (phone, fax, and e-mails) into the same mailbox

An organization increases the odds of hearing from its customers (and thus collects more information) by giving the customers multiple communication options. Having more information lets the company better capitalize on the information it collects.

The challenges associated with moving from a telephone-based call center to a multi-channel communications center are multifaceted and include the key areas of predicting e-mail volume, rethinking staffing requirements, developing a strategy for new technology implementation, and developing service levels appropriate to e-mail and Web-based communications. Brad Cleveland, President and CEO of the Incoming Call Center Institute (bradc@incoming. com), agrees that, "Most call centers, sooner or later, will have to embrace multi-channel communications and this provides challenges to those centers that have provided primarily a phone interface." In this chapter, we present strategies to help you make the transition to an effective multi-channel communications center. Three things are key:

- Fulfilling customer expectations in a multi-channel environment
- Recognizing the communication differences between phone and e-mail
- Motivating call center staff

Fulfilling Customer Expectations in a Multi-Channel Environment

When e-mail messages begin to flow into a call center, they bring with them certain predictable problems: messages getting lost in cyberspace, losing the human touch, and dealing with the time lapse between the initial e-mail and the response. Before you integrate the Web and e-mail into your existing call center environment, you need to address the following three issues:

- **Accessibility.** Make sure e-mails get to the right department.
- **Courtesy.** Train agents to create a positive tone in their e-mail responses.
- **Responsiveness.** Ensure that all e-mails receive a response within a specific time period.

Without careful consideration of these three elements, plus a commitment to maintaining a high level of quality in each one, you won't be able to realize the full value of your call center.

Accessibility: Making sure e-mails get to the right department

Call center technology for routing and responding to incoming phone calls has become very sophisticated over recent years. Live agent interactions are restricted to those callers for whom automated response systems cannot provide answers.

For example, if you call your credit card company to obtain your current balance, it's unlikely that you'll speak with a live agent. The whole interaction is done via technology that, in many call centers, responds to 60 to 90 percent of all inbound calls. Companies are saving money hand over fist.

E-mail technology, on the other hand, is relatively underdeveloped. Most call centers are not yet equipped with automatic routing systems. If a customer sends an e-mail to a general e-mail address, such as `company@xyz.com`, there is a very strong likelihood that the agent who receives the e-mail will not forward it to the correct department. Or, if the message is forwarded to the correct department, there's a high chance that nobody in that department will ever know it's there! If it is seen, it may be ignored.

Whatever the reason for the delivery failure, the customer usually ends up without a response and then fires off another (angry) e-mail message to — yes, you guessed it — the same e-mail address as the first one! Each time this happens, your customer service rating takes a nosedive. You can avoid this problem in three ways:

- ✔ Implement an e-mail routing system
- ✔ Educate your staff
- ✔ Educate your customers

It takes dedication to all three of these points to make sure that your call center is as valuable to your company as it can be.

Implement an e-mail routing system

E-mail routing technology intercepts e-mails that come in from customers, assesses the nature of the message (by recognizing keywords), and then sends it, with a notification, to the agent or department that's best suited to deal with it. An effective e-mail management system can

- ✔ Route e-mails to specific agents or queues.
- ✔ Increase an agent's productivity by displaying both voice and e-mail items so that e-mails can be answered during times of low call volume.
- ✔ Prioritize incoming e-mails based on the sender or the content of the message.
- ✔ Provide a library of suggested responses so that e-mails can be answered faster.
- ✔ Deliver information about the customer to an agent's screen.
- ✔ Track e-mail activity for reporting purposes.

All this automation serves to ensure that your customers never experience any of the frustrations that are too often associated with e-mail communication. Some excellent sources of e-mail solutions for call centers, such as technology integration and updates on new routing technology, include

✔ Brightware (www.brightware.com)

✔ Eon (www.eoncc.com)

✔ Genesys (www.genesyslab.com)

✔ Kana (www.kana.com)

✔ Mindwave (www.mindwavesoftware.com)

✔ Mustang (www.mustang.com)

✔ Lucent (www.lucent.com)

Also, the following associations can provide help in this area:

✔ The Help Desk Institute (www.helpdeskinst.com)

✔ SSPA (Software Support Partners Association, www.sspa-online.com)

✔ ICMI (Incoming Call Management Institute, www.incoming.com)

Even though e-mail routing systems are improving all the time, there is no one slam-dunk solution. No matter how fiendish the algorithms, they cannot yet predetermine the nature of all possible e-mails. For example, a router may not be able to detect if a message is a follow-up to a previous message or recognize from the tone of an e-mail that the customer is very upset and needs an immediate response (possibly by phone). Therefore, regardless of the technology you employ, educating your call center staff on how to monitor incoming e-mail always pays dividends.

Beware the e-gold rush

Getting caught up in the e-hype, as new products promise to simplify and revolutionize all our online commerce needs, is easy. After all, everyone wants to get in on the e-commerce gold rush. It's hard to not dive into a purchase of software that provides, for example, an efficient method for e-mail queuing, prioritization, notification, and routing.

Gerry Barber, Senior VP of Operations at Annexio, (www.annexio.com) a call center solution provider, has twenty years of experience in putting together call centers. He offers this advice: "It's most important to design the system around your customer needs and your priorities. If possible, provide your reps with the same tools and processes that your customers have. For example, call center agents should be able to view the same Web page in the same format as the customer, so they can relate simultaneously. Regardless of what the manufacturers say, there is no out-of-the-box solution, so it's essential to research the subject before you commit; I do extensive reading and then get demos of the products I am considering. Continually attempt to simplify the process. Keep asking yourself, 'What am I trying to accomplish?'"

Educate your staff

In order for call center staff to forward e-mails to the correct people or branches of the business, the staff needs to be educated in what department deals with what incoming e-mail. Some call centers provide online help — often in the form of an intranet Web site — so that agents can educate themselves through a self-service option that doesn't depend on finding the right person at the right time. With proper training, your call center staff can direct inquiries knowledgeably, minimizing the chance of customer frustration. And your staff can use low call volume time to help themselves to at least some of that training.

Educate your customers

Ideally, a customer should be able to send an e-mail to a general address within an organization and receive a reply — regardless of who opens the message. Unfortunately, this isn't yet the case with many companies. Therefore, educating customers as to where they should send specific inquiries can save a lot of torn hair. Many companies publish their specific department's e-mail addresses, such as billing@xyz.com, sales@xyz.com, or support@xyz.com, on their Web site and on all customer materials. Letting your customers know exactly how to contact your company to get the information they need not only empowers your customers, but also demonstrates that you understand their needs.

Courtesy: Training agents to create a positive tone in their e-mail responses

Any call center agent will tell you that customers are very sensitive to the tone of a telephone conversation. Regardless of the words that are being spoken, a customer's perception of the service they're receiving during a call is almost entirely based on the agent's tone of voice.

Less obvious, perhaps, is the reality that customers are also sensitive to the tone of an e-mail response. The way a message is written, regardless of the content, can create a very strong negative or positive impression on the reader. An e-mail message can greatly alter the customer's impression of your company.

- ✔ If the e-mail is sloppy or contains misspelled words or bad grammar, the reader will assume that the writer was in a hurry — meaning the company doesn't care.

- ✔ If the e-mail is short and curt, the reader will assume that the writer isn't friendly — meaning the company doesn't care.

- ✔ If the e-mail has no salutation or greeting, the reader will feel anonymous and unrecognized by the writer — meaning the company doesn't care.

Your business is certain to be affected if your call center agents send out less-than-ideal e-mails. Train e-mail agents to present your company as one that cares by showing them examples of acceptable and unacceptable e-mail responses. For more information on this subject, see Chapter 13.

Responsiveness: Ensuring that all e-mails receive a response within a specific time period

In Chapter 3, we present some frightening statistics regarding response rates for e-mails sent in by customers. The kicker: Less than 7 percent of inquiries receive specific replies. In fact, a poor response rate is one of the biggest complaints that online customers express.

Quality versus quantity

Currently, 69,500 call centers are in the United States. Experts predict that there'll be 78,000 by 2003. These call centers employ 7 million agents with an annual growth rate of 20 percent in new agent positions. Not surprisingly, most of the rapid growth has happened just in the last two years — due largely to e-commerce and the popularity of e-mail and the Web as new and inexpensive communication channels. 25 percent of call center traffic will be on the Web within the year.

Despite all this growth, most businesses don't yet offer customers a broad spectrum of communication options. A recent study by Jupiter Communications shows that only 37 percent of businesses combine three or more customer contact channels on their Web site. (*Customer contact channels* include the phone, traditional mail, faxes, and e-mails.)

A similar study by Servicesoft Technologies, a provider of Internet customer service technology, found that of those people who use the Internet, 73 percent prefer e-mail as the primary way to get online service. However, only 8 percent reported that e-mail consistently met their expectations. The top three problems reported were

- Auto response messages that don't address the customer's specific issues (69 percent)
- A complete lack of reply altogether (65 percent)
- Issues or problems that were never resolved (49 percent)

As customers are increasingly using e-mail to contact companies, the current challenge is for businesses to respond to these e-mails in ways that improve, rather than erode, customer relations.

Auto response is a popular way of letting customers know that you've received their e-mail. An auto response is sent automatically when a message is received. It doesn't require that the e-mail be dealt with immediately by a real person. Many customers don't like auto responses because they are too generic. If you want to score big with your e-mail communications, don't use an auto response. Instead, answer every e-mail quickly and personally. Failing that, be sure that your auto-response messages always contain the following elements:

✔ A thank-you for the inquiry

✔ A time by which the customer can expect a personal response

✔ An alternative method for contact, such as a toll-free phone number

✔ A Web site address where the customer can get more information

An auto response should give the customers some peace of mind by reassuring them that their e-mail did, indeed, travel safely through cyberspace and arrive at its intended destination. It should also set a realistic expectation regarding when the customer can get a personal response.

Moving from a traditional, phone-based call center to a multi-channel call center begins with a shift in perspective. Before you invest in new technology, make sure that you do a thorough purge of any out-of-date notions that call centers are money pits — costing too much and providing too little in return. Because call centers are often the first point of contact between you and your customers, they often determine the level of customer satisfaction — for better or worse.

Recognizing the Communication Differences between Phone and E-Mail

With the (often exciting) arrival of Internet communications, it's easy for call center managers to assume that their strongest agents on the phone will also excel in writing responses to customer e-mails — often a faulty assumption. Individual service agents rarely excel in all methods of communication. Savvy managers assess their staff's strengths and assign them jobs in which they can excel.

Taking telephone cues

Not only are speaking and spelling two very different skills, the actual communication processes are almost opposite. During a phone conversation, a call center agent participates in a dialogue and navigates through the conversation by reacting to ongoing feedback — cues from the customer.

These cues may be answers to specific questions the agent asks, moans or sighs (hopefully not screams), silence, or the customer's tone of voice. A good phone agent is sensitive to these cues and adjusts course appropriately by asking different questions, looking at other options, or simply remaining quiet with the understanding that the customer has more to say.

E-mail templates

E-mail templates are predesigned e-mail forms that you can provide for customers via your Web site. Templates help diminish return or follow-up e-mails to customers because they provide tailored forms, often with pull-down menu choices, that help customers to write e-mails that are concise yet contain all the relevant information you need.

E-mail templates can be designed for all the most common and predictable customer issues. For example, a catalogue company may offer the following e-mail templates (and perhaps many more) to customers who access its Web site:

✔ Overdue Shipment

✔ Wrong Item Shipped

✔ Item Damaged

Each template has menus and spaces for collecting the pertinent information. For example, when the customer opens the Overdue Shipment template, they may find the following:

E-mail Address:_____

Customer Name: _____

Customer Number:_____

Order Number: _____

Would you like

Package Tracking Information

Expected Delivery Date

Other Information

Please enter any other comments in the box below:

Submit

If the customer checks Package Tracking Information, the site links to the delivery company's tracking information page.

If the customer checks Expected Delivery Date, the template is either converted to an e-mail that's received by the call center and responded to or links to a data base that provides the relevant information.

If the customer checks Other Information, he or she is linked to another dialog box that provides several FAQs (Frequently Asked Questions) or he or she is provided with an empty dialog box in which to write a message.

Flying blind with e-mail

An agent's response to an e-mail is a monologue. The interactive process of listening, assessing, and adjusting to the customer is gone.

In a phone conversation, the customer can repeat herself and ask questions to make sure that the agent understands. E-mails offer no such luxury. As such, the e-mail can easily be misinterpreted by the agent, who then sends out an inappropriate response.

Getting background information

In a phone conversation, asking clarifying questions and understanding the background circumstances (whatever they may be) that led to the current situation is easy. When you receive an e-mail message from a customer, however, it's too late to ask him (politely) what he is talking about. Customers often don't include enough, if any, background information in an e-mail.

All of us, in our role as consumers, become so familiar with our service problems that we forget the rest of the world hasn't been sharing our plight. Therefore, we don't even think about attaching relevant documents. Shooting off an e-mail to the copy machine company that reads just "Help! The machine's broken again" is easy — but the message is completely baffling to the person on the other end.

Contacting the customer and asking for more specific information will no doubt be necessary. If the matter is urgent, a phone call may be more appropriate than another e-mail. Be careful not to express any outward signs of frustration towards the customer.

Monitoring quality

"This call may be monitored for quality control purposes" is a phrase that most of us have heard while waiting for a response to our telephone inquiry. Supervisors often listen in on agents talking to customers so that they can monitor call quality and provide pertinent and timely coaching to their agents.

E-mail, however, is not as easy to monitor. Many centers measure e-mail performance by the number of responses generated. Needless to say, in such an environment it's sometimes easy for an e-mail to be sent without an agent paying proper attention to the tone or to a customer's specific needs. Usually, an inadequate response leads to the customer being dissatisfied and sending another e-mail.

To help minimize inappropriate e-mail responses and to maintain message quality, many call centers employ editors to randomly monitor e-mails prior to them being sent to customers.

Having a Great Call Center Staff

The most fundamental and important assets in any call center are the people who work in them. Yet, many managers hang on to the outdated idea that the call center provides employees with little more than a stepping stone for moving on to a better job. Since call center agents are the initial (and often the sole) point of customer contact, you have to value them accordingly. Call center expert Brad Cleveland notes, "We have to stop viewing call center staff as entry-level positions. The call center is the eyes and ears of a company and the staff are the people who are key to us learning about the customers and ways we can be responsive to their needs."

As companies attempt to reduce the high cost of a live conversation by providing online self-service customer support, their Web sites provide more and more product- and service-related information. Call centers are finding that customers who have attempted to access answers via the Web are, as a side effect, more knowledgeable. As a result they tend to ask more sophisticated and complex questions than are asked by those customers who haven't attempted to serve themselves by using information from the Web.

This new breed of knowledgeable customer requires call center agents with in-depth product experience and the commitment needed to resolve issues that are outside the scope of online help. Call center managers who fall victim to the historically high employee turnover rates common in the industry (anywhere between 25 and 35 percent per year) are continually losing agents who have the well-rounded skills needed in a multi-channel call center environment.

A call center manager with a commitment to service excellence *must* have good employees. We've found that those who attract and retain dedicated service agents do so by following these guidelines:

- They hire people with the right attitude.
- They keep the work interesting.
- They define and communicate expected service levels.

> ✔ They set goals and then monitor and coach.
>
> ✔ They provide the right systems and tools.
>
> ✔ They reward and recognize excellent service.

Hiring people with the right attitude

Although considering the job skills of a potential employee is always important, especially when staffing a multi-channel call center, it's ultimately the *attitude* of the individual that determines his or her worth as an effective team member.

Jean Bave-Kerwin (jbaveker@nycap.rr.com), founding President of the Call Center Management Association of New York State and manager of six large government agency centers, confirms the importance of attitude, stating, "High retention and morale is mostly about the attitude of your employees, and that starts before they put a headset on. I've found that it is easier to hire the attitude and be willing to train the rest — rather than vice versa, which is much more difficult. You must hire people that want to help people or your staff will share their misery with coworkers and customers alike."

A call center service agent with a friendly attitude and a genuine desire to help others is the best candidate for presenting a positive company image to your customers. Retaining these key staff members is important because the longer they work for you, the more familiar they become with the goods or services your company offers and the better they can relate this information to your customers. This familiarity translates into a perception, by the customer, that your company cares.

Keeping the work interesting

Look for ways of developing your staff's skills. Too often, we see managers developing staff members for a subsequent position (which is part of the old entry-level perception that some managers still cling to) rather than expanding their skills within the call center. Call center skills *can* be worked on. For example, certain staff members may be eager to improve their writing skills for working with online service requests and others may flourish by developing their analytical skills and working with forecasting, queue analysis, staffing, and so on.

The goal is to find outgoing, empathetic people to staff your call center and then to retain them. By presenting professional development opportunities within your call center, you offer your staff new challenges to keep their work interesting. You want to staff your call center with the most highly motivated, service-oriented agents you can find (or develop!).

Defining and communicating service levels

When coaching staff members about the qualities that are vital to creating a positive customer experience, the service manager's job is to inspire their understanding of why service levels are important. Most people, we have found, are inspired more by values than by tasks. It is incumbent upon managers to continually reinforce service values and to link them to specific skills and job functions. Here is a simple and effective process for reinforcing, say, courtesy, as a service value:

1. **Begin by meeting with your staff (or as many of them as you can take off-line at one time) and ask them to give you some real life examples of times when, as a customer, they have been treated with courtesy. Ask them to give you the specific details.**

2. **Next, ask them to think about times when they have been treated with a lack of courtesy. Ask them to share examples.**

3. **Ask your group what the differences were between the positive experiences and the negative experiences.**

4. **Ask them how, in their job, the customer may be judging the level of courtesy. For example, on a phone call the customer's impressions are formed by how they're greeted. In an e-mail the salutation may be key, and so on.**

5. **Ask them what specific actions they could take that would help ensure that the customer has a positive experience. For example, always offering a friendly "Good morning/afternoon, how may I help you" on the phone or thanking people in an e-mail for their initial enquiry.**

   This step is crucial, as you should end up with a list of specific steps that call center employees can take to enhance service. These are your specific service values.

6. **Recap by explaining why this value is important and how it applies to each of their particular jobs.**

This easy process is great for getting staff involved and interested in a service value. It is powerful because it begins with the value and works down to the specific tactic or action. This is a natural flow and helps prevent the "just another thing to do" response often associated with tactics.

Setting goals, monitoring, and coaching

Use the specific service values from the process above to develop measurable goals for each of your staff. Link these goals to the employee's performance review. Remember that goals will vary depending on each employee's strengths and weaknesses. Jean Bave-Kerwin explains it this way, "It's not about looking for something they do wrong, but coaching them to be the best that they can be. Also, when it comes to how much time each agent should spend with each customer interaction, I have found it more effective to manage this area rather than measure it." In other words, don't give your staff concrete length-of-encounter standards but coach them to stay within generally defined limits, as long as they don't sacrifice courtesy.

The maturity of phone technology makes it easy to monitor real staff interactions with customers. E-mail monitoring technology, being a newer need, is less readily available in most call centers. Using a manual approach, by randomly monitoring e-mail responses is often necessary.

Providing the right systems and tools

Your staff will become frustrated if poorly applied technology makes serving their customers difficult. Make sure, for example, that agents do not have to waste the customer's time by having to access two separate databases when answering a billing inquiry. Regardless of how professional your agents may be, their mood can be negatively affected if they can't prevent customers from getting slow service.

Robert Gray, Vice President of Client Services for ADP (www.csg.adp.com) and manager of over 300 call center staff, has many years of experience integrating multimedia contact points within several call centers. To him, the biggest pitfall is working on each channel separately. "All the new e-mail and Web technology must be integrated with traditional call center channels or there will be inconsistent service. If technologies are not tied together, the information is different on each channel."

Help desk staff must all have access to the same solutions database whether Web-based or IVR (Interactive Voice Response). Let's say a customer calls for help with a GPF error — everyone who uses Windows has received one of these at one time or another! The customer calls in and a tech walks the customer through the solution by accessing the database — but if the solutions database that the tech uses is different from the solutions database available on your Web site, there could be big inconsistency in answers. And this could greatly diminish your ability to effectively resolve the problem. You must have consistency so that all customers get accurate information and the same response regardless of the channel through which they seek a solution.

Rewarding and recognizing

Commensurate with the new agent skill requirements are new agent wage levels. While pay is only part of the retention equation, it does convey a message about how a company regards the importance and worth of call center staff. The two graphs in Figure 6-1 are taken from the Agent Staffing and Retention Study published in the Spring 2000 issue of the *Call Center Management Review* (www.ccmreview.com), an industry newsletter published by the Incoming Call Management Institute (www.incomimg.com). The first graph shows the different types of incentives utilized by call centers and the second graph shows the average hourly wage of entry-level agents and of the top-paid agents. These two graphs reflect the large increase in agents' compensation that has taken place over the past two years.

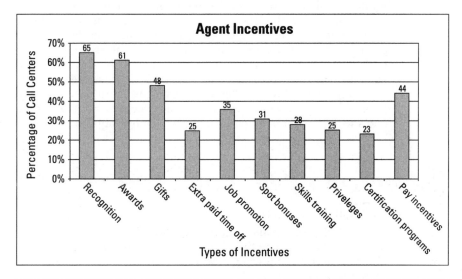

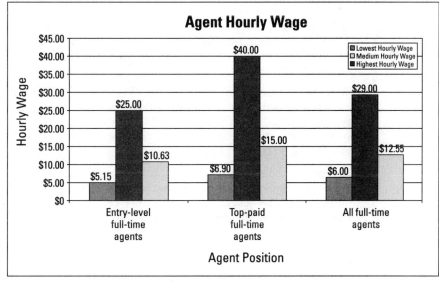

Figure 6-1: Call center reward and recognition graphs.

Paying agents wages that reflect the importance of their job is the first step in rewarding and recognizing your staff. The next step is to reward and recognize your staff for providing exceptional service. Regardless of which incentives you choose, the secret of acknowledging staff is to make it sincere. A heartfelt "thank you" is rarer and worth more than cash to most employees. "Develop a culture of gratitude," advises Jean Bave-Kerwin, "where staff thank each other for help and support." This spirit of cooperation and affection in turn gets passed on to the customers.

Another form of recognition is empowering your staff to take initiative and do what it takes — within specified limits — to keep customers coming back. For example, if a call center agent working with catalogue sales has an unhappy customer, that agent should be empowered to take the necessary actions that will make things right from the customer's point of view. Nobody but the agent who's involved knows what's needed to please the customer, so empowering that agent makes sense. Give her more control over her interactions — be it waiving a charge or making exceptions to the normal process — and she'll give you happy customers while enjoying her own job more.

Outsourcing Your Call Center

For some businesses, outsourcing provides a viable option to an in-house call center, saving set-up and training expenses. However, outsourcing your call center is an alternative that doesn't work for every company. We provide a checklist here to help you gauge how compatible outsourcing may be with your business.

- **Are you doing this just as a way of avoiding an expense?** If your motivation is to offload a problem, think again. Outsourcing a call center requires planning, having a defined service strategy, and ongoing management.

- **What is the purpose of outsourcing?** Will the outsourcer take *all* calls, overflow calls from an in-house center, or specific calls that require less technical knowledge than other calls? For example, a catalogue computer sales company might outsource sales calls but answer more difficult technical support inquiries in-house.

- **Do you have defined service levels for the outsourcer?** For example, you may decide that having 80 percent of the calls answered within 30 seconds is an acceptable level of service. Do you know how long your customers are willing to wait for an e-mail response or hold in a telephone queue?

✔ **After you've chosen a vendor, are you willing to manage the relationship and define incentives and disincentives?** An incentive may be paying the outsourcing center two cents more per call for any hour, day, or week that service levels are exceeded. The same amount is deducted, per call, as a penalty when service levels are not met.

✔ **Are you willing to review call center reports?** Reviewing service levels and complaint logs is a valuable part of call center activity, and not one that you want to lose in an outsourcing arrangement.

✔ **Do you have specific quality standards?** Vendors need to adhere to these standards, let you listen directly to calls for at least thirty minutes every week, and coach them as needed.

✔ **Is the outsourcer conveniently located?** Physical proximity is an advantage for monitoring calls and maintaining a close and continuing relationship.

✔ **Is the vendor experienced in what you are outsourcing?** Remember that part of what you're buying is the vendor's experience in your field, be it catalogue sales, healthcare services, financial advice, and so on.

Chapter 7

Reinventing Your IT Department

*1*t's crucial that your IT department exemplifies your company's commitment to quality customer service in its policies, procedures, and overall mentality. The way in which your IT department functions within your company relates directly to how your company relates to its outside customers.

All the departments of your company use technology and, therefore, need the services of IT. IT comes to the rescue when your PC suddenly refuses to talk to your printer, when you're confused by a new piece of software, or when you need help to recover every e-mail that you just deleted in error (perish the thought!). Even though technology touches all of our jobs, we still find some of the old "us and them" attitude in many companies. *Us* meaning normal folks. *Them* meaning the people who actually — gasp — like and understand computers.

Too often, companies that have even a hint of the "us and them" attitude are tempted to leave IT behind as the rest of the company becomes more customer centric. But IT needs to change too. In fact, we've worked with several Information Technology managers, helping them reinvent their departments to be more customer centric in line with their companies new, customer-centered culture.

We've discovered that much of the "us and them" divide comes from a lack of communication. It's not unusual to find the IT department being used as a scapegoat for anything that goes wrong with a company's network, e-mail, or the technology infrastructure in general — regardless of the real cause of the problem. Regrettably, finger pointing takes the place of collaboration. The various sides retreat to their corners and wait for the next breakdown.

The other driver behind the "us and them" gap has to be blamed on IT staff members. They're so close to the functional aspects of their work that they don't see — or aren't educated about — the big picture. They don't understand service delivery or the part they play in customer service. Too few companies, in our opinion, understand that the quality of service that the external, paying customer receives is proportional to the quality of service that internal customers, the staff within the company, provide to one another.

Each department of your company is a link in the service delivery chain. The service that your company provides is only as good as the weakest link in that chain. For example, your sales department employees may be top-notch. They care about the customer and prioritize customer service. But if their computers are down or they don't know how to use certain applications — because IT dropped the ball — the customer ultimately suffers. As your customer service becomes more and more reliant on using technology, your IT department becomes an even more important link in the service chain.

Reinvent your IT department so that it positively affects every link in your service delivery chain. The three basic steps in doing so are

- ✔ Evaluating the current state of your IT department through an internal survey

- ✔ Developing a mission statement and service standards to define your service goals

- ✔ Creating internal partnerships to facilitate the transition to excellent service

Knowing Where You Are — Surveying Your Internal Customers

The first step involved in reinventing your IT department is to figure out how good it is *right now*. The customers of your IT department are the folks in your company that IT serves. If yours is a relatively small company, informal conversations between IT and department heads may be sufficient to gather the necessary feedback. If your company is larger, we recommend a written survey. (We usually do the survey via e-mail, because an electronic survey is faster and cheaper than a paper survey.) A survey helps ensure that the questions IT asks are consistent and often captures important feedback that may be difficult for some respondents to deliver in a one-on-one conversation.

Designing an IT customer questionnaire

Many factors affect how you design your questionnaire: the nature of your business, what you're interested in finding out, the role that IT plays within your company, and many more. Even though every company's survey should be different, we've found that designing a questionnaire is easier if you have a model to follow. You can use the template in this section as a guide for designing your own survey. We've divided the survey into five sections for clarity — however, feel free to chop and change at will.

In order to get the most comprehensive, meaningful feedback possible, be sure that your questionnaire includes the following elements:

- **Introductory Message.** The introduction states the purpose of the questionnaire, underlines the need for personal feedback, gives contact information in case a recipient has questions, and provides a personal introduction from the individual heading up the survey.

- **Section 1: General Profile.** This provides an overview of your IT department's internal customers (in other words, most of your staff) and identifies the internal customers' level of comfort and ability with computers and software.

- **Section 2: Overall Support and Service.** This section focuses on the opinions that your employees have about your IT department, including how they feel about issues related to responsiveness and follow up.

- **Section 3: Computer Training and Education.** This section identifies the degree to which internal customers feel that they are being provided with the frequency and type of training they need in order to use their hardware and software effectively.

- **Section 4: Communication.** This section assesses the current state of communication between your IT department and its internal customers, as well as the methods of communication these customers prefer.

- **Section 5: Technology.** This section looks at the way the IT department manages existing technology throughout your company.

As you read over the sample questionnaire that we include in this section, let your creative juices flow. Delete, add, or change anything as you make the survey appropriate to your circumstances.

Sample introductory message

Dear _____:

As part of our efforts to ensure that the IT department of XYZ Company is providing you with the quality of service you deserve, we are conducting a survey of our internal customers. The feedback will be used to strengthen the quality of service you receive from IT.

The following customer questionnaire takes about 10 minutes to complete. We are interested in your personal opinion, so please be frank. The report that will be prepared from the findings will be general in nature, tracking trends rather than focusing in on who said what.

> If you have any questions, please give me a call. I appreciate your assistance in this process and look forward to your valued input.
>
> Sincerely,
>
> (Name)
> IT Manager

The friendly, helpful tone of this letter goes a long way toward making survey participants really feel that they have an interest in the outcome of the survey. The letter convinces staff members that they're making a contribution to their company's efforts to improve overall service quality.

Section 1: General profile

Include the questions below to get a sense of how comfortable your staff is with using technology in the workplace. The general profile section of your survey may look like the following:

> So that we may have a better understanding of our internal customers, the IT department would appreciate your answering the following questions:

> 1. What position do you hold at XYZ Company? Please check one:
>
>   ___ Partner
>
>   ___ Management
>
>   ___ Staff
>
> 2. What department do you work in? _____
>
> 3. How long have you worked at XYZ Company? _____
>
> 4. How long have you used a computer? _____
>
> 5. Do you use a computer at home?
>
>   ___ Yes
>
>   ___ No
>
>   If yes, what type do you use? _____
>
> 6. What programs do you use on your XYZ Company PC? Please check all that apply:
>
>   ___ Notes E-mail
>
>   ___ Windows 95
>
>   ___ Excel
>
>   ___ Internet Explorer
>
>   ___ Netscape Navigator
>
>   ___ PowerPoint

___ Calendar Program (which one?) _____

___ Word

___ Other _____

7. For each program that you use, please rate your expertise on a scale from one to six (1 = novice, 6 = expert):

___ Notes E-mail

___ Windows 95

___ Excel

___ Internet Explorer

___ PowerPoint

___ Calendar Program (which one?) _____

___ Word

___ Netscape

___ Other _____

8. What are the main services that you expect the IT Department to provide to you?

_____

Section 2: Overall support and service

By asking the questions in this section (or some variation of them) you can gain key insight into how IT's internal customers perceive the department's effectiveness. Negative feedback that comes up in response to these questions may or may not be justified. However, if your staff perceives that there's a problem, that perception itself is a problem and you need to take action. And the positive feedback that you get in response to these questions provides you with an opportunity to pass along kudos to your IT department for a job well done!

Section 2 of your survey may look something like the following:

In thinking about the service you have received from XYZ Company's IT Department in the past six months, please answer the following:

1. How do you rate the overall service you receive from the IT Department?

___ Excellent

___ Good

___ Fair

___ Poor

2. How do you rate the IT Department's level of responsiveness to your problems and questions?

___ Excellent

___ Good

___ Fair

___ Poor

3. How do you rate the IT Department's ability to solve your problems?

___ Excellent

___ Good

___ Fair

___ Poor

4. How do you rate the IT Department in terms of providing you with a timely resolution to your problem?

___ Excellent

___ Good

___ Fair

___ Poor

5. How do you rate the IT Department at following up on issues that are not resolved on first contact?

___ Excellent

___ Good

___ Fair

___ Poor

6. How do you rate the IT Department's level of communication with you regarding the status of issues that are unresolved?

___ Excellent

___ Good

___ Fair

___ Poor

7. Approximately how often do you call upon the IT Department for help? Please check one:

___ Once a day

___ Once a week

___ Once a month

___ Once every six months

___ Once a year

___ Never

8. When you call the IT Department for help, within what time frame does it usually get back to you? Please check one:

___ Within one hour

___ Within a few hours

___ Within one day

___ Within a few days

___ Within one week

___ Within a few weeks

9. What could the IT Department do to add additional value to the service it is currently offering you?

_____

Section 3: Computer training and education

The information you get from responses to the questions in this section can guide your IT department as it develops training schedules and strategies to empower your staff members to utilize the technology available to them to achieve optimal results and efficiency. It can also provide area managers with some ideas about special training needs for their staff members. This section of your survey may look something like this:

In thinking about the training you have received on your computer/software in the past year, please answer the following:

1. I have received the following types of training at XYZ Company on my computer and software applications. Please check all that apply:

___ PC tutorial

___ Online help

___ Peer/coworker trained

___ Outside training class

___ IT training one-on-one or classroom

___ One-on-one training with an outside resource

___ Training by a friend or family member

___ Training manual

2. Please check the top three methods you prefer for learning how to best use your computer and software applications. Please check three only:

    ___ PC tutorial

    ___ Online help

    ___ Peer/coworker trained

    ___ Outside training class

    ___ IT training one-on-one or classroom

    ___ One-on-one training with an outside resource

    ___ Training by a friend or family member

    ___ Training manual

3. How often do you receive formal training on your computer and/or software applications? Please check one:

    ___ Monthly

    ___ Quarterly

    ___ Yearly

    ___ Never

4. When the IT Department installs new hardware/software, how soon do you receive training on how to use it? Please check one:

    ___ Before installation

    ___ Within the first week of installation

    ___ Within the first month of installation

    ___ Within the first three months of installation

    ___ Never

    ___ Other (please specify) _____

5. When would you prefer to receive training on new hardware/software installed by the IT Department? Please check one:

    ___ Before installation

    ___ Within the first week of installation

    ___ Within the first month of installation

    ___ Within the first three months of installation

    ___ Never

    ___ Other (please specify) _____

6. Who initiates the request for training on your hardware/software? Please check one:

___ I do

___ My manager does

___ The IT Department does

___ Other (please specify) _____

7. How supportive is your immediate manager in your taking time to receive hardware/software training? Please check one:

___ Very supportive

___ Moderately supportive

___ Not very supportive

___ Objects to my taking time for training

8. How supportive would you be of receiving regular required computer and software training? Please check one:

___ Very supportive

___ Moderately supportive

___ Not very supportive

___ Object to training being required

9. How would you rate your current need for more computer and software training? Please check one:

___ Very high

___ High

___ Moderate

___ Low

10. What overall role do you see the IT Department playing in providing you with future training on your computer and software?

_____

Section 4: Communication

Responses to the questions in this section can facilitate a dialogue between your IT department and everyone who depends on its support. Effective internal communications are vital to establishing the company-wide service attitude essential to achieving your service goals. Section 4 of your questionnaire may look like the following:

So that we may have a better understanding of how to communicate with you effectively, please answer the following questions:

1. Please check the top three methods you would prefer the IT Department to use in communicating information to you. Please check three only:

   ___ E-mail

   ___ Internal Web site

   ___ Written memos

   ___ Company brief

   ___ Face-to-face meetings

   ___ Telephone

2. Please check the top three methods you would prefer to use when communicating with the IT Department. Please check three only:

   ___ Suggestion box

   ___ E-mail

   ___ Internal Web site

   ___ Written memos

   ___ Company brief

   ___ Face-to-face meetings

   ___ Telephone

3. How do you rate the IT Department's effectiveness at informing you prior to the installation of new hardware and software that affects your job? Please check one:

   ___ Excellent

   ___ Good

   ___ Fair

   ___ Poor

4. How does most of your communication with IT staff members take place? Please check one:

   ___ Telephone

   ___ E-mail

   ___ Face to face

   ___ Other (please specify) _____

5. How useful would it be for you to spend more face-to-face time with an IT staff member? Please check one:

___ Very useful

___ Moderately useful

___ Somewhat useful

___ Not very useful

6. What could the IT Department do to enhance and improve the quality of its communication with you?

Section 5: Technology

Responses to the questions in this section can help your IT department identify areas where it can improve the quality of the service it provides to your staff. Such information is invaluable to your IT department in its contribution to the overall service orientation of your company. Section 5 of your questionnaire may resemble the following:

So that we may better serve your technology needs, both now and in the future, please rate the following:

1. How do you rate the IT Department's effectiveness at providing you with technology that meets your current business requirements? Please check one:

___ Excellent

___ Good

___ Fair

___ Poor

2. How do you rate the IT Department's effectiveness at soliciting your feedback before it decides on what new technology to implement? Please check one:

___ Excellent

___ Good

___ Fair

___ Poor

3. How do you rate the IT Department's effectiveness at researching the specifics of your job so that it is able to work with you in planning your future technological needs? Please check one:

___ Excellent

___ Good

___ Fair

___ Poor

4. Do you currently have Internet access on your computer? Please check one:

___ Yes

___ No

5. How do you use the Internet in your daily job?

   _____

6. How do you rate the senior management at supporting the stated goal of having XYZ Company be "on the leading edge of technology?" Please check one:

___ Excellent

___ Good

___ Fair

___ Poor

7. What other technology (hardware, software, or other) is needed to make you more effective and productive at doing your job?

   _____

Reporting the survey results

After you've gathered the results of the survey, compile the key points in an executive summary. Like the survey itself, the report on your findings should include information from each of the survey sections. Use the format that follows to get ideas for creating your own survey report.

Calculate your response rate by dividing the number of returned, completed surveys by the number sent out. Use the following guidelines to assess the response rate:

- ✓ 0 to 20 percent: Low
- ✓ 21 to 50 percent: Average
- ✓ 51 to 70 percent: High
- ✓ 71 to 100 percent: Very High

Report introduction

Use the introduction to your report to explain how the survey was conducted, who participated, and any other information that you feel may help readers to understand the significance of the survey. Your introduction may look something like this:

> The results of this survey were gathered from e-mail questionnaires that were sent to all executives, managers, and staff.

> Participation in the e-mail survey was very high. One hundred and eighty-two surveys were sent, one hundred and thirty-six were returned, for a return rate of 75 percent.

Section 1: General profile

Presenting your findings through percentages makes it easy for anyone reading your report to understand the information in terms of your company's big picture. Be sure to include feedback for all of the questions in the survey, as in the following:

> Majority of responses showed that the typical IT Department customer has worked at XYZ Company for an average of ___ years; is computer literate, with ___ percent using a computer at home as well as at work. Majority of respondents use a PC (___ percent) over a Mac (___ percent).

> Questionnaire results indicate that the majority of the IT Department's customers are basic (intermediate/advanced) users, who are somewhat (very) familiar with those programs they need to use daily in order to get their jobs done (Notes, Windows 95, Excel, etc.). Additionally, when asked to rate their expertise on a scale of one (novice) to six (expert) on a series of software programs, the average individual rated themselves as a number ___.

> When asked, "What are the main services you expect the IT Department to provide to you?" the respondents highlighted training and problem solving as key expectations.

Section 2: Overall support and service

Try to report your findings in a positive way. Even if you are presenting a problem, be careful that the tone of your report does not sound accusatory. In the spirit of your company-wide improvement effort, keep your report upbeat, while at the same time giving an accurate account of affairs. Use the following paragraph as an example. (You can substitute the italicized words to suit your own report. For example, change *excellent* to *fair.*)

> *87 percent* of those surveyed rated the IT department as *excellent* at responsiveness to problems and questions. *7 percent* stated that they *get* a call back from the IT Department within *24 hours* of calling.

Where there is *room for improvement* is in the IT department's follow-up. *21 percent* rated the IT Department *good* in terms of follow-up on problems not resolved on first contact and *13 percent* rated it *good* at communicating the status of those unresolved problems.

Section 3: Computer training and education

The feedback you present in the training and education section can be especially helpful for highlighting the need for new training initiatives to empower your staff to meet the challenge of your company's new service goals. The section can also give you feedback that allows you to praise your IT staff members for the wonderful work they're already doing! Use the following as a model. (Again, you can substitute the italicized words to suit your own findings).

Of all the sections highlighted in this report, the area of *training* is by far the *strongest* and the one having the most *positive* impact on the use of technology within XYZ Company. *Praise* about *training* highlighted that the *frequency* of training and the methods used for delivery *do* currently meet the needs of the IT department's customers. *57 percent* of respondents said they receive training *quarterly* while *8 percent* said they have never received any computer training.

13 percent of those surveyed have learned how to use their computer and software through training manuals. However, *74 percent* of those surveyed say they prefer to learn through one-on-one training.

When asked, "What overall role do you see the IT Department playing in providing you with future training on your computer and software?" the response across the board was a desire to see the IT Department take a leadership role in initiating, implementing, and managing a company-wide training program.

Section 4: Communication

Even when you find that you have to report some bad news, try to do so in a positive way and clearly explain the issues, as in the following example:

Communication was the weakest area highlighted in the survey. Two clear problems emerged that are having a negative impact on the IT department's communication within the company.

By far the biggest issue was a lack of follow-through regarding the *status of jobs*. The IT Department, while good at initially responding to customer problems that can be resolved quickly, is not seen as effective at addressing problems that are ongoing or take longer to resolve. This problem is compounded by a lack of keeping its customers in the communication loop on problems that are ongoing.

When asked, "What could the IT Department do to enhance and improve the quality of its communication with you?" respondents expressed a clear desire for a more proactive stance from the IT Department.

Section 5: Technology

As in the preceding sections, try to present your findings as thoroughly as possible. Throwing in some anonymous responses, as in the case below, doesn't hurt.

> Although there are a *few isolated* throughout XYZ Company where *hardware is* an issue, in general *hardware is not* a problem with the IT Department's customers. *61 percent* of those surveyed rated the IT Department *good* at providing technology that meets current business needs.
>
> When asked, "What other *technology* is needed to make you more effective at doing your job?" a significant number of respondents left this question blank! One staff member who did respond hit the nail on the head by writing, "I'm not sure because I don't really know what is available unless I do the research myself."

Conclusions and recommendations

The conclusions and recommendations section of your report could look like the following.

> Today, the IT Department at XYZ Company is functioning as a competent technical support department. The members of the department have sound technical skills and do a good job at being responsive to their customers, when contacted.
>
> Based on the survey results, the IT Department needs to make a transition from being a reactive technical support department to a proactive technology leader with XYZ Company.
>
> Here are some specific recommendations to help this transition take place:
>
> - Hold an off-site meeting for the IT Department. The purpose of this meeting is for the staff and managers of the IT Department to address the issues highlighted in this report and design an overall plan for improvement. Specifics of the off-site should include: a revision of the department's mission statement, creating long term goals for customer satisfaction, and creating short term goals for immediate service improvement.
>
> - Set up listen-and-learn sessions between IT staff members and their customers for the purpose of gathering feedback on the individual needs of each department and how IT can help empower the staff to be more efficient and effective at their jobs. Evaluate staffing levels in IT based on this feedback.
>
> - Develop a certification program on a defined list of software programs to be completed by all staff and managers as a part of their job evaluations.

- Get all staff and managers up and running on the Internet. Include training on how to best utilize this tool for business.

- Create an ongoing and regular IT e-mail update that focuses on upcoming projects, training success stories, future plans, training options, and so on.

- Implement a *bounce back* card system. Every time an IT staff member works with a customer, a card is generated allowing the customer to confidentially evaluate the IT staff member's performance. This feedback should be made part of the IT performance evaluation process, as well as a significant part of any reward and recognition program.

- Implement an internal public relations and marketing campaign aimed at promoting the IT Department's mission, goals, and capabilities to the rest of XYZ Company.

After the report is written, it should be circulated to all IT staff and managers. We recommend setting up meetings between IT and managers so that IT can discuss the report, answer questions, and begin the process of resolving any other issues.

Avoid the temptation to make quick fixes. Applying bandages usually ends up costing more in resources and credibility than a well thought-out solution costs to be implemented.

Developing a Mission Statement and Creating Service Standards

For many IT managers, the next step after getting feedback from internal customers is creating and prioritizing an action list that addresses the key findings of the survey.

However, prior to setting goals and the assigning the accompanying responsibilities and timelines, we recommend revisiting your IT mission statement or, if the department doesn't have one, creating one for your department.

Developing an IT mission statement

A mission statement serves several purposes: It declares the overall purpose of your IT department, underlines the values that your IT department stands for, and provides a framework within which all of the department's goals should fit. Developing a new mission statement — or revising an existing one — is a process of dialogue and consensus building.

The IT mission statement should create a bigger picture than the normal day-to-day activities and deadlines. It should enhance every individual's understanding of the part he or she plays in making your organization more customer centric.

If you'd like a blow-by-blow method for creating a mission statement, look at *Customer Service For Dummies,* Chapter 14.

Here are two examples of an IT mission statement:

- ✔ **Mission Statement #1.** The mission of the IT department is to provide quality customer service through understanding XYZ Company's business and providing technological leadership.

- ✔ **Mission Statement #2.** To enhance XYZ Company's competitive edge and overall services to both internal and external clients by providing:

  - Timely and easy access to data

  - Savings in time and costs across departments

  - Approaches that are open to new technologies

Communicating your IT mission statement

As important as the development of your IT department's mission statement is, letting the other parts of your organization know about the new mission statement is even more crucial. By communicating the IT department's values and intent, you begin the process of change. Your commitment, once declared company-wide, becomes a public promise which everyone then expects you to live up to. By spreading the word about the mission statement, you create a good motivator for keeping the mission alive.

Several methods work well for communicating your mission statement:

- ✔ Company newsletters
- ✔ Staff meetings
- ✔ E-mail

Whatever method or combination of methods you choose, be sure to include the bottom-line benefits that your internal customers can expect as a result of the IT department's renewed focus and direction. The quality of service that your customers receive is directly related to the quality of service that internal departments provide to one another. The benefits of improving internal service are passed on to external customers by improved procedures, better systems, and a team approach to service delivery.

Setting service standards

After the mission statement is created — or remodeled, whatever the case may be — the next step is to develop standards that are consistent with the mission statement.

Standards are sometimes confused with goals, but the two things are actually very different. Standards state *what your customers can count on.* Goals state what your company *will attempt to accomplish.* For example, a worthwhile goal for any organization is

100 percent customer satisfaction

To strive for anything less would be self-defeating. However, this does not mean that your organization *promises* 100 percent customer satisfaction. To do so would be creating an expectation impossible to live up to.

A service standard, on the other hand, can be *promised.* You could have a standard like:

IT will respond to technical assistance calls within 4 business hours

There is no reason why, with everyone working as a team, this standard should not be kept 100 percent of the time.

Standards are important, not only because they allow you to attach hard numbers to your service delivery process, but also because you can use them to measure your IT staff's performance and link performance to employee evaluations.

Creating staff incentive

The performance appraisal of every individual within the IT department must include customer service metrics. Hard measurements, together with compensation, go a long way toward inculcating customer service as a core principal of your IT department.

Bounceback surveys

Bounceback surveys are usually e-mails sent to every customer when a job is completed. A few brief questions usually supply all the information you need to assess performance.

Evaluating the service performance of each employee requires that you set up a simple and effective feedback mechanism that allows each customer to rate the IT staff member's performance. Use the following sample questions to help you get started in developing your own IT bounceback survey:

Did your software developer:

1. Satisfy your requirements?

___ Yes

___ No (If not, please tell us why: _____)

2. Complete the job on time?

___ Yes

___ No

3. Keep informed of any changes or updates?

___ Yes

___ No

4. How satisfied were you with the overall level of service you received?

(not satisfied)   1   2   3   4   5   6   (very satisfied)

5. Were the original requirements changed once the project was started?

___ Yes

___ No

Given the tendency of IT projects to grow and change once the process has started, be sure to include in your surveys and follow-up conversations questions that help clarify the reason a job was not completed on time. Penalizing an employee if the project underwent massive changes that were unseen, and therefore unplanned, when the work commenced is unfair.

Did your software developer:

1. Respond to your request within 4 hours?

___ Yes

___ No

2. Treat you with courtesy?

___ Yes

___ No

3. Complete the job in the time estimated?

___ Yes

___ No

4. How satisfied were you with the overall level of service you received?

(not satisfied)   1   2   3   4   5   6   (very satisfied)

5. Were the original requirements changed once the project was started?

___ Yes

___ No

6. Other comments:

_____

Creating Internal Partnerships

After you have established specific service goals and have devised a method for measuring your staff's service delivery, the time has come for you to create partnerships between your IT department and other departments. Partnering is important so that IT's not working in a vacuum or, worse yet, being used as the sacrificial lamb for projects that go awry — regardless of the cause. Two key strategies will help you create internal partnerships:

✔ Establishing a technology advisory group

✔ Setting up project teams

Establishing a technology advisory group

A technology advisory group (TAG) is comprised of representatives from each of your company's business units and representatives from the IT department. The team should meet once a quarter (or whatever works best for your situation) to update, discuss, select, and prioritize all major IT projects that relate to the day-to-day operations of your business.

Recognizing the benefits of TAG teams

The TAG team's main purpose is to receive and review proposals from the various business units for business process improvements. By passing through a team of cross-department peers, any proposal that is given a go-ahead has the approval of a team and not just one person. Also, any problems or unforeseen roadblocks in the implementation process are brought back to the TAG team for review and for recommendations toward resolution. This team involvement relieves IT of being in the unenviable position of making unilateral and unpopular project decisions.

Another benefit of TAG teams is the valuable integration that occurs when representatives from various departments work together. Whereas a pre-TAG project may have been stalled or delayed because of an unconvinced business unit manager, with a TAG system in place, that business unit now has a voting representative on the TAG team.

Selecting TAG team members

Decide the time and resource commitments required of a TAG team member prior to member selection. We have found that quarterly meetings work well for most companies. Remember that there also may be some extra preparation time required for miscellaneous research or for reading pertinent materials.

Once the "job description" has been finalized, schedule a department head orientation. Because of the difficulties involved with getting everybody together in the same place at the same time, we find that one-on-one conversations work well in helping managers understand the process and answering their questions. Ask the managers to select the best-suited TAG team representative from their department.

Be sure that all members are happy about being on the team. Do not accept team members who are upset or are inconvenienced by their participation on your TAG team. Although they may have been selected because of their many merits, a bad attitude doesn't help build camaraderie

Setting up project teams

For any project that is considered major, say, that will take more than two months to complete (the definition of "major" will vary depending on your company), we recommend that you set up a *project team*. A project team is a partnership between the following three people:

- The IT project manager
- The business sponsor — usually the head of the business group needing the technology work
- A business project manager — committed by the business sponsor and responsible for regularly meeting with the IT project manager

The project team streamlines the communications between IT and its customers; shortening the time it takes for IT to understand, design, and deliver the required services.

Prior to any design or development activities, the IT project manager should meet with the business partner and clarify the project's deliverables. We have the project manager write a letter of understanding that serves as a proposal/contract. It clearly states the specific measurable outcomes and expectations of the project. Work begins once the business partner has signed off on the letter. The business partner and project manager should meet at least once a week and discuss progress, roadblocks, and updates to the project.

Areas to consider when drafting a letter of understanding include

- ✔ How the project will be organized
- ✔ How the implementation plan will be communicated
- ✔ How the existing working processes of the business unit will be reviewed by IT
- ✔ The economic impact of the project
- ✔ The operational impact of the project
- ✔ Platform definition
- ✔ Product selection
- ✔ Vendor identification
- ✔ Proposal solicitation
- ✔ Infrastructure and programming costs
- ✔ Training and support costs
- ✔ Timing and deadlines
- ✔ Fees

In order to understand customer needs, IT project managers must understand the nature of the business they are delivering to and be able to speak in the language of that business. Some of the best IT project managers are former IT customers. Savvy IT managers hire project managers with people skills and project management skills — not just technology skills.

In our experience, most IT departments can greatly enhance their level of customer service by looking for ways to connect with other departments and by remembering that technology is never an end in itself; it is always a means for delivering information faster and easier. This improvement in delivering information, in turn, supports customer service.

Part III
Web Wise and Customer Friendly

The 5th Wave   By Rich Tennant

"Just how accurately should my Web site reflect my place of business?"

In this part . . .

*W*henever customers think of visiting your Web site, they have a set of expectations — your Web site will be easy to find, the pages will load quickly, and navigating through the site will be easy. They also expect that your site will provide them with something of value (usually for free). If this sounds like a tall order to fill, it is. However, the chapters in this part show you how to create, market, and manage your Web site so that you can please even the most discerning customers.

We cover all the essentials you need to know, from how to create a domain name that makes it easy for your customers to find you, to qualities you should look for in a Web developer, to mastering the three Cs of internet success — content, commerce, and community. Providing specific examples and suggestions, this part guides you step by step in building the right brand image for your company and creating a positive online experience for your customers in all phases of their Web interaction.

Chapter 8

The Domain Race in Cyberspace: Winning the Name Game

*A*t its heart, good online service is about creating a positive experience for your customers in every contact they have with your company. Creating a positive experience starts with having a domain name that makes it easy for your customers to find you on the Web and continues to build the right brand image for your business. Your domain name is even more than an invaluable marketing tool. Think of it as the electronic handshake you extend to your online clients. A good name can

✔ **Deliver a message.** The name of Apple's *PowerBook* makes you think of a notebook computer that packs a wallop.

✔ **Tell a story.** *Any Mountain* stores have a name that conveys the message that you can get what you need to take a hike or to climb Everest.

✔ **Make a promise.** *Die Hard* batteries make a commitment to do just that.

✔ **Convey a personality.** www.yahoo.com conjures up an image of fun and excitement. *Yahoo!*

Winning at the name game involves more than just coming up with clever nomenclature; it requires making sure that your chosen domain name is available for use and then protecting it. In this chapter, we show you everything you need to know about creating, registering, and protecting domain names.

Domain Name Basics

A domain name is an alias for an Internet Protocol (IP) address. Your IP address is the string of letters or digits that identifies your particular Web site. Whatever follows the "www" is what constitutes your domain name. Think of it as your Web site's address.

What makes a good name?

A good domain name:

✔ Doesn't resemble, too closely, another company's domain name

✔ Isn't being used by anyone else

✔ Is easy for people to remember

✔ Is easy to understand

✔ Is relevant to your current business

✔ Is easy for people to spell and pronounce

The rules of the game

You do need to keep a few basic rules in mind while sculpting your perfect online name. They are:

✔ Domain names that end in *.com, .net,* or *.org* (called the *extension*) cannot exceed a total of 67 characters, not including the extension

✔ You can only use letters, numbers, and one hyphen in the creation of a domain name

✔ A domain name cannot begin or end with a hyphen

✔ Domain names are not case sensitive

✔ No spaces can be included in domain names

In our experience . . .

When we first created a domain name for our company, Sterling Consulting Group Inc., we tried putting a www in front of the following: sterling, sterlingconsulting, scg, and scginc. Unfortunately, by the time we tried to register these names, they were all taken, and either too expensive to buy or unavailable for sale. In desperation (and without this chapter to guide us!), we chose a hybrid and came up with www.sterconinc.com.

Although the name did meet two of the criteria for a successful domain name (it didn't confuse our company with another and it wasn't being used by anyone else), it didn't pass many of the other requirements of a successful domain name:

- It wasn't easy to remember.
- It wasn't easy to understand.
- It wasn't relevant to our current business.
- It wasn't easy for people to spell and pronounce.

Having seen the error of our ways, we scrapped www.sterconinc.com and created our current domain: www.scgtraining.com.

Creating Your Domain Name

According to the U.S. commercial domain registry, a new company reserves a domain name every two minutes of every business day. The ease of entry to the Web, combined with the relatively low cost of registering a domain name (about $35 per year, per name), has lead to a situation where huge numbers of names are already spoken for. The situation is an evolving one. Naming guru S. B. Master of Master-McNeil (www.naming.com) puts it like this, "It used to be that you wanted to find something short, memorable, and relevant to your business. Today, it is almost impossible to attain a short domain that bears any relation to any words you have ever heard."

Before you put your head on your desk and begin moaning, take a deep breath and read on. True *namesmithing* is an art and a multidisciplinary mix of linguistics, market research, creativity, and psychology — combined with a little bit of luck. Begin by thinking about the two basic strategies you should consider in creating a new domain name:

- **Strategy 1: Short, sweet, and not relevant.** The first strategy is to come up with a name that's short but may not have any immediate relevance to your business. For example, Qualcomm's Eudora e-mail program was named after one of the creator's favorite authors, Eudora Welty, in honor of the short story "Why I live at the P.O." Although interesting and new, the name *Eudora* isn't directly descriptive of the product and required time, energy, and money to become established.

This naming strategy can work if you're well funded and can take the time to turn an unknown and irrelevant name into a known entity.

✔ **Strategy 2: Longer, but with meaning.** The second strategy is to come up with a name that's a bit longer but has some connection to your business. If you're a smaller business and can't or don't want to invest the kind of resources it takes to pursue the first strategy, the wiser course may be to accept a longer name, but one that has a more obvious connection with your business.

Most people only type your domain name in once, regardless of its length. After they've arrived at your site and realized it's the best thing since sliced bread, they will bookmark it and never (hopefully) have to type in the domain name again.

Starting with the obvious

If you have a company name that's already well established and that exact name is available as a domain name, reserve it. You can always let it go later. Using your existing company name makes it easy for your customers to find you. If your company name is not available as is, try using your company's initials or combining your company's name with information that's relevant to your company.

For example, let's say your name is Bob Smith and you own Smith's Automall, a car dealership in Tahoe, California. You went to www.register.com and tried to secure www.smithsautomall.com, but found it was already taken by a car dealership in Slovakia! You might try the following:

✔ www.bobsmithauto.com

✔ www.bsmithauto.com

✔ www.smithauto.com

✔ www.tahoeauto.com

Unless you have an unusual company name, it's unlikely that your company's name or a close variant will be available for registration as a domain name. If this is the case, don't spend too much time bemoaning the name that you can't have, but move on to the namesmithing process outlined in the next section.

If you are an individual, don't assume that your name is so unique that no one else has registered it as a domain. Check, and if your name is available, we recommend grabbing it now! If it's not, try getting something close, such as your first initial and last name, or first name, middle initial, and last name, or try using a hyphen between your first and last name.

The namesmithing process

If you're at ground zero and need to invent an online name, try the three-step namesmithing process outlined in this section. Ideally, it's a group process. A bit later in this chapter, we go over who you should invite. If you've participated in a task team, quality group, or team problem-solving session, you will feel right at home with this format. The three steps involved are

- ✔ **Step one.** Brainstorming words
- ✔ **Step two.** Choosing keywords
- ✔ **Step three.** Putting it together

Even though it's not complicated, this process gets your creative juices flowing and creates excitement about the name with your staff.

Step one: Brainstorming words

The room is set up, the participants are arriving, the excitement mounts. Everyone is sitting down and staring at the facilitator with anxious anticipation as the first session is about to begin. Where do you go from here? Step one is brainstorming possible words for use in your domain name. Brainstorming is the process of generating as many ideas about a given subject as possible. One of the rules of brainstorming is not to evaluate the quality of the ideas put forth. Rather, generate as large a quantity of ideas as possible. Start by listing as many words as you can think of in answer to the following questions:

- ✔ What words represent the product or service you offer?
- ✔ What words represent the values and/or qualities you stand for?
- ✔ What words represent your customers buying criteria? What do they feel is important?

Have the facilitator write the responses down on a separate chart for each specific question. Remember, don't get into evaluation at this point; make it your goal to generate as many answers as possible. Using Smith's Automall in Tahoe, California once again as an example:

What words represent the product/service we offer?

auto

wheels

car

drive

transportation

What words represent the values and/or qualities we stand for?

fair	friendly
easy	local
good price	selection
value	no pressure

What words represent our customers' buying criteria? What do our customers feel is important?

honesty	availability
integrity	style
price	good deals
service	

Forget the Net

Netish sounding domain names are getting harder to come by. ICANN, the name registration authority for the .com domain, has thousands of registered domains that include the terms *web, net, internet,* and *link,* such as www.webauto. com or www.autolink.com.

Wired words are beginning to go out of fashion — victims of their own popularity.

Remember that the more popular these netish sounding names are, the harder it is to differentiate a site from competitors' sites with similar sounding names. At this point, if you're looking for a unique domain name, our suggestion is to forget the net and try picking something more arbitrary but memorable.

Step two: Picking keywords

After you've filled your chart pages and are exhausted from brainstorming a list of potential words, the next step is to begin evaluating and narrowing down the words the group has come up with. Ask yourself or your group, "How do these words feel?" and "How do they sound?" Make sure that all the chart pages are visible and cross off all the words that don't work. For example, the group may decide that *transportation,* while a fine word, is too long and cumbersome to be included in a domain name.

Unlike the first step, which is about quantity, the second step is about quality. This is the time for evaluation. Your goal is to narrow the list down, through group consensus, to a few keywords (between three and six) that you could build your new domain name around.

At some point, the group will begin to move into the consensus phase of this process. Try the *red dot* technique. Give each participant ten self-adhesive red dots, the kind you can buy at your local stationary store. Participants then go up to the charts and put their dots on the keywords that they like the best. The participants have the option of putting all ten dots on one word or spreading them out as they see fit between the keywords that they want to vote for. You add up the dots to see what the most popular words are.

Step 3: Putting it together

Now that you have several keywords in mind, the final step is to come up with a list of possible domain names based on these words. Use the following tips to craft some domain name candidates.

> ✔ **Go plural.** Take a name you like and, to increase the chances of it being available, make it a plural. For example, www.autos.com.

✔ **Make a hybrid.** One of the best ways to use a keyword that is already taken as a domain name is to pair it with a generic word before or after it. This incorporates your original idea and increases the chances of the domain name being available. For example, instead of `www.auto.com`, try `www.yourauto.com`. Some other words to put in front of your keyword include

- the
- about
- my
- get
- find

Some words to put behind your keyword include

- place
- shop
- deals
- info
- central
- zone

For example, `www.autoplace.com`.

✔ **Hyphenate.** Say you're madly in love with the domain name `www.cheapauto.com`, and, unfortunately, the name is not available. Try adding a hyphen to make the domain `www.cheap-auto.com`. Many two-word phrases that are not available can be registered by the simple addition of a hyphen.

✔ **Add geography.** Often a simple, direct, keyword domain name is already taken. Just try registering `www.books.com` or `www.computers.com`. Often, though, the keyword can be incorporated into an available domain name if you add a geographical reference. For example, `www.tahoeauto.com`.

✔ **Combine numbers and letters.** Try combining logical numbers or letters with your keyword in order to make a new domain name. For example, `www.auto4u.com` or `www.auto1.com`.

✔ **Make it fun.** Never underestimate the impact that a fun, silly, or whimsical name can have on your customer. For example, `www.autoparty.com`. Names that are fun are easy to remember and can, over time, generate a brand image that represents positive feelings.

✔ **Make up a word.** Words that are made up or partly made, up such as *google* and *napster,* are unique and have the advantage of distinguishing your company from all others. For example, `www.automeister.com`.

✔ **Use your name.** Consider using your company or personal name in combination with the keyword you want to use. This naming technique can personalize your Web site and make it easy for your customers to remember. For example, `www.bobscars.com`.

✔ **Use a combination of any of the above.** Sometimes, it's the odd combination of words that, when put together, make a great domain name. For example, `www.bobsautoparty.com` combines the owner's name with what the company does and is fun.

Above all, group members should listen to their own inner ear and ask themselves:

✔ How does this name feel in my gut?

✔ Does this name sound right?

✔ Will this name resonate with our customers?

Some experts suggest intentional misspelling (instead of `www.automall.com`, use the improperly spelled `www.automal.com`) or the use of foreign words (instead of `www.auto.com`, try the Hungarian for auto, *kocsi,* as in `www.kocsi.com`) as domain name alternatives. We don't recommend either of these, as this approach can be confusing and frustrating to those trying to find your site.

Making sure your domain name can travel the globe

One of the opportunities created by the Web is the ability to more easily sell your products and services around the world. This means that a domain name that may work well in the United States may be a disaster in another country. To use a non-Internet example, who could forget the Chevy Nova? *Nova* was discovered to mean *no go* in Spanish, but only after the car had been shipped to Latin America.

On the flip side, some names work extremely well in native countries but don't translate well for an American market. For example, in Spain a very successful food product is called *Bimbo Bread.* You'd be asking for trouble if your company tried to place this bread on the shelves of any U.S. grocery store. Although mostly a concern for large multinationals, in this world of increasing global competition every company needs to watch out for innocuous sounding names that are harmless in America but could be obscene, offensive, or downright nasty in another language or culture. If you are concerned, you may want to consider hiring a naming company to do a search for you.

Namesmithing FAQs

Certain criteria exist that help ensure a successful outcome when setting up and running naming sessions. In the sections that follow, we list some of the frequently asked questions about the namesmithing process and our suggestions for how to make your sessions as productive as possible.

Is one session enough? How long should each session be?

Some people want to pull themselves up by their bootstraps, suck in their guts, and barrel through all three steps in one day! While this sounds good in theory, keep in mind that namesmithing is a creative process and uses a lot of brainpower. After a few hours, you get mentally and physically tired. In order to maximize your team's focused attention and creative energy, we suggest scheduling three sessions for namesmithing, one for each step in the process. Ideally, the sessions should be a few days apart. Limit each session to one to two hours. By following this schedule, you maintain a fresh perspective and reduce the tendency for the group to just give in to move on.

Because you want to take full advantage of the participants' talents and energy, we suggest holding the sessions first thing in the morning. This way, people will be fresh and raring to go, before the messages, e-mails, and faxes of the day have worn them down. (Just make sure there's coffee.)

Where should the sessions be held?

Consider holding the sessions off-site, at a nice hotel or meeting facility. If doing so isn't possible, try limiting, as much as possible, the distractions that the participants experience at the office. This makes a big difference in the amount of mental focus they are able to put towards the process.

In today's 24/7 working environment, people are as attached to the cell phones at their sides as the cowboys of the old west were to the guns in their holsters. In order to avoid interrupting the flow of a session, ask everyone to turn off their cell phones and pagers and wait until the breaks to return calls.

How many people should be involved in the sessions?

The sessions work best with a maximum of 15 participant and a minimum of six. Keep in mind that the more people who are involved, the more difficult the session is to manage.

Who should we invite to the sessions and should it be the same people each session?

For the sake of continuity, the same group of participants should attend each session. To get the most creative ideas, you want to involve individuals from different parts of your company and from a variety of backgrounds. Try an eclectic mix of executives, managers, and other staff, including:

You're invited

The way you invite people to the sessions sets the tone for the process.

We suggest a combination of a personal invitation by phone or face-to-face and an e-mail that repeats the invitation and contains the relevant information. A sample e-mail invitation may look something like this:

Dear Irene

Thank you for agreeing to attend our name-smithing sessions on April 7th, April 9th, and April 14th from 9:00 a.m. to 11:00 p.m. The sessions will be held at the Marriott Hotel located at 5466 Highland Street. The phone number there is (898) 767-9999. We will be in the Netmaniac room.

As you know, the purpose of the session is for us to begin the process of coming up with a domain name for our Web site. All supplies will be provided, so just bring your creativity and an open mind. Dress is business casual and lunch will be served following the session.

I look forward to seeing you there,

Eddie

✔ A few people who are close to the customers and can speak from their perspective

✔ One or two people who understand the big picture of sales and marketing in your company

✔ Several individuals who have creative jobs with the company

✔ At least one person who represents the administrative and financial side of your business

How should the room be set up?

The set up of the room has a definite impact on the level and quality of participation. Some of the most important factors include

✔ Making sure the room is well lit. Avoid rooms that are dim or dingy, as they tend to put people to sleep and dull the senses.

✔ Checking to see that no pillars or other obstacles are blocking any of the participants' views.

✔ Evaluating the room for noise levels. Meeting rooms that are next to a kitchen area, an acid-rock band contest, or a busy hallway can often be noisy to the point of distraction.

✔ Ensuring that there is enough space to set the room up seminar style, around a table, so that all the participants can hear and see each other.

✔ Making sure the room you get allows for chart pages to be taped or pinned to the walls — this is critical, so that participants can easily see and review what they've created.

What supplies will we need to run the sessions?

The supplies that you need are (mostly) the same as are required for typical business meetings.

- ✔ Two flip charts with extra pads of paper
- ✔ Box of colored markers
- ✔ A pen and paper for each participant
- ✔ Water glasses and water
- ✔ Masking tape and pushpins
- ✔ Red dots

In addition, we strongly suggest that you have a dictionary and thesaurus on hand, as they're invaluable tools in this process. If all the participants don't know each other, or if you're using a facilitator who doesn't know everyone, we suggest adding nametags to the supply list.

Should we use an outside facilitator for the sessions?

Although these sessions have been successfully facilitated by an internal person, we suggest having an outside facilitator. Someone who isn't from your company is more able to objectively take the group through the process without a hidden agenda or bias towards any department, group, or specific idea. The facilitator need not be an expert at the naming process but should be experienced and skilled at facilitating groups in the brainstorming or problem-solving process.

Take one last look

Before you move on and begin the process of registering your domain name (which we show you how to do later in this chapter), take one last look at your candidate domain names and ask yourself the following questions:

- ✔ Is your domain name logical?
- ✔ Is your domain name appropriate?
- ✔ Does your domain name differentiate you from your competitors?
- ✔ Does your domain name work in other countries where you do business?

If at First You Don't Succeed

If you've tried to create and register a domain name and are just not having any luck, you still have a few options to consider that may help you in acquiring the name of your dreams, including:

- ✔ Checking for expired domain names
- ✔ Hiring a naming company to create an innovative new name
- ✔ Purchasing the name you want

Using any of these methods can get you on the path toward acquiring the domain name of your dreams.

Checking for expired domain names

Every day, countless domain names expire due to nonrenewal, failure to pay maintenance fees, and nonpayment of registration. Dozens of sites list domain names that have become available (although you may have to pay a small fee to see the list). Useful sites include

- ✔ www.tradingzone.com
- ✔ www.dualbytes.com
- ✔ www.unclaimedandexpireddomainnames.com.

Hiring a name guru

If you've tried to solve your naming problem internally and have been unsuccessful, try seeking professional help. We don't mean a therapist for your frustration levels or a plastic surgeon to replace the hairs you've pulled out of your head trying to come up with a suitable name. With the growth of the Internet, a proliferation of naming companies have entered the marketplace that can help you create the perfect domain name for your Web site. Many are one or two person, *soho* (small office, home office) firms. Others are large, multinational companies that have been around a long time and are responsible for some of the most familiar names in play today, names such as *Compaq* (created by Namelab), *Lucent Technologies* (created by Landor Associates), and *Netopia* (created by Master-McNeil).

Factors such as the scope of your project, your budget, and your unique company culture are all things to consider in determining which firm is right for you. If you are in the market for a name guru, check with the above firms or search the Web to find a slew of such geniuses.

Buying a name

If the domain name that you want is taken, you can always contact the owner and make an offer to purchase it. Domain names are owned by individuals, companies, or domain name brokerage firms. You should begin by going to www.allwhois.com and doing some research at this Web site on who owns the domain name you're looking to purchase. Simply type in the URL, and you will be provided with the individual owner or company name, an administrative contact, a mailing address, and, in many cases, an e-mail address.

If the domain name is owned by an individual or a company, go to the Web site that the domain name brings up to see how the Web page is set up and being used. If you're greeted by a home page that says "site under construction" upon arriving at the site, the person or company may be keeping a placeholder on the name but not actively using it. If this is the case, the person or company is probably much more willing to sell the domain name than if the site is fully developed and active.

The next step is to contact the owner or administrator of the domain you want to purchase. Information you should be prepared to provide includes

✔ Your name, company name, and contact information

✔ What you plan to use the site for

✔ What type of business you're in

✔ How much you would be willing to pay to purchase the name

As with all negotiations, a delicate balance must be struck between giving out enough information so that the seller understands who you are and what you want versus giving out so much information that the seller sees gold when they talk to you and adjusts the price accordingly.

Hundreds of domain names for sale by individuals and by companies are listed on www.mindrush.com. Listed in alphabetical order, the entries include pricing information and the e-mail address of the seller.

Many domain names are owned by domain name brokers. These folks are in the business of registering huge numbers of domain names — not for the purpose of using them, but for selling them. Unfortunately, the current domain name feeding frenzy has pushed the envelope on the prices these brokers are charging. Think long and hard before you put down any money to acquire a domain name. Could you create an alternative name that's still available instead?

If you decide to go through with it, the process of acquiring a domain name from a broker is fairly straightforward: You contact them, look up the cost of the domain name you want, and, if you are willing to pay the price, the domain can be yours.

Registering Your Domain Name

Bear in mind that all domain names in the United States are accepted on a first come, first serve basis and that every domain name is unique. For example, there may be hundreds of companies that manufacture doohickeys in the United States, but only one lucky company can have the name `www.dohickeys.com` on the Internet. Even though registering a domain name is a fairly simple process that can be accomplished with a few clicks and a credit card, you should take certain factors into consideration.

The three big guns — .com, .net, .org

You begin the process of obtaining a domain name by applying to a name registration authority, such as ICANN (Internet Corporation for Assigned Names and Numbers). ICANN's designated representatives in the United States are Network Solutions (`www.networksollutions.com`) and Register (`www.register.com`). These two entities handle registration for domains that end in .com, .net, or .org, among others. The big three of .com, .net, and .org are the most popular top level domains (TLD) around the globe. In other words, they're not affiliated with any country and are available to anyone in the general public. Registration for the big three involves a term of one, two, five, or ten years, with the renewal period offering the same timelines.

Don't run the risk of losing your hard-earned name by missing the renewal date on your registration. This blunder happens more often than you would think; in fact, whole sites are dedicated to selling monthly reports on domain names that have become available due to nonrenewal or nonpayment of registration fees. Although the company you registered with should contact you when your domain name is due to renew, keeping track of the relevant dates is ultimately your responsibility.

Although no legal restrictions are placed on the use of these suffixes, they do have a meaning to your customers and the marketplace.

- .com refers to commercial companies
- .net refers to network administration organizations
- .org refers to nonprofit organizations and institutions of all kinds

Other top level domains that are more restricted in their use include:

- .edu, which refers to educational institutions at all levels
- .mil, which refers to military organizations
- .gov, which refers to government agencies

If you submit a name for registration and it's not available, both Network Solutions and Register automatically offer you a list of similar names that are available.

If you just can't seem to catch a break on registering your desired name, you can always take a cybertrip overseas. Register (www.register.com) allows you to register your chosen domain name (if available) ending in a country. For example:

- ✔ .ky — Cayman Islands
- ✔ .ro — Romania
- ✔ .tc — Turks & Caicos Islands
- ✔ .kz — Kazakstan

Beyond domain registration to a trademark

If you want to further safeguard the name you've chosen and prevent it from being co-opted by a competitor, you may want to consider going a step beyond domain registration by registering your domain name as a trademark. Bear in mind that the use of a domain name does not, by default, qualify as trademark use, since trademarks and domain names are recognized by two different organizations. Although this section is not intended as a substitute for legal advice, you need to be aware of the information that follows.

In search of a suffix

Even though .com is the leader of the naming pack, the diminishing number of available top-level domain names has created a need for new endings. ICANN is currently discussing a list of new ones, which may or may not, make the final cut, including:

- ✔ .arts
- ✔ .store
- ✔ .shop
- ✔ .news
- ✔ .sex
- ✔ .firm
- ✔ .law
- ✔ .travel
- ✔ .biz

A *trademark* is an indication of the origin of goods or services. Consider registering your domain name as a trademark to keep others from stealing it in the future. In the United States, you can obtain a trademark by making an application to the U.S. Patent and Trademark Office. From beginning to end, the process takes about twelve to fifteen months to complete.

 For more specific information on trademarks, check out the International Trademark Association (www.inta.org), a nonprofit trade association dedicated to "the support and advancement of trademarks and related intellectual property concepts as essential elements of effective national and international commerce."

Carl Oppedahl, of Oppedahl & Larson LLP, an intellectual property law firm (on the Web at www.patents.com), suggests that it's prudent to follow the three steps below in order to protect your domain name and to keep from violating someone else's trademark:

1. **Coin (make-up) a unique name.** *Kodak* and *Exxon* were unique when they were coined. By following this advice, you drastically reduce the risk that someone else is going to claim that you've violated their trademark.

2. **Conduct a trademark search.** Do this at least in the country where your business is located, and check with a trademark attorney to see that the domain name you want is secure for use.

3. **File a trademark application.** Again, do this at least in the country where your business is located.

You can use a lawyer or do it yourself. Keep in mind that about one hundred countries outside the United States have trademark offices. If you plan on doing business outside the United States, you might need to register a trademark in those countries you plan on conducting business in. Talk to a trademark lawyer for details.

If you want to file the trademark application yourself, you can go to the United States Patent and Trademark Office Web site (www.uspto.gov) and apply online.

Chapter 9

Don't Miss the Hits: Search Engines, Links, and PR

. . . .

In This Chapter

▶ Getting listed with search engines

▶ Maximizing traffic at your Web site

▶ Creating a link exchange program

▶ Spreading the word about your new site

. . . .

*T*he repeated message in the movie *Field of Dreams* is "if you build it, they will come." Although this may be true of a baseball field, it is decidedly untrue of a Web site. The reality is that even if you build the Eiffel Tower of Web sites, you won't get the online traffic you're hoping for if people are unaware your site exists or don't know how to find it.

Research shows that 60 percent of small businesses use the Internet as a sales and marketing tool. One reason the Web is used so often is that you don't have to break the bank on your marketing budget, hire a top notch advertising firm, or commit to an expensive PR campaign to reach a whole new group of potential customers.

In order to maximize your Web site, you must create an overall plan for promoting your site that compels current and potential customers to visit you online. First, determine who you're trying to attract. Ask yourself:

✔ What audience are we trying to reach?

✔ Who would benefit most from visiting our site?

✔ Who do we have the best chance of selling our services and products to?

After you know who your target audience is, the next step is to determine how you're going to reach them. Three of the best ways include

✔ Getting listed with search engines

✔ Establishing beneficial links with other Web sites

✔ Creating a public relations campaign that showcases your Web site

In this chapter, we show you what you need to know to list your site with search engines, to maximize the number of hits your site receives, to establish link exchanges to increase traffic at your site, and to generate interest in your Web site through an effective PR campaign.

Getting Listed with Search Engines

Visitors access your Web site one of three ways. They can type in your URL on a browser, open to your Web site via a bookmark, or find your site on a search engine. Search engines are only one method of attracting visitors to your site, but they are critically important. The benefits of getting listed with a search engine are myriad:

✔ Most search engines list your site for free.

✔ Search engines make it easier for your current customers to find you.

✔ Search engines bring new customers to your site.

Submit your URL and information (your company's name, type of business, Web site address, keywords that describe your business, and so on) to each individual search engine that you want to list your site. Four main ways exist that you can use to do so:

✔ Manual submission

✔ A paid submission service

✔ A search engine submission consultant

✔ Search engine submission software

Manual submission

You can manually submit your URL, as well as specific information for each separate Web page you have, to the individual search engines of your choice. You increase your chances of a higher ranking by completing every field in the submission form with an eye on its maximum potential for matching:

Top search engines

Because new search engines crop up almost overnight, and become popular just as fast, you want to make a habit of regularly surfing the Internet, reading trade publications, and talking to colleagues to see what's new on the scene. Some of the most popular search engines at the time this book was published include

✔ AltaVista (www.altavista.com)

✔ Excite (www.excite.com)

✔ Google (www.google.com)

✔ Hotbot (www.hotbot.com)

✔ InfoSeek (www.infoseek.com)

✔ Lycos (www.lycos.com)

✔ Looksmart (www.looksmart.com)

✔ MSN (www.searchmsn.com)

✔ Webcrawler (www.webcrawler.com)

✔ whatUseek (www.whatuseek.com)

✔ Yahoo (www.yahoo.com)

To register manually at any one of these sites, simply click on the Add URL or Add To Our Site button, found most often on the home page.

✔ Keywords (the words that people search for)

✔ Descriptions (a sentence or two that describes your site)

✔ Content (a description of what is on your site)

✔ Contact information (address, phone, e-mail, and contact person)

The disadvantage to manual submission is that it can be enormously time consuming, making a full-time job of getting listed with all the search engines you've targeted.

If you are going to manually submit your information to a variety of search engines, one way to reduce the time you spend and make the process easier is to cut and paste the information that you use repeatedly. Simply open a file in your word processor and enter the basic information you need to use over again with each new submission. Remember to check the document for spelling errors before you paste the information into submission forms.

Creating this type of master document saves you time. It also helps eliminate grammatical and spelling errors that can occur when you are retyping the same information again and again. Be sure to include the following key information in your master document:

✔ Web page titles

✔ URL title

✔ Keywords

- ✔ A 10-word description of your business
- ✔ A 25-word description of your business
- ✔ A 50-word description of your business
- ✔ Your company's name, address, e-mail, phone, and fax numbers

A search engine is likely to refuse to list your site if you don't provide all the information it requests in exactly the format that it wants. It also may not list your site if your site isn't active enough or, in some cases, if it doesn't like the way your site looks.

Paid submission services

If you have more money than time and you don't want to go through the submission process yourself, you can pay someone else to do it. One advantage of paid submission services is that they allow you to focus on the content of your Web site, while they do the promotional work of listing your site with search engines. Two main types of paid submission services exist.

- ✔ **Automated service.** This type of service submits your information to anywhere between seventy-five to one hundred different search engines in a true blitz fashion. The smear approach is efficient, but not very strategic.

- ✔ **Manual service.** This type of service submits your information to a selective list of the particular search engines that would be most valuable for your business. Of course, this tailored service is a more expensive option than an automated service, but it stands a better chance of producing higher rankings.

Search engine consultants

One result of the new economy is the creation of never-before-heard-of job titles, such as *search engine consultant.* These consultants are experts at getting your site listed and, for a fee, they can help you:

- ✔ Evaluate your site.
- ✔ Design an overall search engine campaign.
- ✔ Design keywords and content to attract visitors to your site.
- ✔ Suggest ways to get high rankings.
- ✔ Maximize every file in search engine submission forms.
- ✔ Submit your site to a targeted list of search engines.
- ✔ Make multiple submission for individual pages of your site.

If you use a paid consultant, you have access to a professional who can look over your keywords and titles and recommend ways to achieve a higher placement within the search engines — so that you attract the greatest number of visitors to your site.

Submission software

An alternative to the above methods is to purchase one of the software packages available on the market today that help you with search engine submissions. Some of these products are better than others, so you need to do some research. Basically, the software works like free submission services. Using submissions software can save you time, but most of them don't allow you to customize your submissions in order to gain a higher ranking.

Achieving the Highest Possible Ranking and Position

The average person who accesses a search engine will only look at about 15 listings before they choose one or move on. Getting your Web site listed with a search engine is only half the battle; the other half is getting it ranked as highly as possible in the search engine results. If you're not in the top fifty results that a user sees after she types in a search, the chances of new customers finding your site are slim to none. You should aim to be in the top twenty.

For example, if you type the keyword "almonds" into the popular AltaVista search engine, you get over *19,000* listings. Among them will be the Almond Event and Tradeshow (who would have guessed), a recipe for Cannelloni with chicken, sausage and almonds, and a site where you can bid on and name your own price for almonds. If you're listing number 18,999, the odds are pretty good that people aren't going to keep perusing the entries until they see yours.

Although we can't make any guarantees, and the rules for ranking seem to change daily, you can probably improve your placement by:

 ✔ Carefully selecting the words you use to describe your site

 ✔ Repeating words in your description for increased frequency

 ✔ Monitoring the status of your site's position

Selecting your words for maximum hits

A simple strategy exists for choosing the best words to describe your site on the search engine submission forms. The strategy involves a bit of research, but the benefit of increased traffic on your site is well worth your time. You don't want to lose Web traffic because you didn't do your homework!

1. **Come up with a list of words and phrases that you think your customers and potential customers are most likely to use when trying to find services and products that relate to the type of business you're in.**

2. **Enter these words into the top ten search engines, and see what the top 10 to 20 sites are.**

3. **Go to each one of these sites and count the number of times that the words and phrases from the list you generated in step one appear on the first page of that site.**

   In addition, view the source code of the page to see what title, keywords, and descriptions have been used to achieve the high ranking.

4. **After you've seen which keywords, when used repeatedly, are giving your competitors an upper hand in the rankings, check your own use of these words in your search engine submission forms and adjust your language as needed.**

In general, the more often a keyword appears on your page, the higher any search engine is likely to rank your site. Be sure to repeat the keywords and phrases that you have determined are the most valuable at least three or four times within the first 100 words of your page.

Monitoring the status of your position

Many individuals and companies simply submit their site to a search engine, do what they can to get a high ranking, and, with fingers crossed, hope for the best. But this isn't good enough if you want to capture as much business as possible with your Web site.

After you've gone to all the trouble of submitting your site — properly using all the techniques available to get you a high ranking — don't waste your hard work. Regularly check the status of your positions and work to improve them. This way, if your position starts to fall, you'll be able to catch it and fix it right away. You can and should stay on top of things by checking your ranking once every few months on each of the top search engines.

Hits versus page views

If you watch any business news program, you have invariably seen some young and upcoming dot-commer puff his or her chest out and proudly announce, "We are getting over 3 million hits per day." While this may sound impressive and make for good PR, the number may be misleading. Web site traffic measures seem to vary greatly depending on who is doing the counting and how the numbers are calculated.

A *hit,* simply put, is made anytime a visitor to your site accesses a file (be it graphic, html, video, or other) contained on that page. To make things more complex, there can be (and frequently are) a number of files contained within a single page. So, a single mouse click can register numerous hits.

For example, if one of your customers accesses your home page and it contains four graphics, the number of hits would be counted as five, one for the html page and one for each of the four graphics. Additionally, if that same visitor goes from your home page to a page you are linked with, even more hits are added to the tally, and on it goes until the visitor exits your site. One visitor can account for dozens of hits on your site.

Page views are the number of pages within your Web site that a user downloads to look at. For example, if a customer visits your site and accesses five pages, this would count as five page views, even if one of the five were the same page visited twice. Each time the customer accesses a page, even if it's a page the customer previously accessed, it counts as a page view.

As you can see, the number of hits you receive on your Web site only tells you part of the story. A useful evaluation of your site should take into account:

- ✔ The number of visitors
- ✔ The number of page views
- ✔ The number of overall hits
- ✔ The length of time visitors stay after they enter your site

These metrics are some of the ways you can measure the effectiveness of your Web site and determine if you're getting the kind of traffic you think you should. Check with your Webmaster to set up a method for measuring these items daily, weekly, or monthly, as appropriate.

Although you may have obtained a high ranking with a search engine when you first submitted your site, your position can slip over time. You'll occasionally be dropped from a search engines database altogether, for no apparent reason. Since your position in the rankings determines how many people find your site, staying on top is as important as getting placed.

Maximizing Your Hits with Link Exchanges

Link exchanges are a good way to promote your site. An exchange is a reciprocal agreement in which you and another site list each other on your respective Web pages. The beauty of a link exchange program is that you can select other companies with whom exchanging links would be a natural fit, mutually beneficial, and inexpensive to boot. The four steps involved with creating a link exchange program are

1. **Defining your audience**

2. **Creating a list of potential partners**

3. **Customizing your contact**

4. **Deciding where to place the links on your page**

Step one: Define your audience

In order to know which sites you could most beneficially link to, you need to identify your *target audience* — the people you want to attract to your site. Generate a list of what types of customer you want to reach, what types of Web sites they're likely to visit, and what related products and services they're likely to buy.

Step two: Create a target list

After you know what types of sites your potential customers may visit, surf the Web to see what sites you may want to exchange links with. Come up with a target list of companies you plan to approach.

Let's say you own a company that sells baskets. You've just come out with a spiffy new kids bicycle basket made of titanium and available in hot pink, black, and the ever-popular chartreuse. Some, but certainly not all, of your natural link exchange partners include

- A site belonging to the manufacturer of kids bicycles
- An online magazine for kids sports
- An online magazine for bicycle enthusiasts
- A site focusing on parenting
- A site dedicated to baskets

Step three: Customize your contact

After narrowing your list of possible link exchange partners, send a customized e-mail message proposing the link. In order to avoid creating the impression that your message is *spam,* a message sent indiscriminately to a multitude of recipients, send your e-mail directly to the decision-maker and make it easy for her to welcome your proposal by including the following information in your message:

- ✔ Your name and position
- ✔ Your company's name and the type of business you are in
- ✔ The types of customers you have
- ✔ The reason you think a link would be mutually beneficial (this is the key!)
- ✔ The reason you think the other company's customers would benefit from a link exchange
- ✔ Your contact information, including phone and address
- ✔ A request that the person get back to you within a specific time range

Step four: Decide where to place links

After you have agreed to exchange links, you need to negotiate the specific placement of your link on your partner's site and your partner's link on your site. Base your decision for determining link placement on traffic. Think of your Web site as real estate. Since your home page represents the most valuable real estate on your site, reserve that space for those links from which you receive the most traffic.

Because determining how much traffic a link will generate at the beginning of a partnership is almost impossible, we suggest that you establish a probation period with any new link exchange partner in order to test the benefits of the link and to determine future placement. If a link exchange isn't working out, a probation period allows you to get out gracefully (unless you are under a legal contract to provide the link).

Pick your partners carefully

Any link exchange you establish reflects on your company; the way your partner company does business can affect your customer's perception of you. Remember that visitors to a Web site assume that a link is an endorsement. Therefore, regardless of potential benefits, never link to a site that will hurt your reputation or credibility. Make sure that any partner company you link up with:

- ✔ Is reputable
- ✔ Has an interesting and well-designed site
- ✔ Provides value on their site
- ✔ Updates their site regularly
- ✔ Shares the business values that your company has

If a company you exchange links with puts you on its home page, you do not need to place its link on your home page. Even if you decide that a link is worthy of occupying the prime real estate of your home page, it should be placed on the bottom of your page so that customers see your information first.

Since the goal is to have your customer stay at your site as long as possible, avoid putting too many links on your site, as doing so increases the chances that your customer will jump from your site to another, and may or may not come back.

Planning a PR Campaign to Announce Your Site

In order for your Web site to serve your company, people have to know about it. The best way to announce the establishment of your new Web site (or a new and improved version of your old site) is to conduct a strategic PR campaign. The five essential parts of planning and executing a successful PR campaign include

- Writing a compelling press release
- Connecting your story to what the media likes to report
- Knowing when to send your press release
- Targeting who should receive your press release
- Giving interviews

Create an effective press release

Don't worry that a media person will consider an unsolicited press release as rude Spam. These folks are in the business of getting information, and expect to be sent releases they haven't asked for. What gets their underwear in bunches, however, is a press release that doesn't follow a professional format. If done properly, a press release is one of the best ways you have of announcing the development of your new Web site to the media. See *Public Relations Kit For Dummies* if you want some guidance on how to write a great press release.

If you are going to send your press release via postal mail, set a professional tone for your release by using letterhead, printing it on a high quality printer (avoid copying), and using matching second sheets.

Small is beautiful

Getting booked on *Oprah* is a lot harder than being on your local cable talk show. The *New York Times* may be more reluctant to cover your story than the *Winnepasaki Weekly* (assuming that you live in Winnepasaki). Too often, though, a PR campaign narrowly focuses on getting the attention of the big hitters.

Although getting the spotlight from the major media is fabulous (and fun) when it happens, don't underestimate the value of getting your story placed in smaller, local media. The whole point of PR is to get your name out there so that potential customers can find your site and are piqued enough to check it out. Remember that you never know where business will come from. Although a local newspaper may not be as sexy as a major daily, it can still be a valuable vehicle for driving traffic to your Web site.

Connect your press release to what the media likes to report

What do the people who read your press release look for? Why a particular story gets picked up for publication, while another lies abandoned, gathering dust on a newsroom floor, can seem like one of the world's great mysteries. Although nothing is certain, you do give yourself an advantage if you can connect your story to a theme that media-types think will sell papers (or attract viewers).

Familiarizing yourself with reporters, both those who are in your own area and nationwide, takes a great deal of time. You must identify what topics appeal to them and know the publications that they work for. Over time, however, the energy you invest to establish a relationship with these people and publications pays off. As they get to know you, they'll begin to use you as a resource again and again when they do a story on their pet topic.

Time your press release

Almost any excuse to send out a press release is a good one. However, certain situations provide the most logical and appropriate time for distributing a release, including:

- ✔ **If you want to make an official announcement about your business.** An official announcement could be presaged by a company accomplishment, the hiring of a new executive, the introduction of new products or services, an award you have won, or an anniversary of your being in business.

✔ **If you are working with a famous person or company.** Although most people and companies are happy to see their name in print, especially, if it's in a positive context, be careful to get permission before you tell the world about your partner.

✔ **If your company is involved in a project, charity, or event.** Let's say you own a paint company and you're sponsoring a production of Shakespeare's *Much Ado about Nothing* at the local high school. As part of your sponsorship, you have provided all the paint needed for the sets, for free! This would make an excellent opportunity for a press release. It promotes your business and it promotes the high school show. Because it's a local event, the story would probably be of interest to your local paper, and as such, would likely be printed.

✔ **If what you do ties into a public holiday or declared event.** Virtually every week is declared either a holiday or special event day in the United States. Small Business Week, National Grandparents Day, Flag Day, and the list goes on and on. Tying your business into one of these holidays or events is a natural opportunity to issue a press release.

✔ **If your company connects with something happening in the news.** From time to time, a news item will break that either relates directly to the business you are in or for which you are an excellent source for commentary. When this happens, speed is crucial. Craft a press release as soon as you can and e-mail it to the various news outlets, either locally or nationally, as appropriate.

Send your press release to the appropriate place

Don't waste your time and abuse goodwill by sending every single press release you craft to every single contact on your media hit list. You'll find that you get much farther if you develop a reputation for being selective in what you send. Carefully identify the audience for whom the content of the release is most relevant.

Most news organizations respect, appreciate, and are looking for releases that are well thought-out and have newsworthy content. In general, you need to target reporters and outlets from within the following categories:

✔ Newspapers

✔ Television

✔ Radio

✔ Magazines

✔ E-zines (online magazines)

Getting help from PR distribution services

Whether you want to send a press release to Lansing or London, a Web-based PR distribution service can help you more easily deliver your message to the right people and places. Rather than hiring a PR firm or taking time from your own busy schedule to do this yourself, the Internet provides a great option for the distribution of press releases to the media. Some resources to check out include

✔ PR Newswire (www.prnewswire.com) is one of the largest services of the bunch. It specializes in electronic delivery of news releases and information directly from companies, institutions, and agencies to the media, financial community, and consumers. In addition to delivery by e-mail, it offers a broad range of services, including broadcast fax and fax-on-demand applications.

✔ GAP Enterprises (www.gapent.com) is an automated press release company that, for a fee (about fifty dollars per hundred releases), can send your press release to over 7,500 media contacts. One advantage of using this service is that, instead of addressing your release to the generic "Dear Editor," they personalize the contact by using specific names.

✔ USA News (www.usanews.net) is a press release network that submits your general press release for distribution to about 20,000 media outlets. The cost is approximately two hundred dollars. This fee also pays to archive your release for one year, so that journalists can search the site and find past releases that relate to a current story.

✔ Xpress Press (www.xpresspress.com) was originally founded specifically to deliver business, computing, Internet, and technology news. Currently, it has expanded its distribution to reach over 9,000 wire and data services, regional and national newspapers, industry specific publications, and radio and televisions outlets. Xpress personalizes each press release distribution list to match your story to the subjects of interest to specific reporters.

Make sure you understand how each service operates so that you can make the best choice as to which one meets your unique press release needs. Some issues to consider include:

✔ Does the service send news releases individually, or does it group them together with other news headlines?

✔ Does the service issue the release to the generic "editor" or to a specific contact person?

✔ Does the service personalize each press release, so that it is distributed to a list that matches your story with a particular type of spin that attracts specific reporters?

✔ Are the media contacts limited to the United States alone, or do they include international media?

Gebbie Press (www.gebbie.com) is an all-in-one media directory where, for less than one hundred dollars, you can purchase a listing of over 10,000 newspapers, radio stations, magazines, and television stations within the United States. In addition, the Web site allows you to search for, and link to, hundreds of magazines and newspapers on the Web, by topic, for free.

Newspapers

A long-time mainstay of the public relations world, newspapers are a great target for your press release because they have to put out copy each and every day. The top ten newspapers in the United States, in order of circulation, are

1. *USA Today*
2. *The New York Times*
3. *Los Angeles Times*
4. *Wall Street Journal*
5. *Washington Post*
6. *Daily News* (New York)
7. *Chicago Tribune*
8. *Daily News* (Woodland Hills, CA)
9. *Newsday* (New York)
10. *Houston Chronicle*

Even if the big papers aren't interested in your story, don't overlook the value of getting your story picked up by smaller, more specialized publications, such as your local paper, trade papers, and newsletters.

Avoid calling newspaper reporters or editors after 3:00 p.m. This is crunch time, and they're often scrambling to meet deadlines and aren't at their most receptive. Instead, try calling either first thing in the morning or early in the afternoon. You stand a better chance of getting their attention.

Television

If you want to get the word out about your new Web site to as many people as possible in a given area, television is the best medium around. If you plan on running a national campaign to promote your Web site, you should focus your efforts on the major television news and talk programs within the top ten media markets. In order, the top ten markets are

1. New York
2. Los Angeles
3. Chicago
4. Philadelphia
5. San Francisco
6. Boston

7. Dallas

8. Washington

9. Detroit

10. Atlanta

Radio

Considering that there are more than 500 million radios in the U.S. alone, and that, on average, people listen to the radio for at least two hours every day, the radio waves are one of the best places to distribute the word about your new Web site.

In the United States, a large city has, on average, one big newspaper and about six television stations. But it has many radio stations looking to fill airtime. Unlike your local newspaper, which broadly targets almost everyone in the city, radio shows (especially talk or news shows) are almost always focused on a certain type of listener. In fact, one of the strongest points in favor of radio PR is that the station has already done much of the work for you by targeting listeners according to certain factors, including age, lifestyle, and areas of interest.

If you need some help figuring out which radio shows have the audience you're looking to target, try going online to `www.rronline.com`. This site is the radio industry's trade publication. You can find radio ratings for different cities. With a little bit of research, you should be able to identify which stations in your area your targeted audience is most likely to be listening to.

One of the best times to announce your site on radio is during morning drive time. *Drive time* is between 5 a.m. and 10 a.m., Monday through Friday. Find out what news or talk shows in your area are on during this time.

Magazines

Getting news of your new Web site placed in a top national magazine is difficult because most magazines have limited space and are published weekly or monthly, as opposed to the daily output of radio and television. In other words, they need less content. You increase your chances of being picked up by a magazine by specifically targeting the publications that you think would be the most interested in your story and customizing your pitch to them. The top ten magazines in the United States, in order of circulation, are

1. *Modern Maturity* (circulation over 20 million)

2. *AARP Bulletin* (circulation over 20 million)

3. *Reader's Digest* (circulation over 13 million)

4. *TV Guide* (circulation over 11 million)

5. *National Geographic Magazine* (circulation over 8 million)

6. *Better Homes & Gardens* (circulation over 7 million)

7. *Friendly Exchange* (circulation over 6 million)

8. *Consumer Reports* (circulation over 5 million)

9. *Family Circle* (circulation over 5 million)

10. *Good Housekeeping* (circulation over 4 million)

E-Zines

The electronic magazine — the *e-zine* — is one of the many inventions caused by the rise of the Internet. E-zines are Web sites that feature full-text articles characteristic of the traditional publication format. Literally hundreds of thee publications are on the Web today. The top ten e-zines, including their number of visitors per month (vpm), are

1. Playboy.com (11,139,966 vpm)

2. Inside Flyer (8,000,000 vpm)

3. Muscle & Fitness (6,500,000 vpm)

4. The Industry Standard (4,000,000 vpm)

5. Soap Opera Digest (3,750,000 vpm)

6. Forbes (3,000,000 vpm)

7. Playbill (3,000,000 vpm)

8. PC World.com (2,250,000)

9. Lodging (2,000,000 vpm)

10. Tuff Stuff (2,000,000 vpm)

Present perfect interviews — the three Ps

Another way to get the word out about your new Web site is to arrange interviews with the media. Reporters, like other professionals, want to work with people who make their lives easier. By following the three Ps listed below, you can win praise (and print space!) from media makers. And if they like you, you may have future opportunities to spread the word about your company.

Be professional

For better or worse, the person interviewing you has the power to get you on air or in print. Occasionally, a reporter, due to other pressures and stories, may be unprepared to interview you. He may not have thoroughly read your materials and may ask you questions that you feel are off the point or even downright stupid.

In this situation, the best strategy is to maintain a professional and polite demeanor. Rather than focusing on the reporter's lack of preparation, be ready to address any question by focusing your answers on the information you want to provide.

Unless you're running for political office or are accused of an unsavory crime, most TV and radio reporters will not say, "You didn't answer my question." They will simply take your answer at face value and move on to the next question, relevant or not!

In general, always practice the basics of professional behavior, including:

- ✔ Being on time for your interview, even if the reporter is late
- ✔ Sending any follow-up materials by the date promised
- ✔ Sending a note thanking the reporter for her time

Be prepared

Do your homework ahead of time by finding out some basic information on the publication, television show, or radio program that will be interviewing you. As much as possible, learn who the audience is and what angle the reporter wants the story to take. Does he want you to talk about how the development of your company's new Web site will bring new jobs to your community? Does he want you to talk about how your company is on the leading edge of technology as you add new features to your site to improve your customer service?

You may want to e-mail the reporter to ask what type of information he would like you to provide. With this knowledge, determine the major points, examples, statistics, and anecdotes you may want to use in the interview. The more focused, specific, and useful that your information is, the more likely you are to end up in print or on the air.

Be to the point

Unless you are an up-and-coming Hollywood star (or a famous defense attorney), don't expect to be booked as the solo guest for an hour of *The Oprah Winfrey Show* or *Larry King Live*. Most television and radio interviews are relatively short. The average interview for a top morning radio or TV show is only 5 to 7 minutes long. If you're giving a newspaper or magazine interview, keep in mind that unless the entire article is dedicated to you or your company, only a small percentage of what you say will be used.

As a result of time restrictions and limited story space, reporters are often looking for answers to their questions that are short and to the point, with stories and specifics to add flavor. One way to train yourself to present your information succinctly is to list all the most important points you want to get across and then practice until you are able to make all your points in 20 seconds or less. If a reporter wants additional details or information, he'll ask.

Chapter 10

The Three Cs: Content, Commerce, and Community

In This Chapter

▶ Attracting visitors to your Web site

▶ Encouraging visitors to purchase at your site

▶ Facilitating communication about your company's products or services

*I*ndustry pundits, Web marketers, and Internet gurus alike agree that getting customers to visit your site more often and to stay longer when they do visit are keys to success on the Internet. The goal is to increase the overall amount of time and attention a visitor gives to your site — often referred to as making you site *stickier* (think of flies stuck on flypaper).

Of course, the longer your customers spend at your site and the more often they return, the better the chances are that they'll buy something. We agree with most experts that the key to making your site stickier is to focus on the three Cs of Internet marketing:

✔ **Content.** The quantity and quality of information available on your site

✔ **Commerce.** The ability to enable visitors to make purchases on your site

✔ **Community.** The means for visitors to share specific ideas and information on your site

Content — Giving People a Reason to Visit Your Site

Given the vast amount of Web sites out there, what could you do to inspire a Web surfer to take the time and effort to visit yours? One answer to this question is to make sure that you've got free, useful, and relevant content. Remember that the Internet was originally a vehicle where scientists and academics could freely share ideas, theories, and findings with each other.

Although e-commerce is a growing part of the Web, the culture of the Internet still values the sharing of information — and emphasizes the "for free" aspect of this sharing. You can add value to your site by featuring useful content in the many forms that we discuss in the rest of this section.

White papers

While *white papers* traditionally refers to reports produced by governments, today it's a generic term used to define a certain type of document that your company has created and posted on its Web site. Similar to research papers, white papers are more detailed and longer in length than how-to articles, which tend to be more of a topic overview.

How-to articles

You can empower your customers by presenting how-to articles that identify common tasks and offer concrete methods to accomplish them. Including how-to articles on your Web site:

- Provides value to your customers by giving them relevant and valuable information in small, bite-size chunks.
- Establishes your company as an expert in its field and, as such, increases your customers' comfort level when buying from you.

The more up-to-date the content on your site, the better. When you regularly add to or update the content on your site, your customers come to know you as a source of consistently current and helpful information. They keep coming back to see what's new and improved.

Relevant links and resources

Links on your Web site to other companies that complement your business add value and convenience for your customer. You can extend the boundaries of your service by anticipating what additional products or services your customers are likely to need and providing links to companies that offer those goods or services.

Make sure that the links you provide direct your customers to vendors whom you know and trust. Customers are very likely to view links as endorsements. (For information on how to set up a reciprocal link program, see Chapter 9.)

Online tools

The content on your site isn't limited to passive print; you can provide your visitors with an online tool as part of the content offering as well. Examples include

- ✔ Questionnaires
- ✔ Surveys
- ✔ Tests
- ✔ Industry specific calculators (for example, to calculate mortgage payments)
- ✔ Real-time stock quotes
- ✔ Syndicated news

TIP

To check out an online tool, log on to our Web site at www.scgtraining.com. You can take an interactive audit that evaluates how customer-focused your organization is and then, based on your score, provides recommended actions.

Advice

If your company has a particular area of expertise or specific information you want to share with your customers, try adding an advice section to your site. Having advice on your site can be as simple as offering a Q&A section, where you post and answer typical questions a visitor may have. If you want to make this section more interactive, you can go to a full-blown advice column (think "Dear Abby") and invite visitors to e-mail you with their questions — to which you promise to respond within a given period of time.

E-mail newsletter

One of the best ways to provide valuable information to your customers and, at the same time, promote the commerce side of your business is to create an e-mail newsletter. Among other things, the newsletter can include

- ✔ Feature stories about your customers and how they are using your products and services
- ✔ How-to articles written by your company's employees and designed to empower newsletter recipients
- ✔ Articles by guest writers on topics relevant to your business and your customers' interests. (You can create an arrangement where writers contribute to your newsletter, in exchange for your listing their Web address.)

Make sure to archive all your past newsletters on your site. Set up a system in which visitors can search your previous newsletters by keywords to find what they are looking for.

Live interview or Web-cast event

A great way to bring people to your site and to provide them with interesting and useful information is to offer a live interview. This is the equivalent of a Q&A session presented in text format. The interview is hosted on your site, set for a specific date and time, and features a guest who is of interest to your audience. A moderator facilitates questions from the online audience.

Alternatively, you can offer a *Web-cast event,* which is more like a live lecture. Web casts are set up in much the same way as a live interview, but have the added features of audio and/or video and are often accompanied by synchronized PowerPoint slides. Both interviews and Web casts can be presented live or prerecorded and made available on demand.

Commerce — Making Purchasing from Your Site Possible

According to one study by the Boston Consulting Group (www.bcg.com), forty-four percent of online shoppers experience technical failure at checkout. The most common reasons given for the problem include

- ✔ Pages taking too long to download
- ✔ Product being out of stock
- ✔ Site not accepting the customer's credit card

The same study found that twenty-eight percent of shoppers who have experienced a failure will not buy from the site again. Another ten percent say that because of their negative experiences, they have stopped shopping online altogether!

The obvious first step toward e-commerce glory is to get your product ready to sell and your technology up and running so that you enable customers to buy from you. But doing so won't automatically put you in the e-commerce Hall of Fame. An overwhelming amount of information is available on how to set up, conduct, and improve your e-commerce capabilities. One search of Amazon.com produces over 600 books with "e-commerce" in their titles!

Although numerous issues exist that are related to conducting commerce on your Web site, we've found that the nine items presented in this section form a good foundation for providing your customers with what they need to purchase confidently from your company. Just follow our advice in this section, and you'll be far ahead of many e-commerce sites.

Make it safe

Even simple e-commerce transactions require buyers to provide a great deal of personal information, including their name, address, phone number, and billing data. Naturally, many consumers are a bit leery about giving this information over the Internet. You can go a long way towards making your customers feel safe in purchasing from you by:

- Using credit-card data encryption
- Promising to keep data confidential (in other words, by not selling it)
- Giving customers the choice of keeping their credit-card data on file at your site or not

Make it convenient

If your purchasing processes aren't quick and easy, you run the risk of not only losing the sale, but potentially losing the customer as well.

Make your purchase processes as easy as possible by:

- Asking your customers to provide you with only the data that's needed to fill their order
- Not making customers enter the same information into the system more than once
- Allowing your customers a means to easily update their information on your system. This can save customers significant hassle on subsequent visits to your site

After you've collected your customer's information, make sure you remember who they are the next time they visit. A couple of good examples of this technology are my.yahoo.com and Amazon.com. Talk to your Web developer for the details.

Confirm order status

When customers place orders over the Internet, they expect an immediate confirmation, either at the end of the order process itself or by e-mail immediately afterwards. To avoid confusion, mistakes, and problems down the line, order confirmations should include

- ✔ A list of the items that were ordered
- ✔ The total cost of the order, including shipping and handling
- ✔ The address the order will be delivered to
- ✔ The date the order will be shipped (if backordered, the expected date of shipment)

If a customer orders a product that has a long lead time or is backordered, e-mailing her weekly updates to keep her appraised of the situation is a good idea. Alternatively, you can provide your customers with a Web link to check on the status of their own order.

Make suggestions

Internet customers have come to expect that Web sites will suggest products and services that may be of interest to them based upon their specific buying patterns. For example, Amazon.com has a section under each book listing called "Customers who bought this book also bought" that lists other, related books the customer may want to purchase. This type of suggestive selling is ideally suited for the Web because it gives customers information about what's available, yet allows them to choose whether to click through.

Offer financial incentives

Consider the success of Cost-Co, Wal-Mart, and outlet stores in general. Everyone loves a bargain! One strategy for encouraging customers to buy from you online is to offer a variety of financial incentives that are only available through purchase via your Web site. You will need to experiment to see which ones work best for your type of business. Some of the incentives to try include

- ✔ **Lowering online prices.** Offer your online customers a lower price than they would get if they purchased through one of your other distribution channels (phone order, mail order, or retail). You may want to explain to customers that when they order online, your costs are reduced — you're able to pass those savings along to the customer in the form of lower prices.

✔ **Limiting the offer time.** Send an e-mail notification to your customer list alerting the customers to a special, limited-time offer. Advertise it on your home page, too. The offer can be a "special of the week," a coupon good for a certain amount off of the customer's next purchase, a gift with purchase, or free shipping and handling. The key to this incentive is to be absolutely clear that the offer is for a limited time only.

✔ **Establishing a bonus program.** A bonus program is based on the idea that every time a customer purchases from you, she racks up points towards a future discount, free merchandise, or a bonus gift. To encourage participation, offer free bonus points just for signing up. Once your customers have an account, they will be more likely to come to your site and purchase.

List recent projects

You can help your customers determine whether your business has what they need and want by posting a "recent projects" section on your Web site. The aim of this section is to demonstrate your company's capabilities to potential clients. This section should list three to six of your past projects in chronological order. Each project description should be no more than a paragraph and should include the following elements:

✔ Client name or type of company

✔ Dates of the project

✔ General project description

✔ Results of project

A sample paragraph may look like this:

> April, 2001: We worked with a large national bank to design and implement a customer relations training program for all 40,000 of its staff and managers. The program focused on teaching day to day customer relations skills that the employees could use with customers face-to-face, over e-mail, and on the phone. Topics included: Dealing with difficult customers, creating rapport via e-mail, team-oriented problem solving, etc. The coordinating management program helped managers understand how to create a day-to-day environment for service excellence with a focus on creating a specific plan for improving service within their work area. Evaluations of the program averaged 4.5 on a 5.0 scale.

Get your client's permission before using its name in association with a particular project. If doing so proves too difficult, you can substitute the actual company name with a general reference to your client's type of business, size, or industry category.

Post testimonials

Nothing is more powerful than a well-placed quote from a satisfied client. Give visitors to your site the option of clicking onto a page or two of testimonials from current and past clients. Knowing what other customers say about you helps to influence a potential buyer's decision to purchase from you. Testimonials should be short and sweet — no more than from three to four sentences — and should be attributed to the name, company, and title of the person giving the quote. As always, get permission before posting the quote on your Web site.

Provide customer lists

Although you don't need to include a complete list of every customer you have or have ever had, a customer list can inspire confidence in potential buyers if they see that others in their industry or well-known companies have purchased from you. You can arrange your customer lists alphabetically or by industry, depending on what best suits your type of business. You may want to give visitors to your Web site some sorting options (alphabetically, by industry, by size, and so on) according to their preferences.

Always make sure that you have your customers' permission before adding them to your customer list.

Show samples of your work

If possible, showcase a sample of your work on your Web site. By all means, toot your own horn! For example:

- ✔ If you're a public speaker, streaming video of yourself delivering a speech
- ✔ If you're a creative writer, a sample of your writing
- ✔ If you're a building contractor, photos of completed projects (maybe before and after shots)
- ✔ If you're an artist, a picture of your art
- ✔ If you're a Web developer, a link to a Web site you've designed
- ✔ If you're a landscape architect, a rendering of a landscape plan you've designed

If your business has recently won any awards or been the subject of positive publicity, post this information on your Web site as well. Anything that can make your company be seen as more competent, trustworthy, and knowledgeable in a customer's eyes is worth putting on your Web site.

Community — Encouraging People to Share Ideas about Your Company

Think of your last trip to a mall near your home on a sunny day. You were probably browsing for the perfect gift for a friend, communing with your fellow citizens, and sipping a Starbucks coffee — ahhhh . . . all was right with the world.

Okay, perhaps we've gone a bit too far. But the point is that today's mall is more than just a collection of stores selling everything from shoes to stereo systems. The shopping mall has become an icon of interactivity, a place for us to meet and greet others in our community. In the online world, your Web site has the potential to be an electronic community, a gathering place your customers will want to visit again and again.

According to Howard Rheingold (www.rheingold.com/associates), author of *The Virtual Community: Homesteading on the Electronic Frontier* (MIT Press), "One value of building community is that on a commercial Web site, it gives you a chance to extend your brand to a new audience. If you do it right, you will empower your customers to become evangelists for your enterprise. . . . The key to creating community on your Web site is to put some kind of mechanism in place that allows visitors to exchange ideas, information, opinions, and resources on the topics relevant to your site."

Consider the success of America Online, which started out as a service provider of value-added information and only brought online shopping into the picture later, after it had a strong community of users already in place. The bottom line is that the greater the sense of community you can create on your site and the more you can tailor your offerings to a specific topic, lifestyle, age, or social group, the stronger the customer relationships you will be able to establish with your visitors.

Although you may find the idea of adding community features to your site overwhelming, in reality there are just a few relatively simple ways to do so.

Message boards

Also called *forums* or *bulletin boards,* a message board allows your visitors to post and reply to messages on various topics. It enables a large number of your visitors to have conversations that take place over a period of time (days, weeks, months, or longer). One of the advantages of this type of community activity is that people don't have to be online at the same time to interact with one another.

Putting a message board on your Web site can also present you with an opportunity to understand how your customers perceive your company. By reviewing the content of these discussions, which remain posted on the board, you can learn a lot about your visitors' interests and concerns. This information helps you identify significant issues and pass useful knowledge on to your customer base.

Chat rooms

A chat room is a live, real-time discussion on a topic. Unlike message boards — where messages are posted and left for others to read, consider, and reply to — messages are typed and immediately responded to by other participants who are online at that moment. One of the keys to a successful chat room is to have a skilled moderator online at all times. The benefits of a chat room are that it is immediate, your customers can hang out in real time, and the tone is generally light and fun.

Broadcast e-mail lists

The simplest of all community building methods, e-mail lists (formerly called *list serves*) are similar to traditional mailing lists in that they go simultaneously to everyone on your list — but they require no postage or printing. You can encourage users who have subscribed to your e-mail list to visit your Web site by sending regular information about what your company is doing, special offers, or any other information your customers may find valuable. Unlike open e-mail lists where anyone can post a message, broadcast e-mail lists are one way and only the host company publishes and sends the e-mails.

Chapter 11

Working with a Web Developer

- -

In This Chapter

▶ Understanding Web site evolution and finding your place in the cycle

▶ Determining your Web site goals

▶ Selecting the person or firm to develop your site

- -

*O*ne of the most important decisions you'll make regarding your business's participation in the Internet is choosing a Web developer — someone you'll entrust with the initial design and ongoing development of your Web site. The person or company you pick to shepherd you through this process can have a dramatic effect on both the commercial success and the user friendliness of your site. In short, your Web developer can make magic or tragic of your online presence.

Finding the right Web developer — someone who fits with your company culture, can provide the expertise you need, and is able to work within your budget — is a process with four key components. They are

✔ Assessing where you are today

✔ Determining your Web site goals

✔ Finding ways to achieve your goals

✔ Engaging the right Web developer for your needs

Assessing Where You Are Now to Know What Kind of Help You Need

An essential truth, drilled into the heads of every business school student and occupying the daily thoughts of most marketing managers, is that all products, businesses, and industries have a lifecycle. They are born, grow, reach maturity, and eventually either transform into something new or go out of existence entirely. Why should the Internet be any different? According to research by dotcom.com (www.dotcom.com), an affiliate of Network Solutions (solutions.com), Web sites have a five-stage lifecycle:

- ✔ Stage 1: Securing an online identity
- ✔ Stage 2: Establishing a Web presence
- ✔ Stage 3: Engaging in e-commerce
- ✔ Stage 4: Practicing customer relationship management
- ✔ Stage 5: Serving as a service application model

By identifying the current stage that your site is in and knowing where you need to go next, you can more easily determine the experience and skill level that the Web developer you hire will need to possess.

For more detailed information and specific statistics regarding these stages, go to www.dotcom.com and look up the article titled "Defining the Dot Com Lifecycle."

Stage one: Securing an online identity

Companies in stage one have registered a domain name, and may have even posted a basic home page, but haven't developed a functioning Web site with useful content, let alone e-commerce capabilities. These sites are essentially a holding place in cyberspace. At this stage, when a user enters the URL, she'll most likely see one of the following:

- ✔ A very simple one to three page Web site
- ✔ A Site Under Construction notice
- ✔ A forwarding notice for moving traffic from this domain to a central one

Although some sites never move past stage one, most stage one sites are the first step toward developing an online presence. They lead to a site with more sophisticated features.

Stage two: Establishing a Web presence

Known in the industry as *brochureware,* stage two sites are usually well developed and act as a company's promotional tool by presenting general information on the services or products available from the company. Most of these sites are focused on one-way information and don't have the technical sophistication to allow customer transactions such as online purchasing. In addition to serving as an online brochure, sites at this stage often feature other useful information and services, such as FAQ pages on products and services, white papers and articles relating to the company or industry, employment opportunity postings, and an option to contact the company via e-mail.

Stage three: Engaging in e-commerce

The vast majority of Web sites up today have not reached the third stage. Those who have made it are still using their site for promotion but have evolved to include selling their products or services on the Internet and allowing their customers to purchase directly from them online. The design of these sites and the technology they employ usually allows such options as online payment with credit cards, a secured payment environment, and an e-commerce shopping cart.

Stage four: Practicing customer relationship management

The essential quality of stage four sites is that they've gone beyond providing simple e-commerce to proactively developing and maintaining relationships with customers. Companies with stage four Web sites have made selected business processes Web based, and are often offering online account management, rewards programs, interactive shopping, and e-newsletter subscriptions. The aim is to make customers' online experiences more personal and more satisfying, thus giving them a reason to visit the site again. (See Chapter 4 for more on customer relationship management.)

Stage five: Functioning as a service application model

Stage five sites are the Rolls-Royces of the Internet. Sites at this stage are at the outermost edge of Internet technology and are offering real-time business processing. They allow visitors to buy and sell goods and services, to store and retrieve information, to check inventory, and to manage portfolios.

Establishing Goals for Your Web Site

Before you log on to the Internet, begin thumbing through the yellow pages, or call your local graphic design firm to look for potential Web developers, spend some time thinking about what you specifically want to achieve with your site. Taking your cue from the five stages presented in the section above, consider what stage your site is at today and what your next steps are. Some questions you may want to ask yourself include

- ✔ What is the purpose of this Web site?
- ✔ Who is the target audience for this site?
- ✔ What are the long-term goals for this site?
- ✔ What are the short-term goals for this site?
- ✔ What is the scope of this particular project?

According to Web development expert Jon Leland, president of Communication Bridges (`www.combridges.com`), knowing what your goals are up front is the key to a good working relationship with your Web developer and a successful Web site. He says, "As with any project, you have to start by being clear about what your objectives are. You should ask yourself, 'What would success on the Web mean for me?' For some people, it is having an effective brochureware site, for others it is generating sales by moving product, for others it is attracting an audience so they can build visibility or interest in what they have to offer."

The more specific the information is that you provide a Web developer, the more accurate an estimate the developer can give you of the time and cost involved in achieving your site goals. Beyond determining what your main objective is, you should be prepared to answer these questions before you speak with a Web developer:

- ✔ Do you already have a domain name or will you need to register one?
- ✔ What specific products or services will be sold on the site?
- ✔ Who do you have in mind to host the site?
- ✔ How do you plan on maintaining and updating the site?
- ✔ Do you have company literature that can be used in the site?
- ✔ How sophisticated a design do you want for the site? (Text, animation, audio, video?)
- ✔ Are you planning on doing interactive features, such as feedback/response forms?
- ✔ What technologies you will need to meet your goals? (Shopping cart, database, animation?)

✔ What is your budget for site creation, maintenance, and marketing?

✔ Are you planning on accepting payments over the site?

One way you can estimate the overall number of pages your site will need is to create a site map, which is essentially a flowchart that represent the structure of your site by showing the main content categories and subcategories you plan to include.

Exploring ways to reach your goals

Now that you know what your site goals are, the last step before sitting down to interview potential Web developers is to decide how you want to divide up the work of the project. For example:

✔ What aspects do you want to hire a Web developer to handle?

✔ What parts of the project will go to other vendors (graphic artists, copywriters, and so on)?

✔ What role do you want your existing staff to play?

Troubleshooting

If you already have a Web site up and you are not getting the traffic or business from it you want, consider hiring a Web developer to investigate these areas and make updates or changes where needed:

✔ Is your site professional looking, when compared to the competition?

✔ Are you currently well positioned in the search engines?

✔ Do you need to freshen up your content to encourage people to come back?

✔ Is your contact information easily found on your home page?

✔ Is your site easy enough to navigate?

✔ Does your site take too long to download due to heavy graphics?

✔ Are you maximizing the use of metatags on all of your pages?

✔ Are you making the best use of title tags, descriptions, and keywords?

✔ Are you using frames? If so, could you get rid of them?

✔ Are you including too much information on one page?

✔ Are you providing something for free to your visitors?

✔ Can you make your site more interactive?

✔ Are you collecting the e-mail addresses of your visitors, so that you can contact them?

✔ Do you have an e-newsletter or e-zine your visitors can subscribe to?

✔ Do you accept credit cards online?

✔ Are your links currently up and working?

The tasks you hire a Web developer to take on will depend in large part on the resources you already have in-house, how much time, energy, and money you have to invest in the project, and the work you may have already put into designing your Web site.

A Web developer can contribute to your site development project in many ways. A developer can

- ✔ Set up all the technology necessary to achieve your site goals.

- ✔ Design, implement, and maintain all aspects of your site.

- ✔ Advise you on ways to implement plans you've already begun to draft.

- ✔ Convert materials, such as brochures, product descriptions, and testimonials, to HTML. Or, a developer can create these materials for you.

- ✔ Create an overall graphic style that represents your business. Or, a developer can transfer your established graphic image to your new Web environment.

Print designers who have limited experience with Web development often make the mistake of thinking that anything they can do in print will translate to the Web. They don't realize the limitations of the HTML environment. For this reason, it's a good idea to hire a graphic designer for general direction, but then supplement that person with a Web designer. Working together, the graphic designer and the Web designer should

- ✔ Develop graphics that are bandwidth friendly.

- ✔ Create interfaces that are user friendly.

- ✔ Design layouts that recognize HTML limitations.

Naming a point person to head the project

Despite the best of intentions and an enthusiastic start, many companies' Web sites fall into a black hole and languish, their potential unrealized. It usually happens like this: The management team goes off on its yearly strategy planning (and golfing) retreat. At the retreat, managers decide to make a presence on the Internet an important part of the marketing mix. Management gets back to the office and announces its intentions, but fails to assign enough time, budget, or staff to the project. The result is a Web site that's birthed but becomes an orphan and does not get the attention and resources it deserves. A sad story, but one that must be told.

A rose by any other name

We asked a number of Web developers which term they felt best described what they do. The three most common answers we got were

✔ Web master

✔ Web designer

✔ Web developer

One thing they all agreed on is that in today's marketplace, these are amorphous terms and are used interchangeably by clients to describe the two critical, yet distinct, components of Web site development: the creative and technical aspects.

All creative aspects of Web site development would be entrusted to a Web designer or developer — the person or company responsible for making the creative decisions concerning your site. Web designers determine how your site will look and feel. Their work may include

✔ Creation of graphic design

✔ Writing of site copy

✔ Design of information architecture

✔ Development of site structure

✔ Determining the proper media mix

✔ Determining the amount of streaming media, animation, and flash to be used

✔ Determining the types and amount of sound to be used

The technical aspects of Web site development are usually considered the work of a Web master — the person or company responsible for the technical decisions and upkeep of your site. Web masters determine how the site will work technically and are often given the job of ongoing maintenance. Their work may include

✔ Programming of HTML and other interfaces

✔ Database design

✔ Development of e-commerce shopping carts

✔ Hosting the Web site

✔ Performing site updates as needed

✔ Dealing with ongoing technical site issues

One way to avoid this too common situation is to assign someone in your organization accountability for the overall Web site project. This is the person who has a "The Buck Stops Here" sign on her desk. The person's duties may include

✔ Developing a budget for the Web site

✔ Screening potential Web developers

✔ Communicating with the Web developer

✔ Putting together the Web development team from in-house talent and outside vendors

✔ Managing the Web development team

Engaging the Right Web Developer

You know your objectives, you have a budget in place, and you have the thumbs up from management. It's finally time to take the big leap and hire a Web site developer. What now? The questions race through your frenzied brain, stimulated by that triple espresso you downed at lunch. Where do I find a Web site developer? How much will it cost to develop my site? How can I make sure they'll do a good job? And on and on.

Unfortunately, many companies don't put the same care, concern, and attention to detail into choosing a Web developer that they would into hiring a graphic designer to create their annual report or an accountant to handle their books. To make matters even more complex, both the job description and the definition of *Web developer* is constantly evolving, making it even more difficult for the average businessperson to determine whom they should hire to develop their site.

The job of putting together a Web site is complex and involves a variety of skills. For this reason, Web developers often have a stable of other experts available who work for them either as employees or on a subcontract basis. Look for a Web development firm that has working relationships with graphic designers, HTML programmers, database programmers, and others who can work together to form a Web development team that can get your job done with the quality you expect.

Evaluating potential Web developers

If you're looking to develop a site that is relatively simple and small, you can probably find all the capabilities you need in a solo practitioner. If your site is going to be mid-sized and offer more bells and whistles, a small Web shop (a company whose business is creating Web sites) can, more than likely, take care of your needs. In general, the advantage of a hiring a solo practitioner or a small Web shop is that your site gets developed by the people you spoke with when you were making the decision on who to hire. Solo practitioners can't really delegate the job to someone else, after all!

If you're looking to develop a large and highly complex site that utilizes leading edge technology, you may need to engage a major Web development firm. The advantage of hiring a large firm is that it employees multitudes of staff who are available to work on your site. Each staff member has specialized knowledge. Regardless of which way you decide to go, certain criteria exist that you can use to evaluate potential Web developers, be they solo practitioners, small Web shops, or large Web development firms.

Technical competence

Ask the developers to describe specific projects they've worked on that incorporate the type of technology you expect to use in your site. For example, if your site is going to be animation heavy, take a look at Web sites that the developers have already created to make sure that they've had prior experience incorporating animation that has the quality you expect. Other technological issues to look for on sites that the developers have created include

- Clear site navigation
- Innovative storytelling
- Appropriate mix of media (audio, video, print, and so on)

In today's rapidly changing business environment, technical competence requires constant updating. Be sure to ask the Web developers what kinds of continuing education they participate in. They should have some method to stay on top of the latest technological bells and whistles in Web site development.

Creative style

In general, you should feel that the sites the developer has created previously are attractive and to your taste, in terms of overall look and graphics. Ask the developer to provide you with a few sites it has created that you can specifically review for overall design quality. If you don't see design concepts that you like, chances are you have incompatible design tastes. Move on and find another developer.

Ongoing maintenance capabilities

One of the biggest complaints clients have about working with Web developers is that, after the site is up and running, getting the developer to respond promptly to changes that need to be made is difficult. One reason for this difficulty is that some developers are strictly in the business of creating the initial site and are not interested in or capable of offering ongoing maintenance. Although hiring one company to do the site development and another to do the maintenance is a perfectly acceptable and common alternative, you want to know beforehand where you stand, in terms of maintenance, with the particular Web developer. Communicating in advance insures that expectations are clear and prevents future problems and frustrations.

Communication skills

Because they've focused most of their attention on honing their technical expertise, many people who develop sites are a whiz at programming — but weak in their interpersonal communication skills. Since the Web developer needs to work hand in hand with you and others, pay attention to how the person communicates in the interview stage. In addition, you may want to call its references and inquire about the following:

- ✔ Was the person's general manner helpful and customer focused?
- ✔ Was the person cooperative in working with others?
- ✔ Did she provide periodic updates on the project's progress?
- ✔ Did she communicate when a problem occurred?
- ✔ Did she let you know if she was going to miss a deadline?

Professional conduct

Because a Web developer is often made privy to the most intimate aspects of your business, including client lists, pricing structure, marketing strategies, and the like, you need to feel confident that the developer will

- ✔ Keep the details of your business confidential.
- ✔ Avoid putting herself in a position to have a conflict of interest between you and any of her other clients.

Many firms ask the Web developer to sign a nondisclosure agreement. Speaking with the Web developer and specifically asking her to tell you if she's currently working with, or has immediate plans to work with, any client where a conflict of interest may exist with your business is a good idea. Dealing with these issues up-front is an important step in establishing a professional relationship with the Web developer. It also helps prevent misunderstandings and problems further down the line.

For the protection of all the parties involved, always get a contract — in writing — prior to the beginning of work. It doesn't matter how great the rapport is between you and your developer. Having a contract protects the developer and ensures that you get what you're paying for. Among other items, the contract should spell out the project scope, the technologies to be used, deadlines, fee arrangements, and payment schedules.

References and credentials

One of the great things about the Internet is that it's given birth to an array of new jobs, including that of Web developer. The downside of this boom is that virtually anyone can hang out a shingle and declare themselves a Web designer, regardless of their background or qualifications. For example, a graphic artist may be great at designing print brochures, have no technical knowledge on implementing an e-commerce site, and declare himself a Web developer! Likewise, a technical-type with outstanding programming skills may decide to go into the Web development business, although he has no sense of how color and design should be used.

Checking the credentials and references of any potential Web developer is critically important in order to insure that the person you hire has the skills necessary to complete the job to your satisfaction. Some issues to consider include

✔ **Has the developer done this type of Web site before?** Given the goals of your project and the various services (including graphic, writing, and technology) you need, is this person qualified? Ask the Web developer to provide you with examples (and URL addresses) of Web sites she has designed that are similar to the type and stage of site you are looking to create. (We write about Web site stages earlier in this chapter.)

✔ **Does this person have any industry or software certifications?** Although being certified doesn't guarantee that the Web developer will be able to get the job done, certification is a good place to start in evaluating the person's knowledge base. However, keep in mind that many top-of-the-line Web developers have no certification, but deliver a high-quality job based on their practical experience and the knowledge gained from self-education.

✔ **How long has the developer been doing this?** The more experience a developer has, the more professional, effective, and unique your Web site will be. Look for someone who has a minimum of three to five years of Web development experience. Remember that the less experience a developer has, the more likely she will be to use templates from an off-the-shelf program. Although a novice developer may only cost you a few hundred dollars, she could leave you with a mediocre site than can cost you thousands of dollars in lost business.

✔ **What do the developer's references have to say about her?** As old fashioned as it may seem, one of the best ways to determine the credibility of a Web developer is to call a few of her clients and ask how their project went. Getting the information straight from the horse's mouth can be invaluable. Don't limit your questions to the person's technical capabilities. To get the big picture, focus your questions on the creative and interpersonal aspects of the reference-giver's relationship with the developer. Consider asking:

  • How easy is the developer to do business with?

  • Did she take a collaborative approach?

  • How was her follow-through on what she promised?

  • Did she get work done on time?

 A good source of information on Web developers is the International Webmasters Association (www.iwanet.org). Among other services, it offers referrals to local resources in your area, certification programs, and white papers on research conducted in the field of Web development.

Where are all the Web designers?

A recent survey by Real Prices Confidential (maintained at www.brennerbooks.com) reported the concentration of Web-services businesses per state. If you live in New York, you have a good shot of bumping into a Web developer every time you go to Starbucks for a double caf, nonfat latté with extra foam. If you live in Tucson, the pickings are slimmer. Fortunately, Web site development is one of the areas where geography is less important than expertise. You can have a perfectly satisfying relationship with a Web developer whom you never see in person. The percentage of all Web developers who live in each state breaks down as follows:

- New York   (14 percent)
- Texas   (12.6 percent)
- California   (8.8 percent)
- Pennsylvania   (8.1 percent)
- New Jersey   (7.5 percent)
- South Carolina (6.4 percent)
- Florida   (3.3 percent)
- Illinois   (3.1 percent)
- Oklahoma   (2.6 percent)
- Connecticut   (2.2 percent)
- Hawaii   (1.8 percent)
- Washington   (1.6 percent)
- Arizona   (1.3 percent)
- Other States   (under 1 percent each)

Calculating the cost

As the old saying goes, "You get what you pay for." This adage is especially true in the area of Web site development. You can get a Web site developed for $500 if you hire a high-school student. You can pay $5,000,000 and hire a great Web development firm. According to a report by Real Prices Confidential, Web site design prices vary from between $10 and $250 an hour in the United States.

The bottom line is that the fair and reasonable price for Web site development is a subjective mater. This being said, the fee you are charged will, more than likely, be determined by a combination of factors. If you're having trouble getting the developer's price to match your budget, try adjusting one or more of these factors:

- The time and effort required to meet the scope of the project
- The level of technical difficulty involved in creating your site
- The likelihood that doing your project will prevent the vendor from pursing others

- ✔ The schedule and time limitations you have determined for the project
- ✔ The fees typically charged in your area by developers with similar credentials
- ✔ The likelihood of future or ongoing business with your firm
- ✔ The level of expertise, experience, and ability of the developer
- ✔ The nature and length of your professional relationship with the developer

Don't ask a Web developer to give you an estimate over the phone of what she thinks your Web site will cost to create. This approach won't result in your getting an accurate estimate and will put the developer in an unfair position. Instead, after the person has had a chance to discuss your goals and needs for the site, ask her to provide you with a formal, written proposal that provides accurate cost estimates, a timeline, and specifies what results will be produced.

Part IV
Essential E-Mail: Building Online Relationships

The 5th Wave   By Rich Tennant

"I like getting complaint letters by e-mail. It's easier to delete than to shred."

In this part . . .

E-mail is so convenient that it's the most widely used communication tool in business today. Its rapid rise in popularity has created new service shortcomings, such as inappropriate messages, an unfriendly tone, and poor response time. Many surveys show that customers feel as if much improvement is necessary before e-mail is a satisfactory means of service communications.

In this part, we show you how to create customer-friendly e-mails that make an impact and produce the results you need. We present the ten most common e-mail mistakes — and how to avoid them. We also show you how to capitalize on e-mail's hidden advantages — building teams and solving problems.

Chapter 12

E-Mail: Making the Most of the Medium

. . . .

In This Chapter

▶ Celebrating the convenience of e-mail

▶ Understanding the one-sided nature of e-mail communication

▶ Minimizing misunderstandings and avoiding negative impressions

▶ Recognizing the limitations of e-mail

. . . .

E-mail is so inexpensive and convenient that it's rapidly becoming the communication channel of choice for many companies and their customers. In our office, we love e-mail. After all, it has all the following advantages:

- ✔ It allows you to communicate with many people simultaneously, by using multiple addresses.

- ✔ It leaves a trail, so that the history of a conversation can be traced.

- ✔ It provides an easy reference to past communications.

- ✔ It doesn't require that our customers be available when we send them a message (a great benefit when working across time zones — you can accomplish things even while you sleep!).

- ✔ It saves us time when we need to communicate with someone, but we don't have time for small talk.

- ✔ It enables us to attach pertinent files that recipients can easily open (usually) without the delay involved with other mail delivery systems.

E-mail communication, although convenient, doesn't always obey the rules of conversation. Electronic messages cannot convey your facial expressions, body language, tone of voice, or other clues to the real meaning of your words. Consequently, e-mail communications are far more likely to be misinterpreted than if you were to have those same communications face-to-face.

Understanding E-Mail as the Medium of Monologue

A dialogue is a conversation between people. In a dialogue, you receive immediate feedback through facial expression and body language, or, if the conversation is taking place over the phone, through tone of voice, pauses, and gasps — of delight or horror. All of these convey a sense of your customer's reaction to what you're saying. This subtle information is very helpful when you're trying to deliver excellent service to that customer. Also, a conversation provides the opportunity for immediate clarification. By asking questions, you can make sure that what you're saying is being understood and that what you're hearing and understanding is accurate.

A monologue, by contrast, is the discourse of a single person. Ultimately, e-mail communications are monologues. No matter how fast and furious the e-mails may fly back and forth, when you write an e-mail message, you are alone. We're in the dark when we write or read e-mails. Without all the accompanying signals, we can sometimes sit and stare at an e-mail message for hours without really knowing what the customer or colleague is trying to convey. For example, imagine receiving the following e-mail message from your boss after a meeting:

> I found the planning and design meeting most interesting this morning and I was happy to see you in attendance. I can always count on you to come up with unusual ideas. I have a few questions about you heading up this project. Let's meet tomorrow so that we can go over the future of this initiative.

What would your impression of this e-mail be? Maybe you'd perceive it as a good message, a vote of confidence in your ability to think outside the box in team meetings. Or, maybe you'd start looking for a new job because the message appears to criticize your contributions at the meeting. In fact, it seems as if the boss was surprised you showed up at all!

In many cases, when you know the sender of an e-mail, you can accurately interpret her intended meaning. Difficulties arise when you are dealing with someone you have never met or spoken to before.

Minimizing misunderstandings

In business, the last thing you want to do is to inadvertently alienate a customer or colleague. Unfortunately, e-mail is a medium where unintended alienation can easily happen, without your even realizing what's going on. Here are some suggestions to help you minimize misunderstandings when you send e-mails to your customers and colleagues:

✔ **Read through your completed e-mail draft before you send it.** Stepping back and looking at your message objectively is useful. If you have doubts about any parts of it, no matter how slight your doubt may be, consider rewriting that part. Trust your intuition.

✔ **Run the message by a friend or colleague.** Ask for her first impressions. If you have to explain what you really meant to say, rewrite the message so that your meaning is clear.

✔ **Check for anything that could be offensive, upsetting, or misconstrued.** Remember that some customers are easily offended or upset. Don't assume that the person to whom you are writing has the same attitude, personality, viewpoint, or sense of humor as you.

✔ **Start with a softener phrase.** Before jumping into the core of the message, create a friendly tone by using a short phrase such as, "Thank you for your recent e-mail" or "I hope this note finds you well."

Avoiding making a negative impression

In addition to the increased possibility of misunderstanding when you communicate through e-mail, you also run an increased risk of making a negative impression. E-mail is so quick and convenient that it's easy to get swept away as you're writing. Then you shoot out an e-mail to an important customer, oblivious to the impact that your message can have on its reader.

You have to be sure that the e-mails you send create a favorable impression — they need to reflect your company's dedication to customer consideration. The following are situations that may not devastate a customer relationship, but can create negative impressions:

✔ **Sending a message that is difficult to read because of poor formatting.** First impressions count, so make sure that your messages don't look like wall-to-wall words with no room for a virtual breath.

Add paragraphs or spacing to your e-mails so that they don't resemble the small print on a life insurance policy. Prior to sending an e-mail, take a look at the overall message and ask yourself "Is there enough white space, and is there room for the customer to take a mental breath?"

✔ **Sending e-mails with numerous spelling, punctuation, or grammatical mistakes.** Spell checkers do not catch every misspelled word, so give your messages a manual once-over after you spell check them. If you do so, you'll catch the *manger* that should be a *manager*.

Interestingly, research indicates that poor punctuation and grammar are not significant to many e-mail recipients in the United States. Even so, assume that your customers do care about preciseness. Customers may interpret grammar and spelling errors as sloppiness — not something that contributes to the image of your company. Read your e-mails through, checking punctuation and adjusting any grammar that reads awkwardly.

✔ **Sending messages that don't explicitly state what the recipient is expected to do — if anything.** When you send or forward e-mails, don't assume that recipients will know how you expect them to respond — nobody can read your mind. Often, messages are forwarded as FYIs to keep colleagues in an information loop. If this is the case, make a point of adding a brief "I thought this would be of interest to you" or simply labeling it as FYI in the subject line or in the text of the message. If, on the other hand, you would like the receiver to take some action, make this clear in a brief note at the beginning of your message. (You can find more information on making e-mail requests that work in Chapter 14.)

✔ **Sending e-mails that don't provide all the background information necessary for the recipient to take any requested action.** Sometimes, when you are very familiar with an ongoing issue, assuming that others have the same intimate knowledge that you do is an easy mistake to make.

If, for example, you've been dealing with a customer issue for the past week and you want to e-mail a co-worker to ask for assistance in the matter, understand that the information you have discovered is probably more in-depth and specific than the information that your co-worker has. Remember to provide the co-worker with all the information she needs to really be of service to you.

✔ **Sending e-mails that have grown tremendously long due to multiple forwardings and replys.** Having to scroll up and down a document dozens of times in order to figure out who said what to whom and when it was said, and to whom you need to respond by when about what is frustrating. When a message has so many parts that scrolling through it is like unrolling wallpaper, consider sending a new e-mail that summarizes all the toings and froings in a simple paragraph or two. By all means, include attachments — but make sure that the body of your e-mail explains what they are and how they relate to the issue at hand.

Recognizing the Limitations of E-Mail

Although e-mail does provide a fast and convenient means of communications, it does not work well for all messages. In the following cases, using e-mail is most often inappropriate:

✔ **When sending messages of a confidential nature.** Because e-mails are not private — in other words, they can be forwarded to the moon and back — don't use them for anything that is of a private nature. Have a face-to-face meeting or use the telephone for topics that are emotional or related to coaching or counseling an employee.

✔ **When sharing big news, such as a takeover by another company.** We once conducted an employee survey for a large company. The overriding feedback was that there was a lack of communication from the top echelons on down.

The executives defended themselves by stating that during the recent takeover by another company, they had sent monthly e-mails to staff to keep everyone informed. The point these executives missed was that most employees want to hear important (potentially life-changing) news from a live person with whom they can interact and ask questions.

✔ **When dealing with time-sensitive issues.** Consider that most people do not check their e-mail as often as their voicemail when they are on the road and away from their desk. Urgent matters, especially when a customer needs a speedy response, should be pursued via the telephone, although you can certainly send an e-mail as well.

✔ **When distressed customers need immediate problem resolution, or at least a sympathetic ear.** Sending an e-mail isn't as personal as engaging in a conversation. When dealing with matters that require empathy and understanding (as well as a resolution), you need to have a dialogue.

Most of us learned to write and use the telephone at an early age, but e-mail is quite new and we do not have the same familiarity with it. The ease with which we write letters and make calls does not translate to e-mails and consequently we tend to make more mistakes when using it. Also, different people have different ideas about what is and isn't acceptable in this medium. Slowly, as we get more used to using e-mail, accepted norms will be established. Until then, make the most of the medium by using it as appropriately as you can.

Chapter 13

The Nuts and Bolts of E-Mail Writing

....

In This Chapter

▶ Recognizing the power of words

▶ Adding rhythm and style to your messages

▶ Discovering the new rules of e-courtesy

....

*A*lthough business e-mails are less formal than business letters, they still represent you and your business. A sloppy e-mail can signify to a customer that you run a sloppy business — that may not be true, but a customer's perception is sometimes more important than reality. So even though you love the ease and speed of e-mail communications, don't get lulled into falsely thinking that this is the new millennium and nobody has time to care about spelling or grammar. Au contraire. We find that as e-mail becomes more universal, people's standards become more sophisticated.

When you're communicating with customers via e-mail — especially in a service environment, where you may have never met the person you're sending an e-mail to — the normal cues of dress, self-carriage, tone of voice, and so on are all absent. Even if you're confident that you can adjust and demonstrate your professionalism through just the words that appear on the screen, what about all the other people in your organization? Do your employees realize that they need to focus and consider myriad issues when they write an e-mail?

Being customer centric online requires that you understand how the language you use in your e-mail communications can enhance or diminish the perception the reader has of your company.

Focusing on Words — Knowing Your Raw Material

It may seem like minutia, but one of the smallest elements of language — the word — can greatly affect your professional image, because customers get either positive or negative impressions from them. The words you choose (and how you present them) can add or detract from the customer's overall feeling of the service you offer. Alright, so a section on spelling makes you feel like you're in fourth grade again. But many successful professionals continue to make serious mistakes in their e-mails, mistakes that cut into the professional image that person has cultivated for years. In the following pages, we tell you everything you need to know to make your e-mails not just correct, but exemplary.

Spelling

Having misspelled words in your e-mails is like having little stumbling blocks sprinkled throughout your message, because misspellings stop the natural flow of your readers' eyes as they scan the page. Every time your readers trip over a spelling mistake, they're momentarily distracted. As a result, your message loses impact because the reader loses focus on what it is you're trying to convey. For example:

> We wood be happpy to visit your showroom and discuss yor spcific needs.

To avoid truly embarrassing spelling errors, use the spellchecker that comes with your software program. As you're writing, go ahead and focus on the content of your message — don't get hung up worrying about correcting spelling. After you've completed your message, go over it with a spellchecker to catch mistakes.

Be sure to read through your message again to find any inappropriate words that may have slipped detection. The following list shows some commonly confused words that you have to watch out for because your spell checker won't identify them as errors:

- Advise/advice
- Affect/effect
- Compliment/complement
- Desert/dessert
- Illicit/elicit

- Moral/morale
- Personal/personnel
- Principal/principle
- Stationary/stationery
- Their/there/they're
- Through/thorough
- Too/to/two
- Whether/weather
- Write/right/rite
- Your/you're

Be sure that your e-mail communications convey the same professionalism you exhibit in all other aspects of your business. For grammar tips to help you avoid common mistakes in your e-mail messages, see the Appendix.

Word choice

Using weak words or including unnecessary words to fluff up your sentences can dilute the impact of your message. Try to choose descriptive words that really say what you mean. For example:

- **Weak:** I *read* the report last night.
- **Strong:** I *studied* the report last night.
- **Fluffy:** I think we have the ability to make a decision regarding making changes to the new call center staffing policy.
- **Concise:** We can change the call center staffing policy.

If you substitute weak words for stronger ones and cut out all unnecessary word fluff, you can convey your ideas with greater impact.

Avoid using fancy words that draw attention to themselves and away from the meaning you're trying to get across in your message. By changing $10 words to $5 words, you get a message that is simpler and more direct. For example:

- **Fancy:** The presentation commenced by demonstrating how to obtain the maximum from the new system.
- **Direct:** The presentation started by showing how to get the most from the new systems.

Also, avoid using vague or general words. Instead, opt for specific words — they add strength to a message because they paint a picture and add character. For example:

- ✔ **General:** Customers reacted strongly to the new color combination.
- ✔ **Specific:** Customers really liked the new orange, green, and pink combination.

The words that you use to begin a sentence have a lot of impact, so choose them carefully. Don't waste this prime location by filling it with phrases such as, *It is, There are, I think, I'm not sure.*

For tips on using word-choice to build rapport through e-mails, check out Chapter 16.

E-mail acronyms

Numerous e-mail–specific acronyms have evolved, and they routinely occur in e-mail communications. Part of the reason may be that people are trying to work as fast as their computers, and a shortened word or phrase may save a nanosecond or two.

If you want to work at Internet speed (or want to appear to be in the know), here's a list of some common acronyms in e-mail communications:

- ✔ FYI (For your information)
- ✔ BTW (By the way)
- ✔ F2F (Face to face)
- ✔ O^3 (One-on-one)
- ✔ GMTA (Great minds think alike)
- ✔ IMHO (In my humble opinion)
- ✔ LOL (Laughing out loud)
- ✔ TNX (Thanks)
- ✔ IOW (In other words)

Too many acronyms make a message difficult to read, so use them sparingly. Also, be aware that using such abbreviated language conveys a very casual tone that may not be appropriate for all business communications.

Capital rules

Ever find yourself typing in the title of a presentation and not knowing which words need capitalizing and which don't? We used to have this problem until we researched the rules about capital letters. Here they are:

- Use capitals on all the main words of your heading.

- Don't capitalize prepositions, for example, *to, of, at.*

- Don't capitalize articles, such as, *the, a, an.*

- Don't capitalize conjunctions, such as, *and, so, but, or.*

- Here's an example: "How to Work Faster and Quieter than Your Computer"

Other capital ideas:

- Never capitalize the seasons.

- Use capital letters for geographic locations and directions only when they are used specifically, for example, *Southeast Asia* or *the West End of London.* When using general terms, keep to lower case, for example, *west coast, southern states,* and so on.

Adding Some Style to Your E-Mails

Well-constructed sentences are easy to read. Although they're concise, they do not resemble quips from Yoda. You should always strive for a balance between getting to the point and creating a friendly tone. This section offers some ideas and strategies for mastering effective e-mail expression.

Note: Although we don't have the space to write about this topic in great detail, you can get more information from *Business Communications For Dummies* (Hungry Minds).

Vary your sentence styles

No one expects your service e-mails to be Nobel Prize–worthy. In fact, customers probably won't consciously pick apart an e-mail, judging whether it's written well or written so-so. However, you can create an impression of dynamism and energy if you add variety to your e-mails. Use different sentence styles to do so.

- **Exclamatory sentences.** These sentences express strong opinions or surprising facts. They, not surprisingly, often end with an exclamation point. For example, "I had to work all weekend!"

- **Declarative sentences.** These are sentences that express facts or thoughts, for example, "I will be in my cubicle by 1 p.m. Monday."

- **Imperative sentences.** These usually are asking for action. They usually begin with a verb. For example, "Take messages for me until I get in, please."

- **Interrogative sentences.** These sentences ask questions. They usually begin with *can, who, why, will, when, have* or *how*. For example, "Will you please get me a double-decaf-mocha-latte-no-foam in a double-cup when you go to the cafeteria at lunchtime?"

- **Stream-of-consciousness sentences.** These sentences don't follow any particular grammar rules. They can be very expressive and often help create an informal and conversational tone. For example, "I can't stay late on Monday afternoon . . . the plumbers coming . . . another back-up . . . Junior's been pushing crackers down the drain . . . I'll need to leave around 4." Although these sentences are fine for informal communication with your friends and family, avoid them at all costs in a service environment.

Use a mixture of sentence styles in your e-mails to make them more expressive. The following two paragraphs contain the same basic message, but the selection of sentences is very different in each:

- **Boring.** Thank you for telling us how much you enjoyed our spring catalog. We enjoy being able to present our customers with new and different fashions each season. We are always happy to receive customer feedback because it let's us know what we are doing well and what we need to improve. We hope you enjoy the summer catalog just as much as the spring one.

- **Interesting.** We were delighted to receive your message about our spring catalog. Have you seen the new summer catalog? We're very proud of it! Letters like yours inspire us to keep doing even better. We'd enjoy hearing from you again if you have any comments about future issues.

The second message, although shorter, contains a mix of different sentence styles. By using the first sentence to express a thought, the second sentence to ask a question, the third sentence to express a strong opinion, the fourth sentence to express another thought, and the last sentence to suggest future action, the writer has added variation and vitality to the ideas being expressed.

Don't try and use every style in every message you write. Keep in mind that your primary goal is clarity.

Vary your sentence lengths

Reading an e-mail message full of sentences that are all the same length can be monotonous. By varying the length of your sentences, you create a more interesting tempo and add impact to your message. The following message presents sentences that are nearly all the same length. An IT service technician is trying to communicate information to internal customers. The words communicate the intended message, but the tempo is flat and even lethargic. The customers, without necessarily knowing why, may get a negative impression of the IT department.

> As you all know, yesterday the network went down for two hours. The cause of the problem was a server that went offline. We are trying to discover why the failsafe back-ups did not switch in. I will let you know more information as I get it. Thank you all for doing whatever was needed to handle the situation.

Compare the same message, but with a few changed words and varied sentence lengths:

> As you all know, yesterday the network was off-line for two hours. A server went down. The backup didn't switch in. We are trying to discover why the failure occurred and I will let you know as soon as I know. You all did a remarkable job. Thank you all for doing whatever it took.

In this second example, the IT service technician who crafted the e-mail not only communicates the necessary information about the network, but conveys it in a helpful, personable way. The varied sentence lengths add a lilt to the message that makes it sound friendlier.

As you vary the length of the sentences in your own e-mails, remember that short sentences are more expressive and energetic in nature, and as such work well for presenting concise thoughts or ideas. For example, "The network is down" or "We closed the deal." Long sentences are more effective for exploring possibilities, elaborating on ideas, or presenting complicated concepts. For example, "We find that most companies understand the importance of customer satisfaction surveys, yet only a few know how to really leverage the information to increase both sales and loyalty."

Very long sentences can be confusing to the reader. If you find that you have a very long sentence, look for a way of separating it into two or three smaller sentences.

Personalizing automated e-mail responses

The use of e-mail management systems is becoming more prevalent in the workplace — leading to customers receiving technical and impersonal e-mails that do nothing to generate loyalty or a sense that the company cares. The problem is growing because of the increasing use of automated e-mail management systems. Many call centers, help desks, and technical support departments have e-mail technology that can "read" incoming e-mails and automatically present a response e-mail with a solution. The agent then forwards this information to the customer. For example, imagine that the technical support department of a software company receives an e-mail from a customer regarding a problem associated with making changes in the preferences window. The automated system scans the e-mail for key words such *as changing, preferences, window* and so on. The system searches the software company's database of known problems and selects the fixes prompted by the keywords.

We have worked with several online service companies, helping them train their agents to add a personal touch and a positive tone to automated e-mail responses. Using the information in this chapter, you can give even the most technical e-mails an individual edge and that will help separate you from the pack.

Select your voice

Active sentences convey your ownership and responsibility to the reader. Passive sentences, on the other hand, tend to avoid responsibility. For example:

- ✔ **Active:** Our accounts payable department promptly handles travel expenses.
- ✔ **Passive:** Travel expenses are handled promptly by our accounts payable department.

In the active example, the subject of the sentence (the accounts payable department) is taking the action (promptly handling travel expenses). In the passive example, the subject (travel expenses) is being done to.

Now and again, it's appropriate to use the passive voice. In the following active sentence, the writer inadvertently diminishes the impact of e-mail by accentuating the role of the call center: "Our call center has seen dramatic changes since the introduction of e-mail."

In a sentence where what is being done (e-mail) is more important than the doer (the call center), the passive approach adds emphasis. For example, "Dramatic changes in our call center were affected by the use of e-mail."

Watch your tone

The tone of your message is the mood that your message conveys to the reader. In a message to a friend, the tone of your e-mail may be informal, light-hearted, tongue-in-cheek, or comical. A message to a colleague, customer, or business associate may be more formal, serious, professional, or analytical. E-mails written to customers should always have a friendly and courteous tone — regardless of how you may be feeling at the time — and should always sound professional.

Reread an e-mail before you send it if you have any doubts about its tone. If you're still not sure, run it by a colleague whose opinion you trust.

Remembering E-Mail Courtesy

Our research shows that the following are the most common courtesy mistakes made when writing and sending e-mails. Remember that people usually read e-mail quickly and the impressions that they form of your writing happen in a flash. Use the following information to insure your message comes across with instant appeal.

Make invitations, not demands

Most of the e-mails that you send are asking somebody to do something. The way you phrase a request can influence how the recipient perceives your tone. Invitations create a friendlier tone than demands. For example, "Could you please give me your order number?" versus "Give me your order number."

To create a friendlier tone in your e-mails, use request words that sound more like invitations than demands.

Invitation phrases connote courtesy and include the following:

- ✔ Could you please . . .
- ✔ I would appreciate . . .
- ✔ Maybe you would . . .
- ✔ How would you feel about . . .
- ✔ What would be the chance of . . .
- ✔ What I will need from you is . . .

Demand phrases are more abrasive:

✔ You will . . .

✔ You must . . .

✔ I must have . . .

✔ You cannot . . .

Use friendly contractions

Contractions are conversational and they make e-mails less stuffy and more informal. However, be careful not to overuse contractions — especially when writing e-mails to customers. Contractions should not be used in a very formal e-mail, although one or two are sometimes a good idea for warming up the tone of an otherwise impersonal message. After the e-mail is written, read it over and ask yourself if the contractions sound natural. If they don't, or you aren't sure, remove them.

Stay away from weird, seldom-used contractions like those in the sentence, "The supervisor'll write a memo stating who should've been responsible."

Focus on the positive

Create a positive tone in your e-mails by focusing on what is possible rather than on what isn't. In those situations where you cannot give customers what they want, for example, focus on giving a *soft no* that offers options and alternatives, rather than a *hard no* that is perceived as unfriendly and unhelpful.

When you're unable to give a customer or colleague what they are asking for, avoid negative phrases such as:

✔ I /You can't do that . . .

✔ I cannot help you . . .

✔ That's not my responsibility. . .

✔ That's not my job. . .

✔ That's not our policy. . .

✔ There's no way!

Use the following positive phrases in your e-mail to refocus your recipient's attention on what is possible:

- ✔ What I can do is . . .
- ✔ It might be possible to . . .
- ✔ I can recommend that . . .
- ✔ I have an alternative idea . . .
- ✔ There is another option . . .

Avoid using negative words and phrases such as: *fail, can't, impossible, no way, neglected to, failed to, you claim, so you say,* and *are you sure?*

Say hello and goodbye

The greeting of your e-mail is the first thing a recipient reads and can help set a positive, friendly tone for the whole message. Customers need a formal, courteous greeting. We believe that writing the greeting acts as a mental reminder that we are speaking to another person rather than just typing words on a screen — something that's easy to forget in today's fast-paced world. The most usual salutation is *Dear,* followed by the recipient's first or last name, depending on your relationship.

Some e-mail correspondents forego the *Dear* altogether and just write the recipient's name followed by a colon. Never do so when writing e-mails to customers, because it can seem curt or impolite to some people.

When responding to customers' e-mails, always use their last name. Also, be sure to use titles if the sender has provided them. An e-mail signed *Dr. Strangelove* is an indication that you should use *Dr.* in your response.

The few words after the salutation also help set the tone for the entire message. They're equivalent to the "Nice to see you" exchange that is the customary opener to any normal face-to-face conversation. Useful e-mail opening lines include

- ✔ Thank you for your e-mail.
- ✔ How are you?
- ✔ I hope this message finds you well.

As with salutations, e-mail sign-offs also convey courtesy. Always use a formal sign-off when you send an e-mail message to a customer. Some suggested formal sign-offs include

✔ Regards (our favorite)

✔ Sincerely

✔ Thank you

When you send e-mails to people outside your organization, be sure to include your name, e-mail address, title, and phone number at the bottom of each message. Most e-mail software programs allow you to compose and save standard signature information that can be inserted with the click of a button. If you decide to include a quote, remember that people will see it every time you send them a message. Keep the quote brief — because even Gandhi's words can get overexposed.

Use the subject line

The subject line is the first impression the recipient receives of any new message arriving in the mailbox. As such, it can effect when or if the e-mail is opened. We work with many professionals who use the subject line as their initial prioritization indicator. If the subject line doesn't look important, the message is put on the back burner, which for some executives is awfully close to the garbage can!

Use arresting subject lines to grab your reader's attention — and to provide an accurate indication about the message's content. Don't concoct lines such as "Never-before-seen-memo" or "Rock-your-world sales projections" just to grab attention. Use a brief subject line (no more than 30 characters, or it will likely get shortened by the receiver's e-mail program) that informs the reader of the content and any action that's needed. If the message is urgent, include *URG* in the subject line, if the message is for information only, include *FYI* at the beginning of the subject line. For example, "URG Updated Sales Projections" or "FYI Response from S. Claus."

Because some people get so overworked or disorganized, they use an *FYI* in the subject line of a received message as a cue for deletion without reading. If you suspect that your recipient only reads e-mails that are directly connected with his or her deliverables, then put the *FYI* at the end of the first paragraph.

Avoid flaming

A *flame* is any e-mail that's inflammatory (hence the name). Flames are most often the result of unbridled anger. The backdrop is usually a difference of opinion that spirals into a full-blown conflict. Normally, Person A receives an e-mail from Person B that contains a remark that Person A doesn't like. Person A then ups the ante by zipping back a snappy, disrespectful reply to

Person B. Keep in mind that e-mail communication makes it easy to be nasty — you're not confronting a person face-to-face. Person B then takes umbrage, and shoots back an e-mail to Person A that's even more hostile or angry. Before you know it, keyboards are hot and tempers are high.

Here's what to do to avoid flame warfare:

1. **First and foremost — never respond to a flame with another flame.**

   Don't take the flame personally. It's how some people blow off steam.

2. **Thank the flamer for the message.**

   Use an empathic phrase, such as, "I can see why you are so upset." If you consider the flame justified, let the flamer know that you agree. If the flamer is not justified, let him know that you appreciate that he's brought the matter to your attention.

3. **Apologize for the inconvenience or problem that the situation has caused the flamer.**

   In this instance, saying "sorry" is not an admittance of guilt but an expression of regret.

4. **Explain the circumstances or history that led up to the current situation.**

   Be sincere and honest. Don't try and discredit the flamer by proving a point.

5. **Offer to take specific actions that will help resolve the issue.**

   If you know that a resolution is already underway, explain this to the flamer.

6. **End the message with another apology and an invitation for the flamer to contact you with any further questions or concerns.**

Never write a message all in capital letters. EVEN IF YOU DON'T MEAN ANYTHING BY IT, THE READER WILL THINK THAT YOU'RE FLAMING HER.

Flaming is especially common in a service environment. Quite often, people send flames to individuals when they're actually upset with the individual's company. For example, say that you're a manager in a company that distributes coffee to corporate break rooms. One of your delivery drivers quits unexpectedly, another wrecks his van, and a third is ill and away from work for a week. Angry customers may send flames your way if their caffeine supply is interrupted — they're not mad at you, really, but they are disappointed in your company. Swallow your pride and try to improve the situation.

Provide background information

An e-mail message can be confusing to the reader if no history or background information is supplied with the message or the recipient is unclear on just what the writer is referring to or what response would be appropriate.

The more familiar you are with an issue, the easier it is to omit important background details when sending an e-mail. Try putting yourself in the recipient's shoes and reread the e-mail before you send it. Ask yourself if anything requires further explanation; should other documents be attached to fill in missing details?

If your message is asking for the recipient to take an action, be sure that the request is specific, well-articulated, and positioned at the front of the e-mail (see Chapter 16 for how to write an effective request). When asking the reader to take several different actions, list them all clearly, possibly using a separate paragraph for each request and its related information. If the e-mail is longer than one page, summarize all the requested actions in the last paragraph.

Understand emoticons

Smileys and emoticons are the little faces that are added to e-mail text by typing out a series of punctuation marks. They help clarify the intended meaning of the message. For example, the following sentence may be misinterpreted if not for the added smiley:

I'm missing my Thursday night water-ballet class to attend this meeting. :-)

The most common emoticon is the sad face made by typing a colon, followed by a dash, followed by a left parenthesis:

:-(

A sad-face emoticon is a casual and light-hearted way of informing the reader that you are sorry or sad about something. For example:

I will miss seeing you at the Sunday morning beer bust. :-(

Only use smileys and emoticons with people you know — and then sparingly. Never use them with customers, because they can appear childish and unprofessional. For example:

The bank has shown remarkable solvency during the past year. :-) I will present a full report to the board in New York next week.

Emoticon madness

If you're interested in seeing every emoticon known to man, go to your favorite search engine and type in "emoticon." One site has 6,500 different listings. If you don't feel the need to see the sad (and often funny) results of people with no apparent life, then here are just a few to sate you:

		=^..^=	Cat
		(8-(I)	Homer Simpson
		: ----)	Person smiling despite long nose
		:-D	Person laughing
		:-D..	Person laughing and drooling
;-)	Person winking	}+ ->	Cycloptic Dracula with one fang
$-)	Person who just won the lottery	: - |	Person confused by emoticon humor

Avoiding Common E-Mail Mistakes

In the example that follows, the writer has made all the common mistakes associated with an unprofessional e-mail (and we mean unprofessional!). Read through the message and see how many mistakes you can spot. You can find the correct answers, with explanations, after the exercise. Have fun!

Common e-mail mistakes exercise

As you read through the message below, you can underline or highlight mistakes if it helps you keep track.

```
To: actng@company.com
From: d.goliath@company.com
CC:    j.beanstalk@ company.com
       l.b.blue@ company.com
       l.r.r.hood@ company.com
       h.dumpty@ company.com
```

Subject: Screw up!

I submitted my expense report last week and I still don't have a check back :-(
I always have problems receiving my checks on time! I know that you have cutoff times and I usually make them, so I don't know what is happening? Is there any way that you could notify people when you don't process thier reports on time? CAN YOU CLARIFY EXACTLY HOW YOUR PROCESS WORKS?- as well as review the policy that you have regarding cutting checks after the standard cut off times? I'd like to get my check Fedexed to me. I realize that TNSTAAFL but there might be a better way to handle this!!!!!! How do you process checks for direct deposit??? Do you have the same cut off times? Can

you process last week's expense report and get it into my Wells Fargo Account as soon as possible? I really don't want to have to wait an extra week on this if at all possible :-(. Please advise. Please don't just me the typical RTM accounting response.

Common e-mail mistakes exercise answers

Here is a list of the biggest mistakes in the message above:

- ✔ **Bad spelling, punctuation, and grammar.** All the misspelled words, missing or inaccurate punctuation, and patchy grammar make the e-mail difficult to understand and create a negative impression.

- ✔ **Obscure acronyms.** Use acronyms sparingly and never use acronyms that your readers are not familiar with. In this exercise, the acronyms are TNSTAAFL, which means "There's no such thing as a free lunch," and RTM, which means "Read the manual."

- ✔ **Unpleasant tone.** This message has an abrupt and unfriendly tone. The subject line alone is an indication of the writer's discourteous attitude.

- ✔ **No salutation.** Omitting a "Dear . . ." or even a short "Hello . . ." is bad etiquette and sets a negative mood for the rest of the e-mail.

- ✔ **No sign-off.** The writer has not closed the message with a "Thank you," "Regards," or even a name.

- ✔ **Unclear subject line.** The subject line is unprofessional and rude. It gives no indication of what the message is about.

- ✔ **Writing words and sentences in all capital letters.** Doing this is considered a big no-no in online communication because it represents shouting. It's the equivalent of getting in someone's face and yelling at them.

- ✔ **Lack of a clear request.** The writer does not make it clear what he specifically wants the reader to do. Make requests clear and easy for your recipient to understand.

- ✔ **No background information.** Given the nature of the issue, the writer may get a speedier response by including background information such as the specific date/number of the last expense report submitted, the dates of other reports that were paid late, and so on.

- ✔ **Inappropriate use of emoticons (smileys).** Some people love smileys, some people hate them. Use them sparingly and only when you know the recipient well. We recommend keeping them away from any e-mails you send to external customers because many people consider them unprofessional.

Chapter 14

Message Mastery: Saving Time for Yourself and Others

....

In This Chapter

▶ Dealing with incoming mail

▶ Cleaning the loose ends from your mailbox

▶ Writing to save time for you and your customers

▶ Sending e-mails that produce results

....

*D*oes your mailbox intimidate you every time you open it? Do you have a hard time locating messages that you sent to customers or verifying that you ever received a response from them? If so, you're not alone. Every month, the volume of e-mails that we send to each other increases. It doesn't take a genius to figure out that this means the volume of e-mails that we have to read also increases — and that our mailboxes are getting harder to control.

Billions of e-mails are sent everyday. With so many messages flying back and forth, and customers increasingly opting for the convenience of e-mail, it's no wonder that you may dread opening your e-mail program — it's like a closet that contains a jumble of disorganized bits and pieces.

On account of the mess, overlooking or losing things is easy — a big no-no when it comes to online customer relations. Not responding to customer's e-mails or responding after a lengthy delay will quickly earn your organization a mediocre reputation, at best, when it comes to customer service.

In order to take back control of your mailbox, you must focus on two areas:

✔ Having a system for dealing with incoming messages

✔ Writing e-mails that efficiently produce the result that you want

The purpose of this chapter is to introduce you to some tools and strategies to help you make e-mail communication as efficient as possible.

Dealing with Incoming Messages

The principles of dealing with incoming messages are very similar to the principles of time management. *Energy* management is the real crux — not in the sense of saving laptop battery power on a long flight, but in the sense of saving your own energy so that you feel energized instead of drained when dealing with e-mails.

Let's revisit the closet we mentioned above. If you don't have a closet that needs cleaning, think of another area of your home or life that needs organizing. Maybe it's a drawer that needs cleaning out, or maybe it's your:

- Checkbook that needs serious balancing
- Car that needs cleaning, repairs, or tow-away service
- Wardrobe that's crammed with clothes that you don't wear but won't dump
- Garage that doesn't have enough room for a bicycle, let alone a car
- Refrigerator that looks like a lab experiment

Are you feeling tired just looking at the list? The point is that any loose end has the potential of making you feel exhausted. This fact becomes very obvious when you consider the opposite situation. Think of the last time you made a to-do list and then went about completing the items on the list. Each time you checked off a completed item, you felt a little jolt of energy as you acknowledged your accomplishment.

Any loose ends or disorganized areas in your e-mail box drain your energy and waste your time. Unlike life, e-mail programs offer us some simple options for getting our acts together. For every incoming message, you have the following options:

- Replying
- Forwarding
- Deleting
- Filing

Replying to e-mail messages

Our research shows that, as customers become more familiar with using e-mail, their expectations change regarding acceptable reply times. While a general "within 24 hours" was an acceptable reply time just two years ago, we recommend that you reconsider what is acceptable to your particular customers in your particular business. As technology develops, the pace of life, business, and communication has quickened. You may need to accelerate your response time to match.

When you reply to a customer's message, always include the note that you are responding to (most e-mail programs have this as a default feature) so that the reader knows what you are referring to.

Avoid replying with attachments whenever possible. Attachments take time to download, use up computer memory, and can be cumbersome to manage. Not adding attachments can save your customers time and stress, and anything you do to help your customers enhances your reputation for being a customer-friendly organization.

Sometimes your response to an e-mail will change the nature of the message. If so, change the subject line accordingly. For example, if you received an e-mail from a colleague with a subject line that reads, "Tomorrow's customer meeting" and the customer had called to tell you that she is no longer able to attend the meeting, change the subject line prior to responding to your colleague's message. A new subject line of "Customer meeting cancelled" will help draw attention to the change.

Forwarding messages

You often receive e-mails that you want to show to other people. Before you forward a message that you have received from a customer or a colleague, consider whether you have permission to forward this message and whether doing so is appropriate. This issue may not be relevant if you're forwarding a message to various members of a team working for the same customer or on the same issue. However, we know of several instances where inter-department issues were inappropriately forwarded to outside departments and companies.

For example, we heard about a manager who created a lot of unnecessary embarrassment and ill-will because of sloppy forwarding. This manager was looking for a person to fill a new position in her department. After interviewing several internal candidates, the job was finally given to an outsider. The manager e-mailed the successful candidate confirming the agreed-upon starting salary. She also accidentally sent the same e-mail to all the unsuccessful candidates!

When you forward an e-mail message, you can avoid confusion by always indicating to the recipients whether or not they need to respond or take any action. Often, the purpose of forwarding is to keep others informed and included in the loop of information. If this is the case, start the first line of your message with *FYI* (For Your Information), which indicates that no action is necessary. If an action is required, make this fact clear in the first part of your message.

Deleting messages

Just as finally cleaning out your messy garage can be enormously satisfying, so can cleaning out your mailbox. We recommend that you delete unnecessary messages when you need a boost of energy. Getting rid of the junk in your mailbox also makes seeing the important messages that are in there a lot easier.

Only delete junk mail and those messages that you can guarantee you'll never need to reference. We have had many conversations with clients where the trail of past e-mail communications was our only reference for tracing the history of complex projects. If you have any doubt whether you may need a message again, archive it.

Filing messages

Establishing an e-mail filing system makes it easy to find past e-mails. You can use various ways to archive and prioritize messages, so you find a system that works for you. Look at how you do business — do you usually work by client name, type of product or service, individual respondents, dates, and so on? Organize your incoming e-mail accordingly. In our business we work with clients, so we archive by client. We create an e-mail folder for each client and we archive all messages to and from that client within that particular folder.

Don't fall into the trap of using "Ignore" as an option for dealing with incoming messages. Anything you are trying to ignore becomes a loose end and a big energy drain. Instead, ask yourself why you don't want to deal with this item. Chances are that whatever your reason, the issue will not be resolved by ignoring it.

Writing E-Mails that Produce Results

Obviously, no guarantees exist that an e-mail you send will produce the result that you want. However, you can improve the odds that you'll get the response you're looking for if you carefully craft the language you use in your messages. These techniques can help make your e-mails more effective:

- ✔ Prioritize your paragraphs
- ✔ Put your request toward the front
- ✔ Trim the fat
- ✔ Use open and closed questions

So that you can become familiar with each of these techniques and practice your skills, we've included a few exercises in this section.

Prioritize your paragraphs

Many of our clients receive more e-mails than they can possibly read — unless they give up weekends and family life. In order to deal with the bulging mailbox problem, many of them read only the first paragraph of all but the most important of messages. This means that if your e-mail does not qualify as an A1, most important, top-of-the-line priority in the reader's eyes, it may never get read. Getting your message across in the first sentence or two is crucial, because anything that follows may not be read and therefore is of questionable worth.

We learned the hard way when we were using e-mail to set up dinner arrangements with a busy executive. Rather than sending an e-mail for the specific purpose of arranging dinner, we simply added the invitation to the end of a business-related message we needed to send him. He always sent very courteous and speedy replies to our other questions, but he never responded to our dinner invitation. Eventually, we figured it out. He wasn't reading beyond the first paragraph. Like it or not, we realized that this was his way of dealing with an overburdened mailbox. As soon as we sent a short e-mail, specifically asking for possible dinner dates, he responded immediately.

We're not suggesting that the you always write one-paragraph e-mails, but it does make sense to make sure that your first paragraph in every message contains the most important information. We call this technique *top-down* writing.

Top-down writing exercise

Practice your top-down writing skills by looking at the following e-mail. We have scrambled the order of the paragraphs. See if you can rearrange them in order of importance. A space at the end of each paragraph is provided for you to write in the number that represents what you think that paragraph's priority should be. You can check your answer in the next section.

> To: all@company.com
> From: J.Jones@company.com
> Re: upcoming meeting
>
> Hello everyone,
>
> I know how hard most of you have worked on preparing your reports. I appreciate all the effort and work put into each of them. Your findings are extremely important to the future of company.com. *(Priority # _____)*

Each report needs to be completed, copied, and bound for presentation. Please do not have any loose handouts, as this will cause confusion. However, for your convenience, the overhead projector will be available. *(Priority # _____)*

Because we have a limited amount of time, I have to ask you to limit your presentation to 2 minutes. We have a lot of material to cover, and by having a short presentation coupled with a copy of each report, we can at least begin the necessary discussions. *(Priority # _____)*

This Thursday's meeting is of utmost importance. In order for us to complete our agenda, I need everyone to be prepared to present their findings within 2 minutes. Please have enough copies of your reports for all 25 participants. *(Priority # _____)*

Two weeks after Thursday's meeting we will all meet again, I expect everyone to have read all 5 reports at that time so that a meaningful discussion regarding the direction company.com needs to go can happen. *(Priority # _____)*

Answers to top-down writing exercise

Priority #1

This Thursday's meeting is of utmost importance. In order for us to complete our agenda, I need everyone to be prepared to present their findings within 2 minutes. Please have enough copies of your reports for all 25 participants.

Priority #2

Each report needs to be completed, copied, and bound for presentation. Please do not have any loose handouts, as this will cause confusion. However, for your convenience, the overhead projector will be available.

Priority #3

Because we have a limited amount of time, I have to ask you to limit your presentation to 2 minutes. We have a lot of material to cover, and by having a short presentation coupled with a copy of each report, we can at least begin the necessary discussions.

Priority #4

Two weeks after Thursday's meeting we will all meet again. I expect everyone to have read all 5 reports at that time so that a meaningful discussion regarding the direction company.com needs to go can happen.

Priority #5

I know how hard most of you have worked on preparing your reports. I appreciate all the effort and work put into each of them. Your findings are extremely important to the future of company.com.

Use concise and meaningful subject lines. Some people judge an e-mail by the subject line alone and delete messages before reading the contents.

Put your request up-front

In the prioritizing exercise, you saw the importance of making the first paragraph count. It follows, therefore, that if your e-mail is asking the recipient to take some kind of action, then your request should be included in the first paragraph of the message.

Once you know to place your request where it is likely to be read, you must do whatever you can to ensure that it produces the results that you want. Obviously, there is no way to guarantee that other people will do what you say or ask (unless you're a hypnotist) but writing a clear request can definitely improve your chances. Here are four factors to think about when you send a request:

- ✔ Describe the specific action that you're requesting.
- ✔ Define a specific time frame for responding.
- ✔ Establish a mutual understanding of the request.
- ✔ Evaluate the competence of the recipient.

Specify the action you're requesting

Make sure the recipient understands exactly what is expected of him or her. For example, you may write something like, "In order to investigate your claim, I will need a letter stating the circumstances."

But you can be even more specific. The recipient of this e-mail could easily respond with a letter that's not detailed enough or with a small phonebook of information.

A better request would be, "In order to investigate your claim, I will need a one- or two-page letter that states the general circumstances."

Set a time frame

When you send a message that requires some action, be sure to state specific time requirements so that no misunderstanding (or missed deadlines) can arise. For example, saying something like, "I need the report as soon as you can get it to me" could be interpreted by the recipient as, "Just send it as soon as you've dealt with all your other, more pressing priorities."

A better request would be, "I need the report by Wednesday at 2 p.m."

Establish mutual understanding

A lot of confusion can arise if the people on both the sending and receiving ends of an e-mail don't completely understand the contents of the message. You may not get the response you're hoping for if the person you're sending the e-mail to doesn't understand all the underlying circumstances. For example, sending an e-mail to your Chicago office (when you're working in San Francisco) requesting a conference call at 4 p.m. might not produce the result you would like — when it's 4 p.m. in Chicago, it's 2 p.m. in San Francisco!

Evaluate the competence of your recipient

Make sure you send your request to a person who is capable of responding satisfactorily. No matter how well formed your e-mail request, if the person you send it to is not competent to fulfill it, then your request won't be answered. For example, sending an e-mail to a newly-hired front-line employee asking her to put together an intranet staff directory would be inappropriate. This new person would not have sufficient knowledge to complete the job quickly or competently.

Trim the fat

Using unnecessary words is a major obstacle to e-mail efficiency. Many of us write the same way that we talk. The problem is that the spoken word is much less tight than the written word; when you write, you ought to be more succinct than when you talk. A customer reading an e-mail has far less tolerance for repetition and unclear phrasing than a customer with whom you're having a conversation.

Also, the spoken word is accompanied by many visual and auditory cues that generate interest and understanding. When you read, you're focused on the words — nothing more. The words alone need to be sufficient to convey your point concisely yet courteously. We include the exercise that follows to give you practice adjusting language to make it tighter and clearer.

Trim the fat exercise

Go through the following e-mail and remove the words that you believe dilute the message. Feel free to add a new word or two if they help make the message more concise.

> To: all@company.com
> From: K.Smith@company.com
> Re: Last Thursday's Meeting
>
> Hello to all,
>
> I just wanted to take a moment to give you my perspective of the very heated discussion that occurred during the first part of last Thursday's lively meeting.

First and foremost, I felt it was not supportive of our teambuilding efforts for all of us to be so defensive about our reports. Let's face it, I believe we all tend to take on a personal attachment to those things that we produce, but rarely are we willing to have the necessary degree of objectivity to be able to discuss it in a positive and open way.

As a result, I feel that some of us felt, to some degree, betrayed by the rather negative comments made by others. Likewise, I personally felt attacked and otherwise not supported for both my content as well as my efforts.

If we are to move forward as a team, then we need to support each other as a team. At this point in time, I welcome any and all discussions regarding my thoughts here as long as they are in constructive form. Furthermore, if any of you wish to meet to clear the air, I would most definitely welcome that as well.

Answers to trim the fat exercise

To: all@company.com
From: K.Smith@company.com
Re: Last Thursday's Meeting

Hello to all,

I ~~just~~ wanted to ~~take a moment to~~ give you my perspective of ~~the very heated discussion that occurred during the first part of~~ last Thursday's ~~lively~~ meeting.

~~First and foremost,~~ I felt it was not supportive ~~of our teambuilding efforts for all of us~~ to be so defensive about our reports. ~~Let's face it, I believe we all tend to take on a personal attachment to those things that we produce, but rarely are we willing to have the necessary degree of objectivity to be able to discuss it in a positive and open way.~~

~~As a result, I feel that some of us felt, to some degree, betrayed by the rather negative comments made by others. Likewise, I personally felt attacked and otherwise not supported for both my content as well as my efforts.~~

If we are to move forward as a team, then we need to support each other as a team. At this point in time, I welcome any and all discussions regarding my thoughts here as long as they are in constructive form. Furthermore, I welcome the idea of discussing this with you further. If any of you wish to meet to clear the air, I would most definitely welcome that as well.

Use open and closed questions appropriately

The way in which you ask a question in your e-mails affects the kind of responses you receive. Sometimes, asking questions that invite the recipients to freely express their opinions or share their knowledge about something is a good idea. The questions that encourage this flowing type of response are called *open-ended* questions and they result in long answers. Open-ended questions usually begin with the following words: *how, when, what,* and *why,* although many other possibilities also exist.

At other times, asking questions that produce one-word answers, either for the sake of clarity or to save time, is a good idea. These questions are called *closed-ended* questions and they usually result in a yes or no answer. Closed-ended questions start with the following words: *are, do, is, can,* and *will,* although, again, there are many other possibilities.

Open-ended questions

Use open-ended questions when you are fact gathering and are interested in discovering the customer's point-of-view. Open-ended questions give people the opportunity to vent their frustration — in the case of a problem — or express their feelings and desires about products or services. Imagine a travel agent receiving the following e-mail from a customer:

> To: spowers@company.com
> From: ttaylor@aol.com
> Re: Disney World
>
> I am planning on taking my grandson to Disney World in the spring and wanted to get your opinion on the best way to do it.
>
> Thanks in advance,
> Tanya

The agent decides to ask a few open-ended questions in order to get an idea of what sort of trip the customer would really enjoy:

> To: ttaylor@aol.net
> From: spowers@company.com
> Re: Reservations
>
> Dear Tanya:
>
> Thank you for the inquiry regarding Disney World. It sounds like a fun trip. In order to plan a wonderful trip for you both, I have a few questions.
>
> How old is your grandson and when are you planning on departing?
>
> What other activities would you and your grandson enjoy doing — when you are not in the park?

I look forward to hearing from you and helping you plan a great trip!

Regards,
Sarah

By asking open-ended questions, the agent provides the customer with an opportunity to let her mind wander and write in a free-flowing fashion about the sort of trip that would make both her and her grandchild happy.

Closed-ended questions

Imagine that a travel agent receives the following e-mail from a customer:

To: spowers@company.com
From: vbrackett@earthlink.net
Re: Reservations

Hello

I need to know what to do with unused airline tickets from a recent trip to Baltimore. I also have rental car vouchers.

I look forward to hearing from you.

Regards,
Vernon

The writer of the above e-mail knows what he wants, but his e-mail needs some clarification. In order to better understand the situation, avoid further confusion, and confirm the facts, the agent sends a response to ask a few closed-ended questions:

To: vbracketts@earthlink.net
From: spowers@company.com
Re: Reservations

Dear Mr. Brackett:

Thank you for your e-mail regarding unused airline tickets. In order to help you, I will need the following information:

Did you complete any portion of the trip to Baltimore?

Did you purchase the tickets through this office?

Can you fax me a copy of the tickets you are holding?

Are the rental car vouchers still valid?

I look forward to receiving the information.

Regards,
Sarah Powers

It's usually a good idea to make use of closed-ended questions when you're seeking clarification from customers whose first language isn't English.

The next time you need fast answers with the minimum of fuss, write your questions in such a way that they evoke a one-word response.

Chapter 15

Problem Solving Online: Teamwork with a Twist

. . . .

In This Chapter

▶ Recognizing the power of consensus

▶ Utilizing a virtual team

▶ Building consensus with e-mail

. . . .

*H*ow well does your company solve customer problems? As you think about this question, go beyond your company's typical, and often predictable, day-to-day problems. Reflect on those issues that require a structured and cross-departmental approach in order to be resolved. Maybe you have a problem with customers receiving inaccurate invoicing. Maybe sales made through your Web site take too long to get processed. Whatever the scenario, being customer centric requires that you have a workable method for solving such problems.

For years, our company has been teaching a team problem-solving technique that's based on all the team members listening to and respecting the opinions of others. Then, through consensus, the team comes up with solutions that are often more innovative and less expensive, over the long haul, than the quick fixes that were originally considered. When teams carefully solve problems by building consensus, they generate an enthusiasm and buy-in that often translates to even better service for customers and clients.

A consensus solution is one that each person on the team can support — even if it isn't the solution that person would have chosen as a team of one. Because consensus encourages input from all team members, fosters ownership in the process, and motivates people to follow through and implement the solution, consensus solutions are generally more powerful than those solutions that are mandated from above.

Utilizing Virtual Problem-Solving Teams

Today, it's something of a luxury for a problem-solving team to be able to sit in the same room together. Sit-down meetings are rare because of time constraints, but also because companies have virtual teams — groups of people who are dedicated to the same project but who live and work in different geographical locations. The digital revolution has made physical location less important than ever before. So how do we problem-solve using the synergy, or collective power, of a group, when the group is scattered across the country or around the world? E-mail, of course.

E-mail is a very effective tool for online problem solving because it provides a forum for brainstorming, for gathering the input of others, and for agreeing on the best course of action. The online problem-solving process presented in the next section produces innovative and cost-effective solutions and motivates everyone involved.

You need to know the three basic ground rules that set the stage for successful online problem solving:

- **Choose a team facilitator.** This person acts as the hub for all e-mail communications by sending, receiving, reading, and consolidating all the e-mail information generated by the group.

- **Invite participants who are knowledgeable about the issue.** Every individual on the team must have a hands-on relationship with the problem being worked on.

- **Make sure that participants feel the problem is worth solving and is solvable.** Every individual on the team must believe that the problem is solvable and have a strong desire to solve it.

Taking Steps to Reach Online Consensus

After the ground rules have been established, the process follows five steps:

1. **State the problem and request feedback on possible causes.**

2. **Publish the possible causes and request cause evaluations.**

3. **Publish the top-voted cause and request feedback on possible solutions.**

4. **Publish the possible solutions and request solution evaluations.**

5. **Publish the top-voted solution.**

Step 1: State the problem and request feedback on possible causes

After the team members have been selected (between four and twelve people works well), the facilitator begins the process by sending an e-mail to all team members. This message contains

- ✔ A description of the problem to be solved
- ✔ A request for the team's input

The facilitator should state the problem as simply and clearly as possible. He should be careful not to state the problem as a solution because this preempts the team's coming up with a different — and probably better — solution. For example, "Should we cancel the interoffice Fruitcake Bake-off?" is better stated as, "We don't have enough volunteers for the interoffice Fruitcake Bake-off." If needed, the facilitator can include a small amount of background information in the e-mail message. Any background information should be kept brief, as most team members should already be familiar with the problem.

Next, the facilitator asks team members to write down what they believe to be the possible causes of the problem. He explains that this is a brainstorming exercise and they should feel free to write down whatever comes to mind without too much editing — that will take place later.

The e-mail may look something like the following:

> Dear Team:
>
> I would like to get your input regarding a problem that we have every year about this time. We do not have enough volunteers for the interoffice Fruitcake Bake-off.
>
> Before we deal with the solutions to this problem, I would like to know from each of you what you believe to be the cause of this problem. Right now, I am interested in getting all your ideas. Please write down anything that comes to mind and e-mail me back before noon on Friday.
>
> I will publish all the results that I receive on the following Monday. Thank you.
>
> Regards,
> Steve

Step 2: Publish possible causes and request cause evaluations

Having received all the e-mails from the group, the facilitator cuts and pastes all the feedback into a new e-mail that is sent to all team members. Each person on the team sees all the ideas submitted by the other people on the team.

This is the online version of writing ideas on a flip chart at the front of a meeting room. The facilitator should remain impartial throughout this process and never edit or paraphrase other people's ideas, because doing so may change the intended meaning. If your organization conducts a lot of online discussions, consider investing in discussion group software, such as Expressions Interaction Suite 3.0 (www.eshare.com) or WebBoard 2.0 (www.oreilly.com).

The second part of the e-mail requests that team members consider all of the contributed possible causes and select which one of them is the root cause of the problem.

Some root causes are very difficult to change in an organization. Try to avoid having the participants agree on a *general* root cause, such as:

- Company culture
- Upper management
- Communication

Obviously, anything goes in online brainstorming. But as the evaluation process begins, facilitators must ensure that any of the general root causes listed above are defined in a more specific manner. The following e-mail shows you how:

> Dear Team:
>
> Thank you for your timely responses to the 'Fruitcake' problem. Here are the causes that you came up with. Please read through them and pick the one that you believe is the root cause.
>
> People hate anything to do with fruitcake
>
> The *60 Minutes* piece on baked goods that can kill has people worried
>
> People are too busy to spend time volunteering
>
> The word *volunteer* reminds people of being in the army
>
> Bad timing — the world shortage of glazed fruit makes the contest politically incorrect

The event has negative PR — last year the winner got into a fight with the runner-up

People don't want to give up their lunch hours

I need to receive your vote for the root cause by end of business on Tuesday. Thanks.

Regards,
Steve

Step 3: Publish root cause and request feedback on possible solutions

After all the evaluations have been received, the facilitator counts the number of votes for each possible cause. After tallying all the numbers, the facilitator publishes the cause with the most votes. This item is considered the real cause of the problem.

Make it clear to all team members that they can add potential causes and new information at any point in the process. Often, as more information is transmitted to each member, new ideas emerge that may be more innovative and effective than the original input.

Now that the real cause has been agreed upon — by group consensus — the next job is to brainstorm possible solutions. To request feedback on possible solutions, send an e-mail like the one that follows:

Dear Team:

Here is the most agreed upon root cause to the fruitcake volunteer situation:

People hate anything to do with fruitcake

Now we need to come up with some creative, cost-effective ways of solving this problem. Once again, I need your input. Please send me an e-mail listing all your ideas for solving this problem. I need your responses by Friday at noon.

Thanks,
Steve

Step 4: Publish possible solutions and request solution evaluations

Having received all the responses back from the team, the facilitator cuts and pastes the feedback into one e-mail that is sent to all team members.

Be sure the e-mail asks each person in the group to evaluate all the suggested solutions and choose the one that he or she thinks will be the most effective. The criteria for a workable solution will vary with your specific circumstances, but usually these areas are important to consider:

- ✔ Financial cost
- ✔ Resource cost
- ✔ Work interruption
- ✔ Management support
- ✔ Implementation time

The message should look something like the following:

> Dear Team:
>
> Here are the solutions the group came up with. They are very creative and I believe we are close to a fruitcake breakthrough!
>
> Use French to disguise the negative fruitcake connotations — something like "Festival de Gateau Fruit"
>
> Publish a list of famous sports personalities who like fruitcake
>
> Change the event to the Fruitcake Hurling Contest
>
> Educate our staff about fruitcakes by setting up a Fruitcake U or an intranet Web page with fruitcake FAQs
>
> Make it a brownie cook-off
>
> Please study this exciting list and vote for the solution that you believe will best solve this annual problem. Please have your responses back to me by Wednesday at noon. Thank you.
>
> Regards,
> Steve

Step 5: Publish consensus solution

The facilitator tallies all the received votes and publishes the most popular solution.

> Dear Team:
>
> Here is the solution that the group unanimously agreed on:
>
> Change the event to the Fruitcake Hurling Contest
>
> There's already an excited buzz about the office. In fact, several people have already volunteered to bake the fruitcakes.

Thank you all for doing an outstanding job. I will contact you next week to get your ideas about the best cake size and weight for hurling.

Regards,
Jennie

This process not only helps strengthen teamwork, but it also lets people know that their input is valuable. By using the synergy of a group, you are sure to end up with higher quality solutions than those generated by one person.

TIP

Overcoming roadblocks

Sometimes teams get bogged down in the details and come to a roadblock in the decision-making process. If this happens, the facilitator may need to coach the group through the stalemate. Coaching via e-mail often takes the form of asking pertinent questions that create dialogue and mutual understanding and get the team back on track. Here is a list of questions that will get you started:

✔ What are the key issues that are holding up the process?

✔ What have you done to try and break the deadlock?

✔ What happened?

✔ What would be a satisfying outcome?

✔ What are the team values that should guide the final outcome?

✔ What decision best reflects these values?

✔ Can the group live with this decision?

✔ What are the next steps in moving on with this decision?

Chapter 16

E-Rapport: New E-Mail Skills for Customer Closeness

*R*apport is defined in *Webster's New World College Dictionary* as "a close or sympathetic relationship." Good customer service requires that you establish rapport with your customers. Having good rapport makes your customers feel like they're more than just a source of income. They'll be much more likely to give you valuable feedback or stick with your company through a few service blunders if rapport has been established. As a business professional, you probably know how to quickly build rapport — look your customers in the eye, make chit-chat, get to know them.

But how do you establish rapport over e-mail? You don't have those long business lunches to bond over. You don't have body language to read, as in even brief face-to-face contacts. You can't even listen carefully to the tone of a customer's voice, as you can over the phone. In this chapter, we give you a few great techniques for establishing what we call *e-rapport*.

We all speak the same language. Or do we? In our workshops, we often get participants to think about language by asking them what comes to mind when we say "orange." Responses include the fruit, the color, the county in southern California, and offbeat ones like "the sweater I wore yesterday." The point is that, although we all use similar words, we each use them in our own unique way. Creating e-rapport requires honing in on the language choices that the other person is making and then responding with similar language. In other words, figuring out the other person's wavelength, and then putting yourself on it.

E-rapport is the skill of using e-mail to get closer to your customers by getting on their wavelength, so that you don't have to fly blind simply because you don't receive visual or auditory cues. Here are two powerful techniques that help insure harmonious relations online:

- ✔ Using sensory language
- ✔ Backtracking key words

Using Sensory Language

Most people, when they speak or write, use words that relate to the senses of seeing, hearing, and feeling. Without realizing it, we often use one sense more than another, and so our e-mail messages contain words relating specifically to that sense. Here are three sentences that say the same thing using different sensory words:

- ✔ I *see* your *perspective* (visual).
- ✔ I *hear* what you're *saying* (auditory).
- ✔ I *feel* that you have a *point* (tactile).

By using sensory words that are consistent with your customers' main style, you add a rapport-building quality to the messages you send. The following sentence is written in neutral language (language that has no sensory relationship):

- ✔ I am interested in knowing more about your products and services.

Now, here is the same sentence translated into language that uses the three primary senses:

- ✔ I *look* forward to *seeing* the information about your products and services.
- ✔ I'd like to *hear* more about the service and products you offer.
- ✔ I'd be happy if you'd get in *touch* with me about the products and services you offer.

All four sentences contain the same basic message, yet the change in sensory language gives each one a different flavor.

Before responding to an e-mail, quickly scan the words in the message to discover which sense dominates the language the sender uses. After you know the writer's sensory preference, reply to the e-mail using a preponderance of those sensory-specific words. The chances are that the recipient will feel a sense of rapport with you — usually without ever knowing the specific relationship-enhancing steps that you have taken.

Crafting visual messages

Writers with a visual preference use words to paint pictures and create images of what they want to communicate. Some words that you can use when communicating with a person who leans toward visual language include

- ✔ Clarify
- ✔ Focus
- ✔ Look
- ✔ See
- ✔ Vision
- ✔ Perspective
- ✔ Clear
- ✔ Observe

The following phrases are visual:

- ✔ I see what you mean.
- ✔ That looks good.
- ✔ I'm a little hazy about that.
- ✔ Let's try and shed some light on this.
- ✔ I have a different view of the situation.
- ✔ I get the picture.
- ✔ I appreciate your insight.
- ✔ I look forward to seeing you.

Incorporating auditory language

Writers with an auditory preference use words and phrases that give tone to what they are saying. Some words that you can use to give an e-mail an auditory style include

- ✔ Sound
- ✔ Hear
- ✔ Say
- ✔ Tell
- ✔ Volume

- Loud
- Listen
- Tone

The following phrases are auditory:

- I'm glad to hear it.
- Let me explain.
- We're in tune.
- Tell me what you hear.
- Everything just clicked.
- That sounds good to me.
- On that note, we should end the discussion.
- That rings a bell.

Using tactile language

Writers with a tactile style use words and phrases that refer to physical sensations when writing a message. Some words that you can use when you want to create a tactile style include

- Touch
- Feel
- Firm
- Pressure
- Relaxed
- Rough
- Solid

The following are tactile phrases:

- It feels right.
- Stay in touch.
- Warm regards.
- It leaves me cold.
- Get a grip.
- Hold on.

Recognizing the Effect of Neutral Language

Neutral language seems formal and very business-like compared to sensory language. Although neutral language can seem cold and impersonal, it's very useful when you want to send a formal response to an official or legal document or when your customer has demonstrated a preference for neutral terms. Some examples of neutral words include

- ✔ Think
- ✔ Seems
- ✔ Know
- ✔ Involve
- ✔ Denote
- ✔ Recall
- ✔ Matter

Responding to upset customers over e-mail

When sending e-mails to customers or colleagues who are upset or angry, use the following tips to help maintain rapport.

Delay sending emotional messages.

If you must send an e-mail about a highly emotional topic (face-to-face or phone conversations usually work much better), compose the note but don't address it or send it. Read it again a few hours later and then revise it, if necessary, before sending it. Make sure you have responded appropriately and not reacted inappropriately.

Soften e-mail messages.

If an e-mail message you're sending sounds too curt or abrupt, add an opening line, such as, "Thank you for the e-mail" or "It was a pleasure hearing from you."

Reread your e-mails.

Before sending an e-mail, reread it from beginning to end and ask yourself if there are any parts of it that could be misconstrued by the reader.

Get a second opinion.

Before sending a sensitive or emotional message, have someone you trust read the e-mail and give you suggestions for making it more customer-friendly.

The following is an example of a neutral e-mail received from a customer. Note that the message creates a feeling of distance rather than of closeness because of the absence of any sensory words.

> Dear Mr. Smith:
>
> Thank you for your acknowledgment regarding the instrument that my institution returned to your company. I am not convinced that this matter has been fully taken care of at your end and request that you forward me the details of the credit return we are expecting.
>
> Sincerely,
> Ms. Jones

Backtracking Key Words

When writing e-mails, people choose specific words and phrases that they think are great ways to describe the situation or that they have a predilection for using. The e-rapport skill of backtracking key words requires you to pick up on the key words that the other person is using. Then, you repeat back some of the key words or phrases. What do you think are the most important words and phrases in the following e-mail?

> Dear Esther:
>
> I strongly suspect that our customers are mystified by the pricing information on our Web site. I would like to meet at your earliest convenience to remedy the situation.
>
> Regards,
> Sarah

The key words are:

- ✔ Strongly
- ✔ Suspect
- ✔ Mystified
- ✔ Remedy

Now use some or all of these key words in composing your response. For example:

Dear Sarah:

I think you are right in suspecting that customers are mystified by the Web pricing. Can you meet me tomorrow morning at 10:30 to work on a remedy?

Regards,
Esther

By using a sprinkling of the senders' words in your response, you mirror back to them something familiar. The more they recognize their style in your response (consciously or subconsciously), the more they feel a sense of rapport and trust.

Part V
The Part of Tens

The 5th Wave — By Rich Tennant

Now take your time and see if you can identify the person who attacked you on e-mail.

In this part . . .

This part of the book contains loads of real-world information for managers, salespeople, and front-line staff. It is a quick and easy way for you to learn specific actions that make the difference between mediocre and world-class customer service, both offline and online.

Chapter 17

Ten Ways to Make Your Online Service Shine

In This Chapter

▶ Establishing successful site navigation

▶ Creating a simple and clean site design

*T*he nature of your customers' online interactions with your company plays an important role in the overall success of your site, the reputation of your company, and the strength of your online brand. If your online customer finds herself confused and frustrated, you've undercut all your other efforts. Underneath the jazzy graphics, clever URL names, and marketing hype, lies the crux of the matter — you are not just creating a Web site, you are creating a customer experience. The following ten tips provide the foundation for making your online service shine.

Make Site Navigation Easy

In order to search any Web site effectively, you need to use a navigation system, a clearly labeled set of buttons that direct you to different parts of the particular Web site you're exploring. The navigation system you establish for your company's Web site is what enables your customers to find the information they're looking for (or frustrates them in their attempts to find that information).

Because you want your site to be as customer-friendly as possible, you need to make exploring the various pages on your Web site as easy as possible. Creative and original design, although aesthetically valuable, is less important than organizing your site in a way that enables visitors to find their way around quickly and easily.

When designing a navigation system for your site, make sure that the site architecture answers more questions than it raises. If you and your Web site designers don't create clear and easy-to-use site navigation, most visitors will become frustrated and leave. Some factors to consider when evaluating your existing site design or deciding on the method that customers will use when navigating a new site include

- ✔ **Providing visual feedback so users know where they are.** If you high-light and reinforce your site's section names, so that users who come to your site know exactly what section of the site they're currently explor-ing, you greatly improve your site's ease-of-use.

- ✔ **Making the site's section names easy to understand.** Because the goal is to make navigating through your site a no-brainer, logical names are more important that cleverness.

- ✔ **Keeping navigation buttons consistent from page to page.** Presenting the same navigation system on every page increases your customers' comfort. Consistency and repetition in the navigation elements prevents your customers from having to search for the buttons on each page.

- ✔ **Making site navigation self-explanatory.** The best navigation systems don't require any thought. The Products button takes you to a page that describes the company's products, the Company Information button takes you to information about the company. Ask yourself if a typical ten-year old could easily navigate the site. If not, the navigation system is probably too complicated.

- ✔ **Using a variety of navigation elements.** Simple links, graphic icons, nav-igation buttons, fancy graphics, photos, and plain old text can all be used in navigating around a site. Use a combination of these elements so that your customers can go to any section of the site they're interested in and easily find their way back to the home page.

- ✔ **Keeping the navigation buttons to the main parts of your site together.** Site navigation tools that send the customer to the main parts of your page should be grouped together. Don't spread them all over the page. They can be placed either at the top, bottom, or side of the page; in general, finding them is easiest if they're placed vertically on the left side of the page.

- ✔ **Giving customers a text description of what the links on your site will provide.** Placing a short sentence underneath each link makes it easy for customers to find what they want. The short sentence helps your customers understand what pages the links connect to.

Offer a Frequently Asked Questions (FAQ) Section

After so many years in business, you know the questions that your customers or potential customers are most likely to ask. Create a Frequently Asked Questions (FAQ) section on your Web site that clearly states, then answers, these questions.

You can further enhance this service by using software that allows your visitors to interact in real time with a customer service representative by e-mail or telephone while viewing your FAQ section. Remember to regularly update the content on your FAQ section to reflect new questions that spring up and to adjust answers that have changed.

Clearly State the Nature of Your Business on Your Home Page

Have you ever visited a Web site and, after a few minutes of looking around, realized that you had no idea what the heck the site was about? The number of sites, especially those of small- and medium-sized businesses, that leave visitors scratching their heads and wondering, "What do these people do?" is amazing — even though a mystifying site is a clear violation of all the rules you learned in Business 101. Make sure that your home page clearly states the business you're in and the types of products and services you offer. Within a few seconds, your visitor should know exactly what your site is about and should have received the main message that you're trying to get across to them.

Offer Something for Free

"Free" is one of the words that have defined the culture of the Internet from the beginning. Even though the Internet is evolving into a hotbed of commercial activity, the attraction of going to a site and finding something for free is still deeply ingrained in the online culture and a big part of what brings visitors to your site.

One of the best and most popular giveaways you can offer is relevant, clear, and useful information in the form of white papers, articles, and company newsletters. Your strategy for service on the Internet should include offering enough information and services for free that you become a bookmark destination for your current and potential customers.

Make Your Downloads Fast

Look around the hurried pace of today's business world and you'll see that your customers have neither the time nor the patience to wait — not in line at the bank, on hold on the phone, or for the Web pages on your site to download. Consider these facts from Zona Research (www.zonaresearch.com):

- ✔ The majority of Web pages take anywhere from 3 to 11 seconds to download.

- ✔ The average viewer will click off a site if a page takes more than eight seconds to download.

- ✔ These click-offs (you can consider them bailouts — when users get tired of waiting and click away from a slow Web page) cost e-businesses an estimated $4.35 billion annually in lost revenue.

Speed does make a difference. You can reduce your customer bailout rate from 30 percent to 8 percent just by reducing your download time by one second per page! Remember that if your site is slow, your customers will go. To decrease the download time of your pages, avoid over-designing the site with too many fancy graphics. In general, photos and graphics with large file sizes take a long time to download.

Begin with high-quality, professional photos. Instead of simply scanning them, try using a software program such as Photoshop to compress the image so that the file size is small enough to load quickly. Be aware that compression may reduce the quality of the image somewhat. We suggest using a professional Web page designer who can help you strike the delicate balance between speed and quality.

Offer Contact Options

Many of the business owners and executives who attend our seminars have told us that customers often see something on their company's Web sites that they're interested in, then want to contact the company to ask a question or to place an order. "Do business with your customers the way they want to do business with you" is one of the principles behind excellent service — meaning you need to make sure that your Web site has an easy to find Contact Us link on the home page. Because some customers won't be accessing your site thorough the front door, you may want to post your contact information on all of the pages within your site.

Too many companies don't provide detailed information on how to contact them, limit the contact information to only an e-mail address, or provide no contact information at all. Your contact section should provide all the possible options for contacting your company, including phone number, street address, fax, and e-mail. Remember to use real e-mail addresses, if appropriate, rather than webmaster@company.com or help@company.com. This reinforces that there are real people behind your Web site.

Don't limit your customers to one method of contacting you, such as e-mail. Rather, give them all the options and let them choose how they want to contact you. Providing a variety of contact options makes you look like a more established business and less like a fly-by-night-company. Providing multiple contact options makes it look like you actually *want* customers to contact you and reflects your company's dedication to excellent customer service

Use Multiple Media

Imagine receiving a brochure from two different companies on the same day. One is all text and the other is a combination of words and images. Which would seem more interesting to you? Create a more dynamic and interactive online experience for your customers by using animation, video, and audio files to enhance the text on your Web site.

As the saying goes, "A picture paints a thousand words." In the online world, pictures can give your customers a feel for who you are and the kind of business you are in. Think about what types of pictures you could put on your site that would help your customers get a better understanding of your business. It could be a picture of yourself, your entire team, or your products.

Video and audio clips are two more good ways to introduce yourself and your company to your customers. They give customers a taste of what you're offering and add value to your site. Be careful that these video and audio files don't take too long to load, though! You could also include an interactive media tool, such as a self-scoring questionnaire, to provide value to your customers by helping them evaluate some aspect of their business or to identify a business need in some relevant way.

Update Your Site Often

After their Web sites are up and running, business owners too often sit down, put their feet up on their desks, wipe their brows, and exclaim with relief, "Whew, I'm glad that's done!" Unfortunately, getting your Web site up is just the beginning of the process of maintaining quality online service. If you want your customers to consider your site a valuable destination, you have to make constant updates.

Visitors are always looking for fresh and new information. In addition to the basics, such as updating your contact information if it changes, removing time-sensitive material, and updating current specials, you can create a What's New section and update it daily, weekly, or monthly, as appropriate.

Keep Your Site Design Simple and Clean

Hundreds of books, magazine articles, and Web sites have addressed the serious business of Web site design. Unfortunately, many businesses don't seem to be paying attention. In their attempts to be unique and cutting edge, they've created Web site design disasters by jamming their sites full of

- ✔ Busy backgrounds
- ✔ Hard to read fonts
- ✔ Too many buttons
- ✔ Jumping, twirling, and spinning animation

Resist the temptation to clutter up your Web site. Go for simple and clean. If you do, you'll have a Web site that's well designed, interesting, and customer focused. A few tips to keep in mind include

- ✔ Although one well-placed *banner* (those little commercial billboards you see on so many Web sites) isn't hard on the eyes, imagine a Web page that has three banners, four Amazon buttons, and a variety of links all competing for attention. You risk making your site look busy, confusing, and unprofessional when you include too many of these banners.

- ✔ A nice, clean background on your site makes text easier to read, looks more professional, and is less distracting than a busy background with some wild pattern that reminds browsers of the bathroom wallpaper they grew up with. Stick with a basic color, that's consistent with the image you want your company to have, for your site background.

- ✔ Graphics make a site visually appealing but, if overused, can leave a poor impression. Remember that your customers (and potential customers) don't like to wait for graphics to download — make sure that any graphics are compressed enough to download quickly.

For more ideas about Web page design, see *Creating Web Pages For Dummies*, 5th edition (Hungry Minds).

Practice E-Mail Excellence

Most of the e-mail you send to customers will probably be responses to their queries. Don't underestimate the impact your e-mail responses have on your customers' perception of the service they receive. Try these four simple, yet effective, ways to ensure that your e-mail creates goodwill and a positive service experience for your customers:

✔ **Be timely.** The sooner you get back to your customer, the better; however, a general rule is to return all e-mail inquiries within 24 hours. If you don't have the information the customer needs within this time, you may want to consider using an automated response system. These systems respond to incoming e-mails with a note saying that the e-mail was received and is being acted on. This note acts to fill the gap until you can get back to your customer with the necessary information.

✔ **Personalize your response.** One of the best ways to add the human touch to your e-mail responses is to use the customer's name in the greeting. Too often, e-mails to customers are impersonal and cold. Although it may seem like a small thing, consider how differently you would feel if you received an e-mail response that began with "Dear Ms. Smith" (assuming that you're a Ms. Smith) than one that started "To whom it may concern" or that had no greeting at all.

✔ **Refer to the original e-mail.** Keep in mind that, not only do you receive hundreds of e-mails a day from your customers, but that your customers also send countless e-mails each day. Make it easy on your customers — include or refer specifically to their original question, comment, or problem in your response. If appropriate, you may want to include the text from their original e-mail. This extra effort on your part saves your customers time and shows that you really are paying attention.

✔ **Have a real person sign the response.** Rather than returning e-mails signed by the ubiquitous "Customer Service Representative" or another generic title, try assigning a real person with a real name to each e-mail correspondence. Also include a phone number and address for this person after their signature. The personal touch goes a long way towards making customers feel that they're dealing with a human organization, rather than cold technology from a corporate monolith.

Chapter 18

Ten Tips for Dealing with Customer Complaints

In This Chapter

▶ Understanding how customer complaints can improve your service

▶ Exploring ways to calm angry customers

*A*s the power and popularity of the Internet grows, business transactions that have traditionally been conducted offline, such as purchasing, making payments, and inquiring about products, are increasingly being carried out online. Whether by mouse or by mortar, you can expect that a certain number of misunderstandings and errors will take place, resulting in customer frustration and complaints. After all, billions of business transactions take place every day, in the United States alone. They can't all go smoothly.

The way you react to these complaints can make the difference between gaining or losing a customer. A study conducted by the Technical Assistance Research Program, Inc. (TARP) found that:

✔ Customers who have a problem with a product or service will voice their objection to the company directly 50 percent of the time. Nine out of ten of these customers will more than likely take their future business elsewhere.

✔ Customers who do voice a complaint to the company are not thoroughly satisfied with the company's effort to resolve the situation 50 percent of the time. These dissatisfied customers will tell, on average, between seven to nine other people about their unsatisfactory experience with the company.

With statistics like this — that show the relationship between customers' unhappiness with service and their taking their business elsewhere — you can't afford to take the issue of customer complaints lightly. Knowing how to deal with customer complaints is an essential part of offering excellent customer service. The ten tips in this chapter help you craft an approach to dealing with complaints that encourages your customers to communicate with you and assures them that you will take quick and reasonable actions to resolve their problems and concerns.

Make It Easy for Your Customers to Complain

One of the things that can drive customers to the brink of hysteria (or into a competitor's arms) is the feeling that they have no outlet for communicating their frustrations to a company that has, in their minds, done them wrong. The TARP study mentioned earlier in this chapter concludes that the three primary reasons customers fail to register their complaints are

✔ They believe it isn't worth their time.

✔ They don't know to whom they should make their complaint.

✔ They feel that complaining will produce no results.

You can minimize the frustration your customers may experience by creating a specific company complaint policy (and making it known to your customers) that, in detail, spells out

✔ How customers can contact you when they have a complaint or problem

✔ Where in your organization to make specific complaints

✔ Who is responsible for dealing with different types of complaints

Remember that the goal is to make communicating with you easy for your customers — even if they are just communicating to tell you about problems. Don't frustrate, confuse, and annoy your customers by making them chase person after person, from department to department, to get their complaints resolved satisfactorily.

View Complaints as Gifts

Even though customer complaints can, at times, be stressful and challenging, they're really a gift. If you're willing to open your mind and listen, complaints can prove to be a great source of information, innovation, and inspiration. They can help you:

✔ Gain valuable ideas for new products or services.

✔ Recover a customer who may otherwise have decided to go elsewhere.

- ✓ Fix problems that could be frustrating to other customers and cause them to leave.

- ✓ Gain a lifelong customer, if you resolve the complaint quickly and efficiently.

Don't think of a complaint as just another problem taking up your time and energy. Think beyond that, and teach yourself and the rest of your company to view customer complaints as valuable opportunities to learn from your customers and to improve your business.

Thank Your Customers for Complaining

Most complaining customers don't expect to be greeted with sincere and heartfelt appreciation. Yet, a simple thank you is one way to let your customers know that you appreciate the time and effort they've taken to inform you about a problem with your company's service or product. In addition to simply expressing thanks for the complaint, let your customers know why or in what way their complaints have contributed to your business. For example, you may want to say:

- ✓ Thanks for your suggestion. It will help us to improve this process in the future.

- ✓ Thank you for giving us a chance to resolve the problem and keep you as a customer.

- ✓ I appreciate your bringing this to my attention so that we can correct the problem.

- ✓ I appreciate your telling me this, because it helps me to do my job better.

Let Your Customers Vent

Unhappy customers want to express their feelings of frustration, anger, and disappointment. Too often, service providers (feeling the pressure to move on to the next customer and the next problem) resent the customer's venting and view listening to it as a waste of time. However, trying to resolve any service problem without first listening to the customer's feelings is a bad idea. It almost never results in a smooth resolution. Only *after* your customers have vented can they start to hear what you have to say; then, the process of problem solving can begin.

If you try to stop customers from expressing their feelings, you push them from annoyed to irate in a matter of moments. Statements that are guaranteed to bring a complaining customer's blood to a boil include

✔ Just calm down.

✔ You don't seem to understand.

✔ You have to . . .

✔ You're wrong.

✔ We won't . . .

✔ We never . . .

✔ We can't . . .

Sincerely Apologize for All Problems

Nothing extinguishes the fires of wrath like a well-timed, sincere apology. Simple enough, right? Yet, many workers resist the idea of apologizing to customers because they don't want to make the company or themselves look bad by admitting a mistake. The problem with this logic is that upset customers already believe that you (or the company) have made a mistake! Strongly professed denials or refusals to apologize just cause more aggravation. A few guidelines for apologizing include

✔ **Don't be stingy with apologies.** An apology is not an automatic admission of guilt; it's a way of letting the customer know that you care and want to right any wrong that has been done.

✔ **Apologize even if you're not the person who made the mistake.** Remember that your customer thinks of you as a representative of the company. She takes your apology as a corporate *mea culpa,* not a personal one.

✔ **Apologize even if the customer is in the wrong.** Say something like, "I'm sorry you're having a problem." What difference does it really make if the customer is right or wrong? Don't waste time trying to figure out who's at fault in a situation. You need to fix the problem, not assign blame.

✔ **Time your apology carefully.** Don't use your apology as a preemptive strike by making it the first thing you say to an upset customer. Instead, give customers time to provide the necessary details so that you can make your apology more personal and specific to their circumstances.

Identify the Elements of the Complaint

In order to resolve a customer's complaint, you need to make sure you understand exactly what's contributing to the dissatisfaction. Although there are hundreds (if not thousands) of ways that customers' expectations are not met, the most common elements found in customer complaints generally include one or more of the following:

- ✔ Billing mistakes

- ✔ Complicated or confusing product or service instructions

- ✔ Delays in delivery of goods or services

- ✔ Failure to fulfill product or service warranties

- ✔ Failure to provide refunds and adjustments as promised

- ✔ Incompetent or discourteous employees

- ✔ Incorrect or misleading information

- ✔ Misleading advertising

- ✔ Misleading statements by sales staff

- ✔ Order filled incorrectly

- ✔ Poor quality repair work

- ✔ Product or service not performing as promised

- ✔ Products are backordered or unavailable

- ✔ Unfriendly user interface

Don't waste your effort (and your customers' time) trying to fix the wrong problem. It's easy to assume that you know what a customer's problem is within the first few sentences of the dialogue — you've probably heard it all a hundred times before. Often, however, the problem changes or becomes unique upon closer examination.

Fix the Problem

Fixing your customer's problem requires an understanding of the elements of the complaint and of your customer's unique perspective on the situation. After you accurately identify the factual part of a problem and your customer's point of view, the next step, obviously, is to fix it. Often, you can quickly remedy the situation by changing an invoice, redoing an order, waiving or refunding charges, or replacing a defective product.

Other times, however, fixing the problem is more complex. The damage or mistake cannot simply be undone. In these instances, you have to reach mutually acceptable compromises. Any solution you come up with should take into account any of the following issues that apply:

- ✔ Contractual commitments you've made or warranties that may be in place
- ✔ Your customer's expectations and any promises you've made to the customer
- ✔ The possible cost of all the potential solutions
- ✔ The value of this customer to your business and the probability of losing the customer's future business
- ✔ What a fair and reasonable action to resolve the problem would be
- ✔ The chances that the problem will get larger if not fixed immediately
- ✔ Your ability to deliver on the chosen solution

You won't always be able to resolve an issue immediately. In such cases, offering a realistic time frame for resolution is important. You should explain why the delay is necessary and what steps you're taking toward resolution.

Give a Care Token

A *care token* is a specific action that you take to let your customers know that you're sorry for the mistake, that you regret any stress or inconvenience they experienced, and that you care about keeping their business. A care token can go a long way toward reestablishing your customers' confidence and doesn't have to be expensive. Examples of care tokens include

- ✔ An airline giving you a coupon for a free drink and movie on your next flight because it ran out of that spicy tomato drink you like by the time the attendants got to your row
- ✔ A restaurant treating you to a glass of wine because you weren't seated for your 7:30 p.m. reservation until 8:00 p.m.
- ✔ The one-hour photo shop giving you a free role of film when it takes longer than an hour to process your holiday snapshots

Follow Up

After you've resolved a customer's complaint, call or e-mail that customer to bring closure to the situation. This follow-up contact ensures that the problem has been completely resolved to the customer's satisfaction and confirms that no further action is required. This personal touch also helps reestablish your company's credibility while reinforcing your sincere hope that the problem has been resolved.

Practice Prevention

The information you gather from customer complaints can provide your company with a valuable source of process-improvement opportunities. In order to capture this information and make sure that you're using it to prevent future problems from occurring, create a formal procedure for recording all incoming customer complaints. The information you record should include

- The date of the complaint
- The name of the person who made the complaint
- The nature of the complaint
- Specific details relating to the complaint
- What actions or follow-up were taken to resolve the complaint

Over time, management or an employee task team can analyze complaint logs to determine patterns, trends, and root causes of recurring problems. In addition, complaint logs allow managers to check the system by making sure that complaints are being handled quickly, fairly, and to the customer's satisfaction.

Chapter 19

Ten Things to Know about E-Mail Privacy

In This Chapter

▶ Recognizing who really owns your e-mail messages

▶ Following your e-mails — wherever they go

▶ Protecting yourself from e-mail abuses

*T*ransacting business over the Internet not only presents security concerns for customers; it also presents new privacy issues for e-businesses. Although scoffing at the news media is easy — who seem to delight in scaring us into thinking that hackers are, at this very moment, trying to get into our hard drives — you need to be aware of some fundamental aspects of online privacy.

Because e-mail is increasingly used as evidence in litigation, getting up to speed in this important area makes sense. This chapter presents the top ten things every e-business employee should know about e-mail privacy.

Personal E-Mails Sent from Work Are the Property of Your Employer

Regardless of the content or recipient of a message, your employer owns all e-mails you send from work. The Electronic Communications Privacy Act of 1986 states that e-mails sent from or received by a closed system (one owned by a company and not for public use) are the property of the system owner — the employer.

E-Mails Sent from Home Belong to You, But . . .

You own the e-mails that you send via a public ISP, such as AOL and Earthlink, and consequently have privacy rights regarding those messages. However, a government agency, such as the FBI or EPA, can access your private records from the service provider's records without having to first notify you, the subscriber.

A Deleted E-Mail Is Not Deleted

Most e-mail programs save all inbox and outbox messages in one file — usually called a PSI file. This means that when you delete an e-mail message from your inbox, you simply remove it from view. The actual file is never overwritten and, consequently, is easily retrievable. Learn to think of e-mail messages as permanent documents.

Your E-Mail Message, Once Sent, Can Become Anyone's Business

There are no guarantees that the person you send an e-mail to won't forward it to another person — possibly a total stranger. Without your knowing it, your message could be forwarded around the world several times. Think of an e-mail message as a postcard that's easily readable by all kinds of people. Remove anything in the message that you would not want a stranger to read.

Also, avoid using your work computer for purposes such as personal banking. You may unwittingly compromise your password or other private information. Keeping private data private — by using your home system for sensitive information — is smart.

E-Mail Is Admissible as Evidence in a Court of Law

A friend of ours recently remarked how much easier his job has become since the widespread use of e-mail. Our friend is a lawyer who noted that "people use e-mail to write things that they wouldn't ever dream of writing in a letter. E-mails have made the collection of evidence much easier." E-mails comprised much of the evidence in the Microsoft antitrust case. Take heed: If it can happen to Microsoft, it can happen to you.

You Can Be Fired for Using the Internet Inappropriately at Work

Although policies vary from company to company, many employers now monitor and record each employee's e-mail and Web usage, focusing in on any sites and addresses that are not related to work. We know of a senior manager who was dismissed because of excessive personal use of the Web. Recent articles in the business press paint a picture of more and more companies making random checks of their employees' e-mails, without any permission being required from the employees.

Copies of Your E-Mails Exist in Places Other Than Your Own Computer

Most of us know how a snail mail letter arrives in our mailbox; however, few of us know how an e-mail arrives in our inbox. Therefore, forgetting that there are probably several copies of your messages, located in a number of places, is easy. A copy of your e-mail could be on servers that were involved in transmitting your original message; copies that were made as an automatic back-up may exist in your company's files; copies may exist on back-up files kept by the recipient's company; and copies are probably on the drives and back-up files of anyone who has been forwarded the message.

E-Mail Recovery Is Big Business

E-mail now plays a central role in many court cases. The use of electronic evidence in court has spawned a new type of company that specialize in e-mail recovery. A company of this type systematically searches for and retrieves e-mails from all the various storage locations where the e-mails could reside.

Privacy Laws Are Being Challenged Every Day

E-mail and Web privacy are high-profile issues that the courts are continually wrestling with. Several advocate groups are working to change the current self-regulating approach to Internet privacy. These groups cite many examples of privacy policies that are either inadequate or have changed without notice. To stay abreast of current issues and changes, you may want to visit the Electronic Privacy Information Center (www.epic.org).

Add a Disclaimer to Confidential E-Mails

When using e-mail to transmit confidential or highly sensitive information, consider adding a disclaimer at the end, after your signoff. Even though a disclaimer doesn't stop an unauthorized recipient from saving, copying, or forwarding your message, it might prevent the e-mail from being used as evidence in a court of law. Ultimately, however, waivers are a deterrent and no guarantee of legal protection. Here are two examples of e-mail disclaimers:

Privileged/Confidential Information may be contained in this message. If you are not the addressee indicated in this message (or responsible for delivery of the message to such person), you may not copy or deliver this message to anyone. In such a case, you should destroy this message and kindly notify the sender by reply e-mail.

Warning! The information contained in this message may be privileged and confidential and protected from disclosure. If the reader of this message is not the intended recipient, you are hereby notified that any dissemination, distribution, or copying of this communication is strictly prohibited. If you have received this communication in error, please notify us immediately by replying to this message and then delete it from your computer. All e-mail sent to this address will be received by the XYZ corporate e-mail system and is subject to archiving and review by someone other than the recipient.

Chapter 20

Ten Ways to Use Voicemail to Enhance Customer Relations

- -

In This Chapter

▶ Recognizing the convenience and efficiency of voicemail

▶ Using voicemail to demonstrate your dedication to quality service

▶ Crafting messages to get the response you need

- -

*A*ccording to a report by International Data Corporation, the number of phone call minutes being transmitted over the Internet (rather than traditional phone networks) is exploding — from 310 million minutes of use in 1998 to an expected 135 billion minutes of use by the year 2004.

The day is coming when you'll be able to leave and retrieve voicemail messages via the Internet, and you'll need to manage voicemail on your computer as well as on your phone system. So for good measure, and with an eye towards the future, we include this section on voicemail.

Voicemail provides a significant interface between your company and your customers, and when it's used well it can improve customer relations, enhance productivity, and facilitate communication between coworkers. This chapter introduces some of the main advantages of voicemail. Voicemail, like any technology, can be a blessing or a curse. Depending on how you use it, voicemail can save you tons of time or it can cause alienation and frustration.

When used effectively, voicemail can enhance service by giving your customers the quick answers they demand in today's fast-paced world. The following ten suggestions help you enhance your voicemail communications, whether you're managing your incoming messages or leaving effective outgoing ones, be it by Internet or telephone system.

Don't Hide Behind Your Voicemail

Whenever possible and practical, answer you own phone or take calls that are forwarded to you by your assistant. Remember that, although many people don't mind using voicemail, most prefer to speak with you directly. Don't sit at your desk, day after day, and let your voicemail system intercept all callers. We ran across one company where people almost never answered their own phones, whether they were at their desks or not. The culture of this company viewed phone calls from customers and coworkers as an interruption! Good customer care requires that you answer your phone, at least, most of the times that it rings. When you do, you send a positive message that you're available and want to help.

Update Your Greeting Regularly

How many times have you called someone, only to be greeted by an out-of-date voicemail message? Say that it's Wednesday, January 17th. You hear a greeting that goes something like this: "Hi. This is Ed. Today is Monday, January 15th and I will be out of the office until Tuesday, January 16th." Besides the fact that this is annoying, what impression do you get of Ed? Do you feel that Ed is well organized and on top of his work? Probably not.

You should always update your greetings to reflect your schedule and provide callers with the best time to reach you. Your callers should be able to figure out an expected timeframe for a return call by the greeting you leave. Additionally, if you are going to be out of the office, away on vacation, or away from your phone for a prolonged period of time, let your callers know when you'll return and provide the name and number of a coworker who can assist them in your absence.

Record all greetings in a noise-free environment. Background conversation, honking horns, barking dogs, and the like, all create a negative impression and communicate to your listener that you're unprofessional. If your work environment in noisy, try getting in early or staying late to record your message — when less noise is likely.

Respond to Messages Promptly

One common complaint that customers have about voicemail is the potential for a delayed response. If your callers don't receive a response from you within a reasonable period of time (usually a day or two), they will begin to think that voicemail is an ineffective way of communicating with you. Remember that callers feel secure and comfortable leaving you voicemail messages only if you consistently get back to them in a timely fashion.

Get in the habit of checking for messages at least three times a day, including every time you return to your office from lunch or a meeting. After you receive a message, you should act immediately. Choose one of these options:

- ✔ Reply immediately.
- ✔ Forward the message to someone else for action.
- ✔ Save or write down the message for reply at a later date.
- ✔ Delete the message.

When forwarding a voicemail message to another user, be sure to add an introduction that explains when the message was originally left, why you are forwarding it, and what actions, if any, you want the other person to take.

Encourage Your Callers to Leave Effective Messages

The more specific the information that callers leave, the better the chances are that you'll be able to get back to them with a response or take the action they need. Encourage your callers to leave more effective messages. Craft your voicemail greeting so that you ask for:

- ✔ The reason for the call and any specific information that you need to know.
- ✔ An e-mail, if necessary, that conveys any additional, helpful details.
- ✔ The caller's phone number. Many people, in the rush to leave a detailed message, forget to leave their number. Consider incorporating a statement like, "Please leave your phone number, even if you think I already have it," into your greeting.

Give Callers the Option of Skipping Your Voicemail Greeting

Nothing is more frustrating than being forced to listen to a voicemail greeting you've already heard at least ten times. You can set up most phone systems so that your caller can bypass your greeting by pressing the pound (#) key.

The caller then goes straight to leaving a message. Although you may need or want to leave a lengthy greeting to provide important information, enable frequent callers (who presumably already know the information that you put in your greeting) to skip it. Likewise, if your system allows, give your callers the option of pressing 0 to reach a company operator.

Plan and Prepare Your Return Calls

You can save time and effort by carefully planning your return calls. Making specific notes on what you want to cover in the call, rather than relying on memory, can reduce the amount of time you spend on the phone when you return a call.

You can also make your calls more efficient by stating a time frame, for example, "Bob, I wanted to get back to you with this information, but I only have about five minutes to talk."

The best times of day to return phone calls are ½ hour before lunch and ½ hour before the end of the day. People have less time to chat at these times and are more focused on getting the job done so that they can leave for lunch or go home.

Provide a Context for Your Call

Breakdowns in voicemail communication that lead to telephone tag, unnecessary phone calls, and frustration most often occur because of three mistaken assumptions on the caller's part. You can instantly improve your voicemail messages by keeping the following in mind:

- ✔ **Don't assume that the person you're calling recognizes your voice.** No matter how well you think he knows you or how many times you've spoken with him on the phone, assuming that the person you're calling on business will recognize your voice is a mistake. Always state your name at the beginning of your message. Doing so keeps the receiver from having to listen to your message a dozen times to figure out who the heck called.

- ✔ **Don't assume that the person you're calling has your phone number handy.** Make it easy for the person you're calling to respond to your call by including your phone number in your message. Don't make him do the extra work of looking up your phone number. Remember that he may be away from the office and not have your number with him or he may have lost your number.

> ✔ **Don't assume that the person you're calling knows what you're talking about.** When responding to a voice message, don't assume that the person you're calling knows which message you are referring to. Instead, introduce your response with an opening that explains why you are calling. For example, "Hi, Cheshta. This is Ginger. I'm getting back to you on the message you left me regarding your billing problem."

Keep Your Outgoing Messages Short and to the Point

Americans who work in corporations receive an average of 175 fax, e-mail, telephone, and voicemail messages per day. Don't add to this burden by leaving rambling messages. Limit the length of your voice messages to between twenty seconds and two minutes. After a couple of minutes, you risk annoying or even losing your listener. Likewise, you want to avoid unfocused messages that obscure the purpose of your call.

Before you leave a message, know the points you want to cover and focus on one topic per message. If you group several topics together into one message, the person you're calling may wait until she can address all the topics before taking action or responding. In addition, single-topic messages are easier to forward.

If you're calling to ask a question, ask it directly. Rather than saying, "Hi. This is Cynthia. I have a question. Call me back," leave your actual question on the voicemail. By doing so, the recipient can prepare an answer before calling you back, saving both of you time and effort.

Specify the Response You Expect

Giving the people you call some guidance on how you would like for them to respond makes things easy on them. If your call is simply an FYI and you don't expect a response, say so. If you want them to take action, be specific:

> ✔ Please let me know that you received this message.

> ✔ Please call or e-mail me back with your response.

> ✔ Please take care of this immediately.

> ✔ I need this item by next Tuesday; please let me know if you can do this.

Many voicemail systems give you the option of marking a message as urgent. Use this feature sparingly! You don't want to run the risk of becoming the voicemail equivalent of the boy who cried wolf. Marking too many voicemails as urgent can lead to a situation where you send a message that *really* needs immediate attention, but based on your frequent use of the urgent feature, it's automatically sent to the bottom of the return pile.

Take Security Measures

Unauthorized entry into your voicemail can potentially cause anything from embarrassment to disaster for you and your company. Take the following measures to increase your mailbox security:

- **Use 5 to 10 digits for your security code.** The more numbers you use, the harder it is for someone to figure out the code.

- **Avoid overly simple or obvious codes.** Obvious numbers, such as your birth date, anniversary, or repetitious numbers such as 2222, are too easy to figure out. Choose a code that's not obvious to reduce the risk of your voicemail being broken into.

- **Memorize your code.** Don't keep your code written in the phone directory of your time management system or on a slip of paper you carry in your wallet. Instead, take some time to commit it to memory.

- **Change your code.** Just to be safe, occasionally change the access code that you use for voicemail. Doing so is especially important if an employee who knew the code has left the company or if you think the code has been compromised in any way.

Chapter 21

Ten Ways to Evaluate Your Online and Offline Service

. . . .

In This Chapter

▶ Using the Internet and e-mail to get feedback from your customers

▶ Conducting surveys

. . . .

*T*o have a customer-focused company, you must understand what your customers want and expect from your business, then evaluate how well you're meeting those desires and expectations. Become customer focused by:

✔ Gathering specific feedback about how satisfied your customers are with the level of service they receive

✔ Providing an initial benchmark against which you can measure future progress

✔ Making changes, based on your research, to the way you do business

To get the most accurate picture of your customers' online and offline service experience, use a combination of the methods that we show you in this chapter. For example, combine focus groups and written questionnaires, or combine telephone interviews and Web-based surveys. Either combination gives you a mix of general and specific feedback and qualitative and quantitative data.

Focus Groups (Online or Offline)

Using a traditional focus group to evaluate your service means inviting a number of your customers (usually 8 to 10 people) to get together to have a general discussion about some aspect of your company's service or products. Due to the power of the group dynamic (the more people in the room focusing on an issue, the more ideas that get tossed around for consideration), focus groups usually provide a lot of rich feedback in a relatively short period of time. A few tips on conducting your own focus group:

- ✔ Allow 60 to 90 minutes for the session.
- ✔ Invite attendees by letter, then follow up with a phone call.
- ✔ Expect that 50 percent of the people you invite won't come, so invite more people than you want to attend.
- ✔ Call participants a few days before the session to confirm attendance.
- ✔ Serve breakfast, lunch, or light refreshments as a courtesy.
- ✔ Ask questions that are general in nature to serve as discussion starters.
- ✔ Choose an off-site location, such as a hotel meeting room.
- ✔ Hire a trained facilitator or moderator to run your focus group.

To conduct a focus group online (a cost-efficient alternative), invite 8 to 10 of your customers to join you in a designated chat room for a set period of time (60 to 90 minutes). Just as with the offline focus group, you should have a professional moderator conduct the session with a predetermined set of questions ready to ask the participants. Many companies allow participants to view relevant text, video, and streaming media during the session to facilitate discussion. One advantage of the online focus group is that you can create a transcript of the session and make it available hours, or even minutes, after the session is completed.

The success of any focus group (online or offline) depends largely on the skill of the facilitator. The facilitator can be an external consultant or someone from inside your company. The facilitator makes sure that all participants have an opportunity to speak, keeps the group on track, and probes for in-depth feedback.

Web-based Surveys

Web-based surveys are an easy, effective, relatively inexpensive way to measure your customers' online service experience. You can hire professional companies to design your survey and evaluate the results, or, if you have the time and resources, you can design and evaluate a survey in-house. The three basic types of Web-based surveys include

- ✔ **E-mail invitation.** Start by sending out an e-mail invitation to a designated group of customers, asking them to participate in a survey. Embed a link for customers to click if they decide they want to complete the survey. Upon clicking this link, they are electronically whisked away to your survey.

✔ **Pop-up window.** A pop-up window survey counts the number of visitors who come to your site. At a predetermined number (for example, every two hundred visitors) it opens a window that asks the user if she is willing to fill out a short online survey. If the visitor chooses not to complete the survey, she can click No. The window disappears and she can go on her merry way. Clicking Yes takes her to the online survey.

✔ **Feedback or survey buttons.** Try to avoid using a feedback or survey button. Similar to the "tell us what you think" survey cards found in most hotel rooms, feedback buttons tend to draw feedback from extreme customers — either extremely satisfied or extremely upset. Feedback buttons don't provide a representative sampling of your customer population. Additionally, response rates for feedback buttons tend to be very low (less than 1 percent), so your survey results are not statistically valid.

Written Surveys

If your company has never conducted a survey or hasn't done one in a long time, start with a general written survey. Randomly select a certain number of your customers and send them a questionnaire that asks them to evaluate the service they receive from your company. Most written surveys have a response rate of between 30 to 60 percent, so remember to distribute more surveys than you expect to get back. The typical written survey is one to three pages in length and poses a series of specific questions, usually presented in one of the following ways (or a combination of the three).

Yes-or-no questions

Yes-or-no questions are closed-ended questions, meaning that they are phrased in such a way that they prompt a simple yes or no answer. These questions are most commonly used to gather general information. The respondent simply circles or checks the appropriate responses. For example:

Do you have a living will?	Yes	No
Is your current life insurance sufficient?	Yes	No
Do you own your own home?	Yes	No

Poor – excellent questions

Poor-to-excellent questions usually begin with the words "how" or "what" and ask respondents to rank their responses on a scale from poor to excellent. Respondents simply answer the questions by circling the word or number that best reflects their opinions. For example:

How would you rate the overall service you received from our technical-support staff?

> Poor   Fair   Good   Excellent

What is your overall evaluation of our technical-support group? (Circle one)

> (Poor)   1   2   3   4   5   6   (Excellent)

Degree questions

Degree questions usually start with the words "did," "does," "do," or "to what degree." They usually refer to specific experiences or events and ask respondents to rate their responses by choosing one of four specific descriptive phrases. For example:

To what degree did our Web site answer your questions about our company? (Choose one)

    ___ To a large degree

    ___ To a moderate degree

    ___ To a small degree

    ___ Not at all

Similarly, you can present statements that offer a scale of possible answers that range from "strongly agree" to "strongly disagree." Respondents simply choose the phrase that best reflects their opinions. For example:

Our accounting department provides you with accurate and timely billing. (Choose one)

___ Strongly agree

___ Agree

___ Disagree

___ Strongly disagree

The salesperson I dealt with was very knowledgeable about the product. (Circle one)

(Strongly Agree)   1   2   3   4   5   6   (Strongly Disagree)

 If you are using a numbers format and want to avoid "middle of the road" answers, use a series of numbers that ends with an even number, such as 1 to 6, rather than a series of numbers such as 1 to 5 that ends with an odd number. By using an even amount of numbers, you remove the middle number option and the respondent has to get off the fence and express a preference in one direction or another.

Customer Panels

 Of all the survey methods we use with our clients, we find that customer panels make the greatest impact on our clients. Something about hearing the information straight from the horse's mouth is both powerful and undeniable. One disadvantage to customer panels is the amount of time they take. Nonetheless, we think the results they produce make the effort well worth it.

Before the panel

Personally telephone a small number of your customers (usually no more than from 3 to 6 people) and invite them to participate on a customer panel. Carefully consider the customers you choose to be on the panel — pick people who are willing and able to give you balanced feedback. Establish a date, location, and time for your panel to meet (for 60 to 90 minutes) and reiterate that you are looking for balanced feedback on both the positive and negative aspects of the service your company provides. In addition, explain to you customers that approximately 10 to 25 of your company's managers and staff will attend to hear what the panel has to say.

During the panel

Set up the room in a U-shape with a table up front for the panel to sit at. Each participant should have a nametag, pen, paper, and water. The moderator asks a single question and gives each participant five minutes or so to answer, then moves on to the next question. Some general questions may include

✔ What, in your perception, is Company X's biggest strength? Biggest weakness?

✔ How well does Company X keep you informed?

✔ How easy is it to do business with Company X?

✔ Against the expectations that you have, how do Company X's products and services perform?

✔ How well does Company X meet its commitments? Does it deliver what it promises?

✔ What would Company X need to do to exceed your expectations?

Allow the audience to address a limited number of questions to your panelists, so that the audience can be perfectly clear on what the panelists are saying. It is critical that the audience not argue with the panelists' comments, try to explain something the panelist has misunderstood, try to fix the problem then and there, or become defensive in any way. The idea is to *listen* and learn what your customers have to say. Address any issues that arise during the panel's discussion after the panel is adjourned.

After the panel

Personally call and thank each panelist for participating. If issues arose during the panel relating to that particular panelist, set up a follow-up meeting to discuss the specifics of the problem or to outline the steps you are taking to resolve the problem. Although not necessary, some companies send a thank-you gift to panel participants.

Customer Exit Surveys

At one time or another, you've probably been stopped as you leave a department store or get off an airplane by an enthusiastic person holding a clipboard and asking if you have a few moments to answer some questions. A long-time method for gathering customer feedback, exit surveys are conducted on the spot and provide immediate feedback while the service experience is still fresh in the customer's mind. One disadvantage to exit surveys is that they interrupt busy people who are often in a hurry and who may not be willing to stop to answer questions. You can overcome this to some degree by making the questionnaire short (no more than one page long) and by making questions easy to answer (present check boxes instead of asking people to write answers). If you have a building where customers physically visit your business, consider including this method in the measurement mix.

Employee Surveys

Nothing puts a bad taste in a customer's mouth faster than dealing with employees who have resentful attitudes about their jobs or your company. An employee survey (where you gather information from your staff) can help highlight common problems and put them on the table for discussion and resolution. This type of survey is almost always implemented through a confidential written questionnaire that is sent out to all staff and managers. Among other topics, a typical employee survey covers three areas that are critical to your company's ability to provide excellent service to your customers:

- ✔ Your staff's job-satisfaction rate
- ✔ The effectiveness of communication within and between departments
- ✔ The extent to which employees feel that they're part of a team and that teamwork is valued company-wide

Lost-Account Surveys

If you want to know why you've lost a particular customer or group of customers, then lost-account surveys are the technique for you. A lost-account interview is conducted (usually by telephone) with a customer who has stopped doing business with your company. The call usually begins by letting the ex-customer know that you are sorry that she is no longer doing business with you and that you are interested in learning from your mistakes. Explain how understanding her reasons for leaving will help you make improvements for future customers. Although this is not the purpose of the call, one great side benefit of lost account surveys is that you may have the opportunity to take some corrective action and regain this person as a customer.

Telephone Surveys

If geography, time, or financial constraints make it difficult to interview your customers face-to-face, try telephone surveys. Phone surveys are relatively inexpensive (compared with focus groups), but still allow you to engage in a dialogue with your customers. The most effective telephone surveys utilize two complimentary techniques: *ask-and-answer* and *discussion*.

Ask-and-answer

The ask-and-answer technique is built around a set of predetermined questions. The interviewer, after explaining the type of rating scale the customer should use to evaluate the questions, reads each question to the respondent and makes a note of the answers.

For example: "Using a scale of one to six, where one means poor and six means excellent, please respond to the following question: 'How would you rate the courtesy of the service technician who checked in your car?'"

Discussion

The discussion technique is built around probing questions. It is generally more spontaneous and exploratory than the ask-and-answer format. The interviewer asks an open-ended question and listens carefully to discover specific issues that the client has. This technique allows the interviewer to pick up on part of an answer and then ask the respondent for more details. For example:

Interviewer: What was your impression of our Web site?

Customer: It was okay.

Interviewer: What could we do to make it better?

Customer: Well, it was kind of hard to find the prices on the items I wanted.

Interviewer: Why was that?

Customer: The prices are not listed next to the item — you have to click on each one to link to the pricing section. This required me to go back and forth between pages. It was a waste of my time and annoying.

Mystery Shoppers

Mystery shopping uses detective work to measure your company's service performance. The first thing to do is contract with a professional market research firm that offers mystery shopping. The company then sends employees to your store to pose as your customers. After observing your company's service in action, your contractor puts together a report that offers feedback on your service performance, using a combination of quantitative scoring and anecdotal information. You can also apply the mystery-shopping method to evaluate your online service.

Communicate the Results

Regardless of the methods you employ to measure the effectiveness of your company's customer service, you are not taking full advantage of the feedback unless you follow through. Once your company has taken the initiative to actively invite feedback, you have an ethical responsibility to take some action to address the issues that you have discovered. Remember: If you don't want to know, don't ask!

Going to the effort of gathering information and then not doing anything about the problems you identify is a waste of time and resources. It also increases the skepticism of your staff and customers regarding how serious you are about service improvement. Closing the loop by communicating the results of your survey to the people who provided you with the feedback via e-mail, newsletter, or personal meetings is critical. Be sure to thank them for their participation and let them know the basics of what you learned and what actions you plan to take to improve the service that your company provides.

Grammar Reminders for E-Mail Perfection

· ·

S ome sophisticated grammar and spelling software packages are available that are stand-alone products and can be used in conjunction with any e-mail or word-processing program. This appendix offers grammar tips to help you craft excellent messages on your own, so that you're not reliant on software and can catch mistakes that computers can't.

Turning Words into Plurals

Sometimes the simplest mistakes create a bad impression. Even though most of us learned about plurals in school, it's easy to forget the basics. Here are the rules for turning the one into the many.

- ✔ Words ending in a *y* that is preceded by a vowel become plural if you add an *s* to the end of the word. For example, *pays, attorneys, ploys.*

- ✔ Words ending in a *y* that is preceded by a consonant become plural if you drop the *y* and add *ies.* For example, *quality* becomes *qualities, query* becomes *queries, fantasy* becomes *fantasies.*

- ✔ Words ending in *s, ch* or *x* become plural if you add *es.* For example, *lunch* becomes *lunches, box* becomes *boxes, loss* becomes *losses.*

- ✔ Words ending in *um* or *on,* such as *addendum* or *medium,* become plural if you drop the *um* or *on* and add an *a,* for example, *addenda* or *media.*

- ✔ Make a number or an acronym plural by adding a small *s,* for example, *VIPs* and *1990s.*

Adding Suffixes to Words

A suffix is any ending that you add to a word. Suffixes are often added to change a word's part of speech. For example, the word *entertainment* (a noun) is made of the word *entertain* (a verb) plus *ment* (the suffix). When you use suffixes, you need to follow some basic rules:

- ✔ When adding suffixes to words that end in a *y,* remember to change the *y* to an *i.* For example, *friendly* becomes *friendliness, identify* becomes *identifiable.* The exception to this rule is when you add the suffix *ing,* in which case you keep the *y* and do not change it to an *i.* For example *querying, pacifying, identifying.*

- ✔ When adding a suffix that begins with a consonant to words that end in an *e,* keep the final *e.* For example, *polite* becomes *politeness, achieve* becomes *achievement.* When adding a suffix that begins with a vowel, drop the last *e.* For example, *achieve* becomes *achievable, argue* becomes *arguable.* As an exception, the final *e* usually stays when the last *e* comes after another *e* or an *o, c,* or *g.* For example, *manage* becomes *manageable, agree* becomes *agreeable.*

- ✔ When adding suffixes that begin with a vowel to words that end in consonants, have two syllables, and the accent is on the first syllable, the last consonant remains unchanged. For example, *question* becomes *questioning, standard* becomes *standardize.*

- ✔ When adding suffixes that begin with a vowel to words that end in consonants, have two syllables, and the accent is on the second syllable, the last consonant is doubled. For example, *remit* becomes *remittance, defer* becomes *deferring.*

Knowing When to Use "Me," "Myself," or "I"

Lots of people get confused on whether to use *I, my,* or *myself* in sentences. Sometimes, the confusion comes about when people are talking about themselves and others in the same sentence. For example, "My boss and I/me often make visits to our clients." To figure out the correct word, imagine that the other person is not included in the sentence and read it as if it were you alone. The above example would read like this, ". . . I/me often make visits to our clients." The correct word is *I,* so the sentence should read, "My boss and I often make visits to our clients."

Here is another example, "Please call my boss or I/me to schedule a conference call." Using the same rule, remove the other person and the sentence
reads, "Please call I/me to schedule a conference call." The correct word to
use is *me,* so the sentence should read, "Please call my boss or me to schedule a conference call."

Use the word *myself* in sentences where you are both the person who takes
an action and the person who has a reaction. For example, "Sometimes I
really crack myself up," or, "If I want something done properly, I do it myself."

Using Punctuation to Add Rhythm

Punctuation adds to your e-mails the timing, rhythm, and other subtleties
that are conveyed by body language and voice tone in a person-to-person
conversation. The basic punctuation survival kit contains the following
items:

- ✔ Commas
- ✔ Apostrophes
- ✔ Ellipses
- ✔ Dashes
- ✔ Colons
- ✔ Semicolons
- ✔ Parentheses

The comma

Small yet powerful, the comma's main purpose is to separate one part of a
sentence from another. This section presents a few of the comma's more popular uses.

Making a quick pause

Add commas to a sentence where you want the reader to take a slight pause.
If you are unsure whether a comma is required, use the following technique:
Read the sentence quickly to yourself, without a pause where you're thinking
of placing the comma. If it sounds confusing to you, add a comma. If it doesn't
sound confusing, then omit the comma.

Separating a group of items

Use commas to separate words or phrases that are written one after the other. For example, "Our survey discovered that customers care about location, price, courtesy, and experience." Note that the last item, the word *experience,* is separated by a comma. That comma is optional, and many writers prefer not to include it.

Separating transitional words

Transitional words or phrases, such as *however, additionally, for example,* and *on the other hand,* are often used at the beginning of sentences. Always use a comma to separate them from the words that follow. For example, that's one example. Here's another: "Additionally, we should all get Mondays off."

Replacing "and" before a noun

When using a series of descriptive words (adjectives) that all relate to the same subject (noun) use commas instead of the word *and.* Using *and* in the following sentence is redundant and awkward. "The power failure created some ugly scenes at the call center. You should have seen our red-faced and hair-tearing and totally-crazed supervisor." Replacing *and* with commas creates a sentence that's easier to read. "The power failure created some ugly scenes at the call center. You should have seen our red-faced, hair-tearing, totally-crazed supervisor."

Separating independent thoughts from dependent thoughts

Use a comma to separate an independent thought from a dependent thought when they are in the same sentence. In the following sentence, there are two separate thoughts, "I enjoy working with other employees, especially the friendly ones." The first part of the sentence, "I enjoy working with other employees," is an independent thought because it is not reacting to another phrase or clause in the same sentence. The second clause, "especially the friendly ones," is reacting to the first clause and is therefore dependent on the first clause.

Separating nonessential asides

Often when writing, we add small comments or asides that make a message more personal, but that are not essential to the basic meaning of the message. When adding such phrases, separate them from the main body of the sentence by using commas. For example, the essential message may be, "Our vendors promise that the new system will be up and running in two days." You add your own comment, separated by commas, such as, "Our vendors promise, just like they did last week and the week before, that the new system will be up and running in two days."

The semicolon

Semicolons are part comma and part period. They are used to separate different parts of a sentence and signify a longer pause than a comma. Here are some guidelines for using semicolons correctly in your e-mails:

✔ Use semicolons to separate a list of items that are already separated by commas. For example, "Our customers view us as helpful, skilled and friendly; our employees view us as caring, fair and responsive; our vendors view us as professional and experienced."

✔ Use a semicolon to separate two closely-related parts of a sentence when a comma isn't strong enough and a period creates too much separation between the two clauses. For example, "Our salespeople are very committed; they spend a fortune on clothes alone."

The apostrophe

The apostrophe serves two purposes: It works with an *s* to form the possessive of a noun, such as "Angelo's computer," and it forms contractions, such as "Customers can't (cannot) always get what they want."

Many people have a hard time knowing exactly where to put the apostrophe in a possessive situation, so here are the rules:

✔ Place an apostrophe before an *s* whenever you want to signify that the object belongs to a person or thing. In the sentence, "I thought that Amber's design was the best," the design belongs to Amber. Therefore, the apostrophe is inserted before the *s.*

✔ Place an apostrophe after the *s* when the noun is a plural and ends with the letter *s,* for example, "Not all the employees were excited about the managers' training." *Managers* ends in an *s* and is a plural. If it were only one manager in the sentence, the word would read *manager's.*

One thing to watch out for: *Its* is a possessive form and *it's* is a contraction. For example, "It's too cold outside to play baseball" and "The team won its last game."

The ellipsis

The ellipsis is enjoying a revival due to e-mail because it provides a natural and conversational transition between different thoughts in the same e-mail sentence. For example, "The office is busier than ever . . . I'm as slow as ever . . . some things never change." In this example, the ellipsis signals a pause similar to a comma.

The other, more official, use for an ellipsis is to signify missing words in quotations. For example, "If music be the food of love . . ." or "Everyone in the doctor's waiting room suddenly started singing 'Some enchanted evening . . . across a crowded room." Don't use ellipsis in sentences where the quote is obviously only a part of the original. For example, "After the negotiations, the chairman told us of the new merger and how it was 'going to make life easier for all of us.'"

The long dash or short hyphen

There are two dashes available to you on most keyboards. The most common is the short one that lives at the top right of your keyboard, between zero and plus. It works well for joining words, such as, "We're inviting our top customers to an all-encompassing, ten-day tour of our multi-channel call center."

The other dash is longer and doesn't have its own key on the keyboard. Known as an *em dash* (because it is as wide as the widest letter, *m*) it can usually be written by pressing the option key along with the normal dash key.

A long, em dash, is used in e-mails to accentuate a thought, such as "We invited customers to the office party — boy, was that a mistake." It can also interrupt a sentence with an aside, such as "The day after the party we received several calls from customers — I'm surprised they could talk — asking for the date of the next one."

You can easily overdo dashes, so use them sparingly.

The colon

When writing e-mails, most people use colons after the salutation, such as, "Dear Michelle:" Another use of a colon is for the introduction of a list. For example, "Every customer who accesses our Web site must type in the following: their name, date of birth, mother's maiden name, favorite color, blood type, and next of kin." A colon can also introduce a quote. "The sales clerk looked up at the ceiling and said: 'Let me see, I think we stopped selling those about fifteen years ago.'"

Parentheses (at last)

Parentheses are very useful for adding asides or explanations that you don't want as part of your main message. "The senior executives (bless their hearts) agreed with my plan," is a sentence in which the parenthetic is an aside. Parentheses can also be used to include important details without making the message too confusing. "At the awards dinner, we would like you to sit with your team. This means that the green team (the team with the cucumbers) will sit at the green table (closest to the stage), and the orange team (the team with the carrots) will sit at the orange table (near the piano). We look forward to a fun evening."

If you write a complete sentence within parentheses, end it, as you would normally, with a period. (This is an example.) In all other cases, place the period outside of the parentheses. For example, "Our service levels for e-mail response are all over the place (but better than last year)."

Never have parenthetical statements that are so important or distracting that they take attention away from the message of the sentence. Also, consider rewriting the sentence if you find that your parenthetical statement is longer than the sentence it is sitting in.

Be patient with e-mails from people whose first language is not English. If you find yourself getting annoyed with their improper use of English, imagine yourself writing a note in their native language!

Index

• D •

• *F* •

Notes

Notes

Notes

Notes

Notes

Notes

Dummies Books™
Bestsellers on Every Topic!

GENERAL INTEREST TITLES

BUSINESS & PERSONAL FINANCE

Title	Author	ISBN	Price
Accounting For Dummies®	John A. Tracy, CPA	0-7645-5014-4	$19.99 US/$27.99 CAN
Business Plans For Dummies®	Paul Tiffany, Ph.D. & Steven D. Peterson, Ph.D.	1-56884-868-4	$19.99 US/$27.99 CAN
Business Writing For Dummies®	Sheryl Lindsell-Roberts	0-7645-5134-5	$16.99 US/$27.99 CAN
Consulting For Dummies®	Bob Nelson & Peter Economy	0-7645-5034-9	$19.99 US/$27.99 CAN
Customer Service For Dummies®, 2nd Edition	Karen Leland & Keith Bailey	0-7645-5209-0	$19.99 US/$27.99 CAN
Franchising For Dummies®	Dave Thomas & Michael Seid	0-7645-5160-4	$19.99 US/$27.99 CAN
Getting Results For Dummies®	Mark H. McCormack	0-7645-5205-8	$19.99 US/$27.99 CAN
Home Buying For Dummies®	Eric Tyson, MBA & Ray Brown	1-56884-385-2	$16.99 US/$24.99 CAN
House Selling For Dummies®	Eric Tyson, MBA & Ray Brown	0-7645-5038-1	$16.99 US/$24.99 CAN
Human Resources Kit For Dummies®	Max Messmer	0-7645-5131-0	$19.99 US/$27.99 CAN
Investing For Dummies®, 2nd Edition	Eric Tyson, MBA	0-7645-5162-0	$19.99 US/$27.99 CAN
Law For Dummies®	John Ventura	1-56884-860-9	$19.99 US/$27.99 CAN
Leadership For Dummies®	Marshall Loeb & Steven Kindel	0-7645-5176-0	$19.99 US/$27.99 CAN
Managing For Dummies®	Bob Nelson & Peter Economy	1-56884-858-7	$19.99 US/$27.99 CAN
Marketing For Dummies®	Alexander Hiam	1-56884-699-1	$19.99 US/$27.99 CAN
Mutual Funds For Dummies®, 2nd Edition	Eric Tyson, MBA	0-7645-5112-4	$19.99 US/$27.99 CAN
Negotiating For Dummies®	Michael C. Donaldson & Mimi Donaldson	1-56884-867-6	$19.99 US/$27.99 CAN
Personal Finance For Dummies®, 3rd Edition	Eric Tyson, MBA	0-7645-5231-7	$19.99 US/$27.99 CAN
Personal Finance For Dummies® For Canadians, 2nd Edition	Eric Tyson, MBA & Tony Martin	0-7645-5123-X	$19.99 US/$27.99 CAN
Public Speaking For Dummies®	Malcolm Kushner	0-7645-5159-0	$16.99 US/$24.99 CAN
Sales Closing For Dummies®	Tom Hopkins	0-7645-5063-2	$14.99 US/$21.99 CAN
Sales Prospecting For Dummies®	Tom Hopkins	0-7645-5066-7	$14.99 US/$21.99 CAN
Selling For Dummies®	Tom Hopkins	1-56884-389-5	$16.99 US/$24.99 CAN
Small Business For Dummies®	Eric Tyson, MBA & Jim Schell	0-7645-5094-2	$19.99 US/$27.99 CAN
Small Business Kit For Dummies®	Richard D. Harroch	0-7645-5093-4	$24.99 US/$34.99 CAN
Taxes 2001 For Dummies®	Eric Tyson & David J. Silverman	0-7645-5306-2	$15.99 US/$23.99 CAN
Time Management For Dummies®, 2nd Edition	Jeffrey J. Mayer	0-7645-5145-0	$19.99 US/$27.99 CAN
Writing Business Letters For Dummies®	Sheryl Lindsell-Roberts	0-7645-5207-4	$16.99 US/$24.99 CAN

TECHNOLOGY TITLES

INTERNET/ONLINE

Title	Author	ISBN	Price
America Online® For Dummies®, 6th Edition	John Kaufeld	0-7645-0670-6	$19.99 US/$27.99 CAN
Banking Online Dummies®	Paul Murphy	0-7645-0458-4	$24.99 US/$34.99 CAN
eBay™ For Dummies®, 2nd Edition	Marcia Collier, Roland Woerner, & Stephanie Becker	0-7645-0761-3	$19.99 US/$27.99 CAN
E-Mail For Dummies®, 2nd Edition	John R. Levine, Carol Baroudi, & Arnold Reinhold	0-7645-0131-3	$24.99 US/$34.99 CAN
Genealogy Online For Dummies®, 2nd Edition	Matthew L. Helm & April Leah Helm	0-7645-0543-2	$24.99 US/$34.99 CAN
Internet Directory For Dummies®, 3rd Edition	Brad Hill	0-7645-0558-2	$24.99 US/$34.99 CAN
Internet Auctions For Dummies®	Greg Holden	0-7645-0578-9	$24.99 US/$34.99 CAN
Internet Explorer 5.5 For Windows® For Dummies®	Doug Lowe	0-7645-0738-9	$19.99 US/$28.99 CAN
Researching Online For Dummies®, 2nd Edition	Mary Ellen Bates & Reva Basch	0-7645-0546-7	$24.99 US/$34.99 CAN
Job Searching Online For Dummies®	Pam Dixon	0-7645-0673-0	$24.99 US/$34.99 CAN
Investing Online For Dummies®, 3rd Edition	Kathleen Sindell, Ph.D.	0-7645-0725-7	$24.99 US/$34.99 CAN
Travel Planning Online For Dummies®, 2nd Edition	Noah Vadnai	0-7645-0438-X	$24.99 US/$34.99 CAN
Internet Searching For Dummies®	Brad Hill	0-7645-0478-9	$24.99 US/$34.99 CAN
Yahoo!® For Dummies®, 2nd Edition	Brad Hill	0-7645-0762-1	$19.99 US/$27.99 CAN
The Internet For Dummies®, 7th Edition	John R. Levine, Carol Baroudi, & Arnold Reinhold	0-7645-0674-9	$19.99 US/$27.99 CAN

OPERATING SYSTEMS

Title	Author	ISBN	Price
DOS For Dummies®, 3rd Edition	Dan Gookin	0-7645-0361-8	$19.99 US/$27.99 CAN
GNOME For Linux® For Dummies®	David B. Busch	0-7645-0650-1	$24.99 US/$37.99 CAN
LINUX® For Dummies®, 2nd Edition	John Hall, Craig Witherspoon, & Coletta Witherspoon	0-7645-0421-5	$24.99 US/$34.99 CAN
Mac® OS 9 For Dummies®	Bob LeVitus	0-7645-0652-8	$19.99 US/$28.99 CAN
Red Hat® Linux® For Dummies®	Jon "maddog" Hall, Paul Sery	0-7645-0663-3	$24.99 US/$37.99 CAN
Small Business Windows® 98 For Dummies®	Stephen Nelson	0-7645-0425-8	$24.99 US/$34.99 CAN
UNIX® For Dummies®, 4th Edition	John R. Levine & Margaret Levine Young	0-7645-0419-3	$19.99 US/$27.99 CAN
Windows® 95 For Dummies®, 2nd Edition	Andy Rathbone	0-7645-0180-1	$19.99 US/$27.99 CAN
Windows® 98 For Dummies®	Andy Rathbone	0-7645-0261-1	$19.99 US/$27.99 CAN
Windows® 2000 For Dummies®	Andy Rathbone	0-7645-0641-2	$19.99 US/$27.99 CAN
Windows® 2000 Server For Dummies®	Ed Tittel	0-7645-0341-3	$24.99 US/$37.99 CAN
Windows® ME Millennium Edition For Dummies®	Andy Rathbone	0-7645-0735-4	$19.99 US/$27.99 CAN

Dummies Books™
Bestsellers on Every Topic!

GENERAL INTEREST TITLES

FOOD & BEVERAGE/ENTERTAINING

Bartending For Dummies®	Ray Foley	0-7645-5051-9	$14.99 US/$21.99 CAN
Cooking For Dummies®, 2nd Edition	Bryan Miller & Marie Rama	0-7645-5250-3	$19.99 US/$27.99 CAN
Entertaining For Dummies®	Suzanne Williamson with Linda Smith	0-7645-5027-6	$19.99 US/$27.99 CAN
Gourmet Cooking For Dummies®	Charlie Trotter	0-7645-5029-2	$19.99 US/$27.99 CAN
Grilling For Dummies®	Marie Rama & John Mariani	0-7645-5076-4	$19.99 US/$27.99 CAN
Italian Cooking For Dummies®	Cesare Casella & Jack Bishop	0-7645-5098-5	$19.99 US/$27.99 CAN
Mexican Cooking For Dummies®	Mary Sue Miliken & Susan Feniger	0-7645-5169-8	$19.99 US/$27.99 CAN
Quick & Healthy Cooking For Dummies®	Lynn Fischer	0-7645-5214-7	$19.99 US/$27.99 CAN
Wine For Dummies®, 2nd Edition	Ed McCarthy & Mary Ewing-Mulligan	0-7645-5114-0	$19.99 US/$27.99 CAN
Chinese Cooking For Dummies®	Martin Yan	0-7645-5247-3	$19.99 US/$27.99 CAN
Etiquette For Dummies®	Sue Fox	0-7645-5170-1	$19.99 US/$27.99 CAN

SPORTS

Baseball For Dummies®, 2nd Edition	Joe Morgan with Richard Lally	0-7645-5234-1	$19.99 US/$27.99 CAN
Golf For Dummies®, 2nd Edition	Gary McCord	0-7645-5146-9	$19.99 US/$27.99 CAN
Fly Fishing For Dummies®	Peter Kaminsky	0-7645-5073-X	$19.99 US/$27.99 CAN
Football For Dummies®	Howie Long with John Czarnecki	0-7645-5054-3	$19.99 US/$27.99 CAN
Hockey For Dummies®	John Davidson with John Steinbreder	0-7645-5045-4	$19.99 US/$27.99 CAN
NASCAR For Dummies®	Mark Martin	0-7645-5219-8	$19.99 US/$27.99 CAN
Tennis For Dummies®	Patrick McEnroe with Peter Bodo	0-7645-5087-X	$19.99 US/$27.99 CAN
Soccer For Dummies®	U.S. Soccer Federation & Michael Lewiss	0-7645-5229-5	$19.99 US/$27.99 CAN

HOME & GARDEN

Annuals For Dummies®	Bill Marken & NGA	0-7645-5056-X	$16.99 US/$24.99 CAN
Container Gardening For Dummies®	Bill Marken & NGA	0-7645-5057-8	$16.99 US/$24.99 CAN
Decks & Patios For Dummies®	Robert J. Beckstrom & NGA	0-7645-5075-6	$16.99 US/$24.99 CAN
Flowering Bulbs For Dummies®	Judy Glattstein & NGA	0-7645-5103-5	$16.99 US/$24.99 CAN
Gardening For Dummies®, 2nd Edition	Michael MacCaskey & NGA	0-7645-5130-2	$16.99 US/$24.99 CAN
Herb Gardening For Dummies®	NGA	0-7645-5200-7	$16.99 US/$24.99 CAN
Home Improvement For Dummies®	Gene & Katie Hamilton & the Editors of HouseNet, Inc.	0-7645-5005-5	$19.99 US/$26.99 CAN
Houseplants For Dummies®	Larry Hodgson & NGA	0-7645-5102-7	$16.99 US/$24.99 CAN
Painting and Wallpapering For Dummies®	Gene Hamilton	0-7645-5150-7	$16.99 US/$24.99 CAN
Perennials For Dummies®	Marcia Tatroe & NGA	0-7645-5030-6	$16.99 US/$24.99 CAN
Roses For Dummies®, 2nd Edition	Lance Walheim	0-7645-5202-3	$16.99 US/$24.99 CAN
Trees and Shrubs For Dummies®	Ann Whitman & NGA	0-7645-5203-1	$16.99 US/$24.99 CAN
Vegetable Gardening For Dummies®	Charlie Nardozzi & NGA	0-7645-5129-9	$16.99 US/$24.99 CAN
Home Cooking For Dummies®	Patricia Hart McMillan & Katharine Kaye McMillan	0-7645-5107-8	$19.99 US/$27.99 CAN

TECHNOLOGY TITLES

WEB DESIGN & PUBLISHING

Active Server Pages For Dummies®, 2nd Edition	Bill Hatfield	0-7645-0603-X	$24.99 US/$37.99 CAN
Cold Fusion 4 For Dummies®	Alexis Gutzman	0-7645-0604-8	$24.99 US/$37.99 CAN
Creating Web Pages For Dummies®, 5th Edition	Bud Smith & Arthur Bebak	0-7645-0733-8	$24.99 US/$34.99 CAN
Dreamweaver™ 3 For Dummies®	Janine Warner & Paul Vachier	0-7645-0669-2	$24.99 US/$34.99 CAN
FrontPage® 2000 For Dummies®	Asha Dornfest	0-7645-0423-1	$24.99 US/$34.99 CAN
HTML 4 For Dummies®, 3rd Edition	Ed Tittel & Natanya Dits	0-7645-0572-6	$24.99 US/$34.99 CAN
Java™ For Dummies®, 3rd Edition	Aaron E. Walsh	0-7645-0417-7	$24.99 US/$34.99 CAN
PageMill™ 2 For Dummies®	Deke McClelland & John San Filippo	0-7645-0028-7	$24.99 US/$34.99 CAN
XML™ For Dummies®	Ed Tittel	0-7645-0692-7	$24.99 US/$37.99 CAN
Javascript For Dummies®, 3rd Edition	Emily Vander Veer	0-7645-0633-1	$24.99 US/$37.99 CAN

DESKTOP PUBLISHING GRAPHICS/MULTIMEDIA

Adobe® In Design™ For Dummies®	Deke McClelland	0-7645-0599-8	$19.99 US/$27.99 CAN
CorelDRAW™ 9 For Dummies®	Deke McClelland	0-7645-0523-8	$19.99 US/$27.99 CAN
Desktop Publishing and Design For Dummies®	Roger C. Parker	1-56884-234-1	$19.99 US/$27.99 CAN
Digital Photography For Dummies®, 3rd Edition	Julie Adair King	0-7645-0646-3	$24.99 US/$37.99 CAN
Microsoft® Publisher 98 For Dummies®	Jim McCarter	0-7645-0395-2	$19.99 US/$27.99 CAN
Visio 2000 For Dummies®	Debbie Walkowski	0-7645-0635-8	$19.99 US/$27.99 CAN
Microsoft® Publisher 2000 For Dummies®	Jim McCarter	0-7645-0525-4	$19.99 US/$27.99 CAN
Windows® Movie Maker For Dummies®	Keith Underdahl	0-7645-0749-1	$19.99 US/$27.99 CAN

Dummies Books™
Bestsellers on Every Topic!

GENERAL INTEREST TITLES

EDUCATION & TEST PREPARATION

Title	Author	ISBN	Price
The ACT For Dummies®	Suzee Vlk	1-56884-387-9	$14.99 US/$21.99 CAN
College Financial Aid For Dummies®	Dr. Herm Davis & Joyce Lain Kennedy	0-7645-5049-7	$19.99 US/$27.99 CAN
College Planning For Dummies®, 2nd Edition	Pat Ordovensky	0-7645-5048-9	$19.99 US/$27.99 CAN
Everyday Math For Dummies®	Charles Seiter, Ph.D.	1-56884-248-1	$14.99 US/$21.99 CAN
The GMAT® For Dummies®, 3rd Edition	Suzee Vlk	0-7645-5082-9	$16.99 US/$24.99 CAN
The GRE® For Dummies®, 3rd Edition	Suzee Vlk	0-7645-5083-7	$16.99 US/$24.99 CAN
Politics For Dummies®	Ann DeLaney	1-56884-381-X	$19.99 US/$27.99 CAN
The SAT I For Dummies®, 3rd Edition	Suzee Vlk	0-7645-5044-6	$14.99 US/$21.99 CAN

AUTOMOTIVE

Title	Author	ISBN	Price
Auto Repair For Dummies®	Deanna Sclar	0-7645-5089-6	$19.99 US/$27.99 CAN
Buying A Car For Dummies®	Deanna Sclar	0-7645-5091-8	$16.99 US/$24.99 CAN

LIFESTYLE/SELF-HELP

Title	Author	ISBN	Price
Dating For Dummies®	Dr. Joy Browne	0-7645-5072-1	$19.99 US/$27.99 CAN
Making Marriage Work For Dummies®	Steven Simring, M.D. & Sue Klavans Simring, D.S.W	0-7645-5173-6	$19.99 US/$27.99 CAN
Parenting For Dummies®	Sandra H. Gookin	1-56884-383-6	$16.99 US/$24.99 CAN
Success For Dummies®	Zig Ziglar	0-7645-5061-6	$19.99 US/$27.99 CAN
Weddings For Dummies®	Marcy Blum & Laura Fisher Kaiser	0-7645-5055-1	$19.99 US/$27.99 CAN

TECHNOLOGY TITLES

SUITES

Title	Author	ISBN	Price
Microsoft® Office 2000 For Windows® For Dummies®	Wallace Wang & Roger C. Parker	0-7645-0452-5	$19.99 US/$27.99 CAN
Microsoft® Office 2000 For Windows® For Dummies® Quick Reference	Doug Lowe & Bjoern Hartsfvang	0-7645-0453-3	$12.99 US/$17.99 CAN
Microsoft® Office 97 For Windows® For Dummies®	Wallace Wang & Roger C. Parker	0-7645-0050-3	$19.99 US/$27.99 CAN
Microsoft® Office 97 For Windows® For Dummies® Quick Reference	Doug Lowe	0-7645-0062-7	$12.99 US/$17.99 CAN
Microsoft® Office 98 For Macs For Dummies®	Tom Negrino	0-7645-0229-8	$19.99 US/$27.99 CAN
Microsoft® Office X For Macs For Dummies®	Tom Negrino	0-7645-0702-8	$19.95 US/$27.99 CAN

WORD PROCESSING

Title	Author	ISBN	Price
Word 2000 For Windows® For Dummies® Quick Reference	Peter Weverka	0-7645-0449-5	$12.99 US/$19.99 CAN
Corel® WordPerfect® 8 For Windows® For Dummies®	Margaret Levine Young, David Kay & Jordan Young	0-7645-0186-0	$19.99 US/$27.99 CAN
Word 2000 For Windows® For Dummies®	Dan Gookin	0-7645-0448-7	$19.99 US/$27.99 CAN
Word For Windows® 95 For Dummies®	Dan Gookin	1-56884-932-X	$19.99 US/$27.99 CAN
Word 97 For Windows® For Dummies®	Dan Gookin	0-7645-0052-X	$19.99 US/$27.99 CAN
WordPerfect® 9 For Windows® For Dummies®	Margaret Levine Young	0-7645-0427-4	$19.99 US/$27.99 CAN
WordPerfect® 7 For Windows® 95 For Dummies®	Margaret Levine Young & David Kay	1-56884-949-4	$19.99 US/$27.99 CAN

SPREADSHEET/FINANCE/PROJECT MANAGEMENT

Title	Author	ISBN	Price
Excel For Windows® 95 For Dummies®	Greg Harvey	1-56884-930-3	$19.99 US/$27.99 CAN
Excel 2000 For Windows® For Dummies®	Greg Harvey	0-7645-0446-0	$19.99 US/$27.99 CAN
Excel 2000 For Windows® For Dummies® Quick Reference	John Walkenbach	0-7645-0447-9	$12.99 US/$17.99 CAN
Microsoft® Money 99 For Dummies®	Peter Weverka	0-7645-0433-9	$19.99 US/$27.99 CAN
Microsoft® Project 98 For Dummies®	Martin Doucette	0-7645-0321-9	$24.99 US/$34.99 CAN
Microsoft® Project 2000 For Dummies®	Martin Doucette	0-7645-0517-3	$24.99 US/$37.99 CAN
Microsoft® Money 2000 For Dummies®	Peter Weverka	0-7645-0579-3	$19.99 US/$27.99 CAN
MORE Excel 97 For Windows® For Dummies®	Greg Harvey	0-7645-0138-0	$22.99 US/$32.99 CAN
Quicken® 2000 For Dummies®	Stephen L . Nelson	0-7645-0607-2	$19.99 US/$27.99 CAN
Quicken® 2001 For Dummies®	Stephen L . Nelson	0-7645-0759-1	$19.99 US/$27.99 CAN
Quickbooks® 2000 For Dummies®	Stephen L . Nelson	0-7645-0665-x	$19.99 US/$27.99 CAN

Dummies Books™
Bestsellers on Every Topic!

GENERAL INTEREST TITLES

CAREERS

Cover Letters For Dummies®, 2nd Edition	Joyce Lain Kennedy	0-7645-5224-4	$12.99 US/$17.99 CAN
Cool Careers For Dummies®	Marty Nemko, Paul Edwards, & Sarah Edwards	0-7645-5095-0	$16.99 US/$24.99 CAN
Job Hunting For Dummies®, 2nd Edition	Max Messmer	0-7645-5163-9	$19.99 US/$26.99 CAN
Job Interviews For Dummies®, 2nd Edition	Joyce Lain Kennedy	0-7645-5225-2	$12.99 US/$17.99 CAN
Resumes For Dummies®, 2nd Edition	Joyce Lain Kennedy	0-7645-5113-2	$12.99 US/$17.99 CAN

FITNESS

Fitness Walking For Dummies®	Liz Neporent	0-7645-5192-2	$19.99 US/$27.99 CAN
Fitness For Dummies®, 2nd Edition	Suzanne Schlosberg & Liz Neporent	0-7645-5167-1	$19.99 US/$27.99 CAN
Nutrition For Dummies®, 2nd Edition	Carol Ann Rinzler	0-7645-5180-9	$19.99 US/$27.99 CAN
Running For Dummies®	Florence "Flo-Jo" Griffith Joyner & John Hanc	0-7645-5096-9	$19.99 US/$27.99 CAN

FOREIGN LANGUAGE

Spanish For Dummies®	Susana Wald	0-7645-5194-9	$24.99 US/$34.99 CAN
French For Dummies®	Dodi-Kartrin Schmidt & Michelle W. Willams	0-7645-5193-0	$24.99 US/$34.99 CAN

TECHNOLOGY TITLES

DATABASE

Access 2000 For Windows® For Dummies®	John Kaufeld	0-7645-0444-4	$19.99 US/$27.99 CAN
Access 97 For Windows® For Dummies®	John Kaufeld	0-7645-0048-1	$19.99 US/$27.99 CAN
Access 2000 For Windows For Dummies® Quick Reference	Alison Barrons	0-7645-0445-2	$12.99 US/$17.99 CAN
Approach® 97 For Windows® For Dummies®	Deborah S. Ray & Eric J. Ray	0-7645-0001-5	$19.99 US/$27.99 CAN
Crystal Reports 8 For Dummies®	Douglas J. Wolf	0-7645-0642-0	$24.99 US/$34.99 CAN
Data Warehousing For Dummies®	Alan R. Simon	0-7645-0170-4	$24.99 US/$34.99 CAN
FileMaker® Pro 4 For Dummies®	Tom Maremaa	0-7645-0210-7	$19.99 US/$27.99 CAN

NETWORKING/GROUPWARE

ATM For Dummies®	Cathy Gadecki & Christine Heckart	0-7645-0065-1	$24.99 US/$34.99 CAN
Client/Server Computing For Dummies®, 3rd Edition	Doug Lowe	0-7645-0476-2	$24.99 US/$34.99 CAN
DSL For Dummies®, 2nd Edition	David Angell	0-7645-0715-X	$24.99 US/$35.99 CAN
Lotus Notes® Release 4 For Dummies®	Stephen Londergan & Pat Freeland	1-56884-934-6	$19.99 US/$27.99 CAN
Microsoft® Outlook® 98 For Windows® For Dummies®	Bill Dyszel	0-7645-0393-6	$19.99 US/$28.99 CAN
Microsoft® Outlook® 2000 For Windows® For Dummies®	Bill Dyszel	0-7645-0471-1	$19.99 US/$27.99 CAN
Migrating to Windows® 2000 For Dummies®	Leonard Sterns	0-7645-0459-2	$24.99 US/$37.99 CAN
Networking For Dummies®, 4th Edition	Doug Lowe	0-7645-0498-3	$19.99 US/$27.99 CAN
Networking Home PCs For Dummies®	Kathy Ivens	0-7645-0491-6	$24.99 US/$35.99 CAN
Upgrading & Fixing Networks For Dummies®, 2nd Edition	Bill Camarda	0-7645-0542-4	$29.99 US/$42.99 CAN
TCP/IP For Dummies®, 4th Edition	Candace Leiden & Marshall Wilensky	0-7645-0726-5	$24.99 US/$35.99 CAN
Windows NT® Networking For Dummies®	Ed Tittel, Mary Madden, & Earl Follis	0-7645-0015-5	$24.99 US/$34.99 CAN

PROGRAMMING

Active Server Pages For Dummies®, 2nd Edition	Bill Hatfield	0-7645-0065-1	$24.99 US/$34.99 CAN
Beginning Programming For Dummies®	Wally Wang	0-7645-0596-0	$19.99 US/$29.99 CAN
C++ For Dummies® Quick Reference, 2nd Edition	Namir Shammas	0-7645-0390-1	$14.99 US/$21.99 CAN
Java™ Programming For Dummies®, 3rd Edition	David & Donald Koosis	0-7645-0388-X	$29.99 US/$42.99 CAN
JBuilder™ For Dummies®	Barry A. Burd	0-7645-0567-X	$24.99 US/$34.99 CAN
VBA For Dummies®, 2nd Edition	Steve Cummings	0-7645-0078-3	$24.99 US/$37.99 CAN
Windows® 2000 Programming For Dummies®	Richard Simon	0-7645-0469-X	$24.99 US/$37.99 CAN
XML For Dummies®, 2nd Edition	Ed Tittel	0-7645-0692-7	$24.99 US/$37.99 CAN

Dummies Books™
Bestsellers on Every Topic!

GENERAL INTEREST TITLES

THE ARTS

Art For Dummies®	Thomas Hoving	0-7645-5104-3	$24.99 US/$34.99 CAN
Blues For Dummies®	Lonnie Brooks, Cub Koda, & Wayne Baker Brooks	0-7645-5080-2	$24.99 US/$34.99 CAN
Classical Music For Dummies®	David Pogue & Scott Speck	0-7645-5009-8	$24.99 US/$34.99 CAN
Guitar For Dummies®	Mark Phillips & Jon Chappell of Cherry Lane Music	0-7645-5106-X	$24.99 US/$34.99 CAN
Jazz For Dummies®	Dirk Sutro	0-7645-5081-0	$24.99 US/$34.99 CAN
Opera For Dummies®	David Pogue & Scott Speck	0-7645-5010-1	$24.99 US/$34.99 CAN
Piano For Dummies®	Blake Neely of Cherry Lane Music	0-7645-5105-1	$24.99 US/$34.99 CAN
Shakespeare For Dummies®	John Doyle & Ray Lischner	0-7645-5135-3	$19.99 US/$27.99 CAN

HEALTH

Allergies and Asthma For Dummies®	William Berger, M.D.	0-7645-5218-X	$19.99 US/$27.99 CAN
Alternative Medicine For Dummies®	James Dillard, M.D., D.C., C.A.C., & Terra Ziporyn, Ph.D.	0-7645-5109-4	$19.99 US/$27.99 CAN
Beauty Secrets For Dummies®	Stephanie Seymour	0-7645-5078-0	$19.99 US/$27.99 CAN
Diabetes For Dummies®	Alan L. Rubin, M.D.	0-7645-5154-X	$19.99 US/$27.99 CAN
Dieting For Dummies®	The American Dietetic Society with Jane Kirby, R.D.	0-7645-5126-4	$19.99 US/$27.99 CAN
Family Health For Dummies®	Charles Inlander & Karla Morales	0-7645-5121-3	$19.99 US/$27.99 CAN
First Aid For Dummies®	Charles B. Inlander & The People's Medical Society	0-7645-5213-9	$19.99 US/$27.99 CAN
Fitness For Dummies®, 2nd Edition	Suzanne Schlosberg & Liz Neporent, M.A.	0-7645-5167-1	$19.99 US/$27.99 CAN
Healing Foods For Dummies®	Molly Siple, M.S. R.D.	0-7645-5198-1	$19.99 US/$27.99 CAN
Healthy Aging For Dummies®	Walter Bortz, M.D.	0-7645-5233-3	$19.99 US/$27.99 CAN
Men's Health For Dummies®	Charles Inlander	0-7645-5120-5	$19.99 US/$27.99 CAN
Nutrition For Dummies®, 2nd Edition	Carol Ann Rinzler	0-7645-5180-9	$19.99 US/$27.99 CAN
Pregnancy For Dummies®	Joanne Stone, M.D., Keith Eddleman, M.D., & Mary Murray	0-7645-5074-8	$19.99 US/$27.99 CAN
Sex For Dummies®	Dr. Ruth K. Westheimer	1-56884-384-4	$16.99 US/$24.99 CAN
Stress Management For Dummies®	Allen Elkin, Ph.D.	0-7645-5144-2	$19.99 US/$27.99 CAN
The Healthy Heart For Dummies®	James M. Ripple, M.D.	0-7645-5166-3	$19.99 US/$27.99 CAN
Weight Training For Dummies®	Liz Neporent, M.A. & Suzanne Schlosberg	0-7645-5036-5	$19.99 US/$27.99 CAN
Women's Health For Dummies®	Pamela Maraldo, Ph.D., R.N., & The People's Medical Society	0-7645-5119-1	$19.99 US/$27.99 CAN

TECHNOLOGY TITLES

MACINTOSH

Macs® For Dummies®, 7th Edition	David Pogue	0-7645-0703-6	$19.99 US/$27.99 CAN
The iBook™ For Dummies®	David Pogue	0-7645-0647-1	$19.99 US/$27.99 CAN
The iMac For Dummies®, 2nd Edition	David Pogue	0-7645-0648-X	$19.99 US/$27.99 CAN
The iMac For Dummies® Quick Reference	Jenifer Watson	0-7645-0648-X	$12.99 US/$19.99 CAN

PC/GENERAL COMPUTING

Building A PC For Dummies®, 2nd Edition	Mark Chambers	0-7645-0571-8	$24.99 US/$34.99 CAN
Buying a Computer For Dummies®	Dan Gookin	0-7645-0632-3	$19.99 US/$27.99 CAN
Illustrated Computer Dictionary For Dummies®, 4th Edition	Dan Gookin & Sandra Hardin Gookin	0-7645-0732-X	$19.99 US/$27.99 CAN
Palm Computing® For Dummies®	Bill Dyszel	0-7645-0581-5	$24.99 US/$34.99 CAN
PCs For Dummies®, 7th Edition	Dan Gookin	0-7645-0594-7	$19.99 US/$27.99 CAN
Small Business Computing For Dummies®	Brian Underdahl	0-7645-0287-5	$24.99 US/$34.99 CAN
Smart Homes For Dummies®	Danny Briere	0-7645-0527-0	$19.99 US/$27.99 CAN
Upgrading & Fixing PCs For Dummies®, 5th Edition	Andy Rathbone	0-7645-0719-2	$19.99 US/$27.99 CAN
Handspring Visor For Dummies®	Joe Hubko	0-7645-0724-9	$19.99 US/$27.99 CAN

YOUR ONLINE RESOURCE
WWW.DUMMIES.COM

Discover Dummies Online!

The Dummies Web Site is your fun and friendly online resource for the latest information about *For Dummies* books and your favorite topics. The Web site is the place to communicate with us, exchange ideas with other *For Dummies* readers, chat with authors, and have fun!

Ten Fun and Useful Things You Can Do at www.dummies.com

1. Win free *For Dummies* books and more!
2. Register your book and be entered in a prize drawing.
3. Meet your favorite authors through the Hungry Minds Author Chat Series.
4. Exchange helpful information with other *For Dummies* readers.
5. Discover other great *For Dummies* books you must have!
6. Purchase Dummieswear exclusively from our Web site.
7. Buy *For Dummies* books online.
8. Talk to us. Make comments, ask questions, get answers!
9. Download free software.
10. Find additional useful resources from authors.

Link directly to these ten fun and useful things at
www.dummies.com/10useful

SURF THE NET
WWW.DUMMIES.COM

For other titles from Hungry Minds,
go to **www.hungryminds.com**

Not on the Web yet? It's easy to get started with *Dummies 101: The Internet For Windows 98* or *The Internet For Dummies* at local retailers everywhere.

Find other *For Dummies* books on these topics:
Business • Career • Databases • Food & Beverage • Games • Gardening
Graphics • Hardware • Health & Fitness • Internet and the World Wide Web
Networking • Office Suites • Operating Systems • Personal Finance • Pets
Programming • Recreation • Sports • Spreadsheets • Teacher Resources
Test Prep • Word Processing

Hungry Minds™

FOR DUMMIES
BOOK REGISTRATION

Register This Book and Win!

We want to hear from you!

Visit **dummies.com** to register this book and tell us how you liked it!

✔ Get entered in our monthly prize giveaway.

✔ Give us feedback about this book — tell us what you like best, what you like least, or maybe what you'd like to ask the author and us to change!

✔ Let us know any other *For Dummies* topics that interest you.

Your feedback helps us determine what books to publish, tells us what coverage to add as we revise our books, and lets us know whether we're meeting your needs as a *For Dummies* reader. You're our most valuable resource, and what you have to say is important to us!

Not on the Web yet? It's easy to get started with *Dummies 101: The Internet For Windows 98* or *The Internet For Dummies* at local retailers everywhere.

Or let us know what you think by sending us a letter at the following address:

For Dummies Book Registration
Dummies Press
10475 Crosspoint Blvd.
Indianapolis, IN 46256

...FOR DUMMIES™

BESTSELLING BOOK SERIES